Peter McWilliams
Personal Electronics
Book

Prentice Hall Press • New York

Published by Prentice Hall Press
A Division of Simon & Schuster, Inc.
Gulf+Western Building
One Gulf+Western Plaza
New York, NY 10023

PRENTICE HALL PRESS is a trademark of Simon & Schuster, Inc.

Library of Congress Cataloging-in-Publication Data
McWilliams, Peter.
    Peter McWilliams Personal Electronics book.

    1. Household electronics--Purchasing.   I. Title.
II. Title: Personal electronics book.
TK7870.M398   1987   621.38   87-22030
ISBN 0-13-657354-1

Manufactured in the United States of America
10 9 8 7 6 5 4 3 2 1
First Edition

This book is for

John-Roger

without whom none of it
would have been probable.

Acknowledgments

To Phil Pochoda, my publisher. When I first conceived the idea of this book, I could think of no one in publishing I would rather work with than Phil. Our deal was a phone call away. His support, trust and enthusiasm has been constant.

To Roger Lane, who offered expert council and advice. (And I happily accepted.)

To Christopher Meeks, who helped with editing and, especially, product reviews.

To Christopher McMullen, for necessary (and a few unnecessary) distractions, and for his help in product reviews.

To Daniel & Toni Will-Harris, and their especially useful book, *Desktop Publishing With Style* (And Publishing Co.), an invaluable guide for any desktop publisher.

To Alexis Bernard, for lending her hawkeye and helping hands.

To Dan DeLeon, for keeping it together.

To Gary Leong, for gathering the products to review.

To Bill and Anita Fitelson, for the courage to get a VCR and a CD player in the *same month*, and for their constant love.

To Beatrice Wayne Godfrey, for the portrait of St. Teresa and for the funny phone calls.

To Maurice Grosser, who loved personal electronics, and who I loved.

To Virgil Thomson, who mistrusts personal electronics, but allows others to use them in his behalf.

To Melba Colgrove, just for being Melba.

To Bill Buckley, for his friendship.

To Ron Gold, for his P. R.

To my brother, Michael McWilliams, for doing a complete copy-edit on the finished book (which is more than I did for his book).

And to Mary Toarmina McWilliams Fadden ("mom" for short) and her roommate Larry Fadden, for trying out — eventually — whatever personal electronics I sent them. (I wanted to see what would happen if middle America went digital. Results: Not bad.)

To all of you, thank you.

Table of Contents

Part Three

Part Four

Peter McWilliams

Personal Electronics

Book

INTRODUCTION

Are You Ready for the Nineties?

ave you tried buying a TV recently? I did (about a year ago). It was the first time I had to actually *shop* for a TV in almost twenty years.

The last time was in 1968. Relatively fresh out of high school, I was about to buy my first color TV. I took the job with utmost seriousness. I read all the reports and visited all the stores. To everyone's surprise, especially my own, I chose a 13-inch Sony Trinitron over the top-rated-by-everyone 100-dollars-cheaper 19-inch Zenith. The Sony simply had a better picture, and back then 13 inches was as large as they came.

Over the years, the only difficulty in buying a new television was coming up with the money. The choice was easy: get the biggest Trinitron around.

Until last year. My buy-a-Sony habit was challenged by TV's with larger screens, TV's with higher resolution and TV's promising "greater color fidelity." (Whatever that was.)

What to do? While pondering this, my five-year-old CD player broke. More choices. Five years earlier it was either

3

a CD player or it wasn't; it either played Compact Discs or it didn't. Now I had a choice of how many lasers I wanted (as many as four), how many discs it would hold (as many as ten), and how much I wanted to spend (as much as $2,800).

Then my VCR went south. The repair cost would be "around $300" ($5 for parts, $295 for labor). They would have to order parts so it might take "about two weeks." I'd had enough electronic things repaired to know that "about two weeks" means "sometime this year, providing it's not yet July."

A new Video Cassette Recorder was clearly in order, but which one? A VHS or a Beta? Should I get SuperBeta or Clark Kent Beta? Hi-Fi VHS or Lo-Fi VHS? And let's not forget 8mm.

I was doing what I always do when confused (nothing) when my landlord told me I'd be moving to Los Angeles. (When your New York City landlord tells you he is not renewing your absurdly low-rent lease and is throwing you out to compete for limited living space with two-lawyer-income families and retiring Arab oil sheiks, he's basically saying, "You're moving to L.A.")

When moving 3,000 miles, one must question everything one owns. "Is this worth packing and moving, or should I just get a new one in L.A.?" I had to reevaluate my Mr. Coffee, my vacuum, my stereo (component by component), my microwave, my ice cream maker, my shaver, my electric toothbrush, my popcorn popper . . .

Then it dawned on me: it's not easy buying this stuff. Deciding "Do I need it?" then deciding "Which one?" then deciding "Is it worth it?" then deciding "How do I get one (as cheaply as possible)?" was never an easy process, but somehow, in just the last few years — what with microchips and Japan, Inc. and Korea Co. and the U.S. manufacturers' response to Japan, Inc. and Korea Co. — the process of choosing almost any electrical gadget has become downright *staggering*.

So I staggered around for a few months and discovered that, amid the confusion, there was a lot of great stuff out there. (And a lot of irredeemable trash, too.)

4

Introduction

I found myself enthusing to friends about certain gadgets and warning them about others. "Can't we talk about something that doesn't plug in?" they would ask. "Sure!" I would say, and tell them about all the battery-operated things I had seen.

It soon became clear, as it had with computers seven years earlier: If I wanted to keep my few remaining friends, I had better start writing about electronics. (If I write about something I tend not to talk about it.)

Hence this book.

It's called *Personal Electronics* because we'll be looking at electrical things we *personally* use to perform some useful task, or just to entertain. (Personally, I consider entertainment one of the most useful tasks electronics — or anything else — can provide.)

We'll explore TV's, VCR's, CD's, DAT's (Digital Audio Tape) Hi-Fi's, car stereos, small appliances, and a miscellaneous category I call Stuff. There's some general information (a series of primers) and specific product reviews. There are tips on what to buy and how to buy it. I praise the praiseworthy and trash the trash.

Come along. You'll have fun — and the undying gratitude of my friends.

Chapter One

A Brief, Incomplete and No Doubt Inaccurate History of Personal Electronics

 lectricity entered the home with the new century.

It had to be something immensely practical to justify running all those wires to and through the house, for we were a practical people. (We're still a practical people; now we're just practical about frivolous things.) And a practical thing was found: the electric light bulb.

Edison did not so much invent the electric light as he invented the system by which the electric light was invented — the research laboratory. That an electric light was going to be invented was a given, and most scientists of the day knew roughly what it was going to be like — a glowing coil within some kind of vacuum. What the coil would be made of, what size the coil would be, how much electricity it would take to make the coil glow and a dozen other variables were questions Edison was uniquely prepared to answer.

In 1876 Edison took his profits from the invention and manufacturing of stock tickers and set up an industrial re-

7

search laboratory in Menlo Park, New Jersey. Prior to this, inventors worked alone, in basements and garages, on weekends and at night. The idea of gathering craftsmen, engineers, designers, clockmakers and other specialists under one roof with a common goal — "Invent Stuff; Practical Stuff" — was one of Edison's most brilliant (and often unheralded) inventions.

Inventing the light bulb was for the 1870's what getting to the moon was for the 1960's — everyone knew it could be done, everyone believed it would be done, the only questions were "Who?" and "When?"

The smart money was on Edison, "The Wizard of Menlo Park," just as the smart money in the moon race was on the United States, "The Land of the Free and the Home of Technology."

Immediately after setting up shop, however, Edison, almost by accident, invented the phonograph. The electric light was an *expected* invention; the phonograph, completely unexpected. A *machine* that records and plays back *sound*? Unbelievable. Inconceivable. Edison had drawn a rough sketch and handed it to his chief engineer. The first model brought to Edison worked, much to Edison's surprise.

It's obvious he didn't expect that first phonograph to work. If he had expected it, don't you think he would have chosen more, well, significant words than, "Ha, ha, ha. Mary had a little lamb, its fleece was white as snow, and everywhere that Mary went, the lamb was sure to go. Ha, ha, ha."?

Neil Armstrong had a pretty good idea he'd make it to the moon, so he thought real hard and came up with, "One small step for a man, one giant leap for mankind." If only Armstrong were around to help Edison. The first recorded words might have been, "One small sentence for a man, one large voice for mankind."

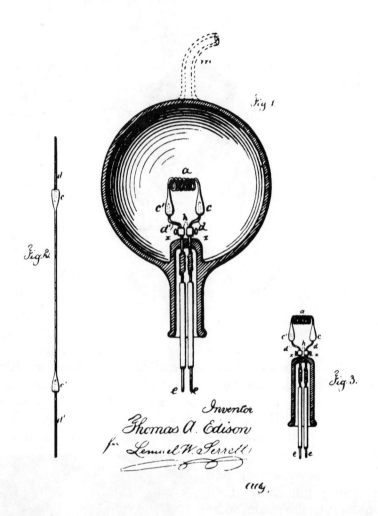

Inventor

Thomas A. Edison

f. Lemuel W. Serrell

There is a theory. It states that new ideas do not come to just one person at a time; a new idea trickles down into dozens of minds, and whoever acts upon the idea first gets the benefits of it.

Almost simultaneous with Edison's invention of the light bulb, a man named Joseph Swan invented almost exactly the same bulb. If Edison had lingered over the phonograph an extra month, "Swan" and "Electricity" might now be synonymous. Consolidated Edison would have to be called Consolidated Swan, or Con Swan, for short.

Ironically, the inventor of the phonograph was, due to a childhood illness, nearly deaf.

The phonograph distracted everyone at Menlo Park from the light bulb for a year or two. "Edison's Talking Machine" had to be perfected and marketed, and Edison himself had a grand time demonstrating it to presidents, royalty and heads of state. Edison also personally approved every singer, song and cylinder to roll off his production line.

But by 1878, it was time to get to work again on the incandescent light bulb. Edison had already taken $50,000 (and that was 50,000 1878 dollars) from, among others, Cornelius Vanderbilt and J.P. Morgan to form The Edison Electric Light Company. There was only one small technicality — there was no Edison Electric Light.

Inventing the light bulb was rather dull work, especially after the excitement of the phonograph: try one kind of filament, put it in a vacuum, put a current to it, see how long it burned. One after another, for fourteen months. He finally settled on a carbon filament, which was one of the first filaments he had tried and, for some reason, abandoned.

Soon his Menlo Park laboratory ("The Invention Factory," he called it) was aglow with incandescent lights and overrun with reporters. Three years later he opened his first electric generating station on Pearl Street in New York.

Edison's electricity was direct current (DC). George Westinghouse, of You-Can-Be-Sure-If-It's-Westinghouse fame, favored the European method of alternating current (AC). The public battle between these two giants deserves a place in American history beside William Jennings Bryant's conflict with Clarence Darrow and The Devil's altercation with Daniel Webster.

Although alternating current is more practical for distribution over long distances, it is also more dangerous than direct current. Edison and his comrades exploited the danger of AC shamelessly. Edison traveled around the country electrocuting animals using a Westinghouse generator. In one particularly funny newsreel, Edison electrocuted an elephant. (Granted, it was not very funny to the elephant.)

In what the pro-DC forces hoped would be a *coup de grace*, the legislature of New York deemed Westinghouse's AC method of electrical generation the state's official form of execution.

It didn't work. Westinghouse lost the PR battle but he won the war. AC became the electrical standard for the United States, and Edison remained bitter over his defeat the rest of his life — which went on sixteen years longer than Westinghouse's. (The battle between the companies they founded — Westinghouse's Westinghouse and Edison's General Electric — continued long after both went on.)

During the great AC-DC battle, Edison discovered something that would have even more far reaching effects on personal electronics than the type of electricity used to power them. It was, in fact, the seed of the most important discovery in the history of personal electronics as we know them.

In 1883, while working on an improved version of the light bulb, Edison noticed that current flowed from a filament to a positively charged plate within the bulb. He didn't know what to make of this, but he dutifully recorded his observation (he filled 3,400 notebooks in his time), named it "The Edison Effect" (he named everything after himself; if he thought it might prove harmful to humanity he probably would have called it "The Westinghouse Effect"), and forgot about it.

What Edison discovered was the basis of the electron tube, which was the basis of the transistor, which eventually became the microchip. He lived to see The Edison Effect revolutionize personal electronics and, less significantly, Life on Earth.

Let's divide personal electronics in the twentieth century into four time periods, each period spanning roughly twenty-five years. I named each quarter-century segment after the most significant underlying cause for change in personal electronics during that period. They are. . .

1900-1924: The Electric Motor and the Glowing Coil

1925-1949: The Electron ("Vacuum") Tube

1950-1974: The Transistor

1975-1999: The Microchip

1900-1924: The Electric Motor and the Glowing Coil

As I mentioned before, in order to justify the expense and trouble of bringing electrical wires to and through the home, electricity had to do something *practical*. The first quarter of this century was made up exclusively of products doing just that.

The light bulb (a glowing coil) replaced kerosene lamps and gas jets. Most homes were wired only for lights — if you wanted to plug something in, you had to screw the "plug" into a light socket. As late as the 1930's, when purchasing electronic devices, you had a choice: plug in or screw in.

(Edison's bulb eventually became the Mazda lamp, a design that continued for years. Some of them are still in use. I wrote this book under the pleasant glow of one, just for luck.)

A glowing coil not contained in a vacuum provided heat. Smokeless, odorless heat could be brought to any

room with no need for venting and no fear of asphyxiation. Electricity's glow also heated electric irons, waffle irons and hair curlers.

Electric motors were practical, therefore popular. Pumping water, washing clothes, powering sewing machines, and even washing dishes were gradually taken over by electricity.

Keep in mind that none of the entertainment devices in the first two decades of the century used electricity, although, looking back, one wonders why.

Phonographs, even expensive councils, were windup affairs. Player pianos required pumping. One wonders why a motor wasn't attached to these — at least to the top-of-the-line models — before the mid-1920's.

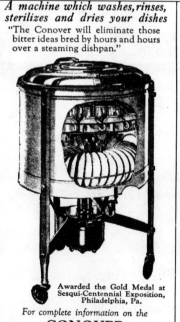

1925-1949: The Electron ("Vacuum") Tube

In 1906, Lee De Forest invented the electron tube. It was a variation of Thomas Alva's "Edison Effect" light bulb. It amplified weak electric signals, and the degree of amplification could be controlled. This one advance would change the world.

Dr. De Forest with his electron tube.

The first place De Forest used his tube was radio. Back then it was called "wireless," as the telephone did everything the wireless did, it just required a wire. Wired "broadcasting" was quite popular in Europe in the late 1890's. At the turn of the century in Budapest, for example, there were 6,500 "wired" subscribers who heard music, news, stock market reports and "dramatic presentations" fourteen hours a day. It took almost seventy years before "cable broadcasting" caught on again.

By 1923, wireless radio, thanks to De Forest's vacuum tube, was on its way. The early tube sets used DC batteries for power, but by 1926, AC models that plugged into the wall (or, more commonly, screwed into a light socket) were available.

Bell Telephone had a desperate need for De Forest's invention. The longest long distance they could muster was Boston to Chicago. The Bell engineers took De Forest's design and improved it. The vacuum tube made not just transcontinental telephone service a reality, it vastly improved local telephone service as well.

Thus began the "personal telephone." Prior to vacuum tubes, telephones were primarily a business tool. You had to shout hard at one end and listen hard at the other. (Alexander Graham Bell preferred the greeting "Ahoy!" over "Hello," because "Ahoy!" was easier to yell.) Telephones were large boxes mounted on the wall. None of this lent itself to casual conversation.

Improved transmission and reception, as well as the dial candlestick telephone, led to "chatting" and the overwhelming personal use of the telephone from 1925 on. (It was 1929 before there was a telephone in the Oval Office.)

The vacuum tube also ushered in electronic recording. Prior to amplification, performers had to crowd around a single "horn," which was connected to a needle, the vibrations of which "cut" the record. This was known as "acoustic" recording.

Caruso's drawing of himself making an acoustic recording.

With electronic recording, microphones could be placed at various locations throughout the recording studio or concert hall. Electronics also improved the frequency response, and allowed strings to be recorded properly for the first time. (The early orchestrations — heavy with brass, woodwinds and percussion — were a result of the limitations of acoustic recording.) The electrical process permitted performers a subtler, more intimate approach. Farewell, Caruso. Hello, Crosby.

The vacuum tube changed home phonographs as well. Amplification permitted better, louder sound. And, as long as they had to plug it in, manufacturers added a motor to turn the records around.

Car radios were introduced in 1927, as was coast-to-coast radio broadcasting. Bell Labs demonstrated TV transmission between New Jersey and New York, and the first talking motion picture, *The Jazz Singer,* was made. All of these would have been impossible without De Forest's electron tube. (While recording the first sound cartoon, *Steamboat Willie*, Walt Disney, the voice of Mickey Mouse, coughed into an open microphone. A vacuum tube on the recording device exploded.)

Television, a tube medium if there ever was one (probably the only vacuum tube in most people's homes anymore is the TV picture tube), went on sale in 1939. It promptly stalled due to World War II. World War II gave us magnetic recording tape, however, courtesy of the Germans. Prior to tape, the only methods of recording at home were records (some players permitted record making) and wire recorders. (Anybody remember wire recorders?)

FM broadcast began in 1941. By the end of the war (1945) there were 9 TV stations, 46 FM stations and 943 AM stations on the air.

In 1945 there were 10,000 television sets in the United States. By 1951, thanks to Milton Berle, there were 10,000,000. Eight years later, 50,000,000. Now more homes have television than indoor plumbing.

A History of Personal Electronics

1950-1974: The Transistor

In 1947, Bell Labs demonstrated the transistor. It was, in a sense, a small vacuum tube that required very little power and no vacuum. After inventing it, the Bell Labs all but abandoned it. The transistor, however, captured the imagination of our latest technological trading partner, Japan. (Bell Labs, which perfected the vacuum tube but did not invent it, invented the transistor but did not perfect it.)

In 1954, the first "transistor pocket radio" was marketed in the United States. It cost $49.95. Within a few years it cost less than $10 and caused a sensation.

When I remember the fifties, I think of hula hoops, Eisenhower and the transistor radio. Those little radios had roughly the same impact on the fifties as the Walkman had on the seventies. Everyone, it seemed, owned one (except for parents, of course) and the sound of music was everywhere. Rock 'n' roll was beginning then, and I like to think the transistor radio — cheap, portable and everywhere — had something to do with rock's success.

To the electronics industry in the United States, the transistor radio was a toy and the transistor a fad. The radios had a cheap, tinny sound. (It was, in fact, the little speaker that sounded so bad.) And it was only purchased by teenagers. (The buying power of teenagers would be discovered in later decades.)

The domestic electronics industry kept itself happy with the long playing (LP) record (1948), color TV (1954), and the stereo LP (1958). It also sold a lot of stereo phonographs to people who just bought mono phonographs and a lot of color TV's to people who just bought black & white TV's. The more things change, the more they stay the same.

The Japanese, on the other hand, took the transistor seriously. Very seriously. When Japan began marketing portable TV's and stereo amplifiers that were every bit as good as "tube types" — only cheaper, cooler, and longer lasting — the stateside electronics industry began to take Japan, Inc. — and its miniature Trojan Horse, the transistor — seriously.

"Would you like to see my transistor?"

Thus began the days of Solid-State. After years of ridiculing the transistor, the American manufacturers couldn't very well do an about-face and advertise, "Transistorized for your safety and comfort." They devised the term "solid-state." Why "solid-state" is beyond me. No one referred to vacuum-tubed equipment as being "flaccid-state."

But the days of solid-state electronics were on. By 1967 solid-state color TV's were the latest and greatest (if you were to believe the ads), and by 1973, solid-state television dominated the market. By 1975, transistorized components also dominated the stereo, radio and tape recorder market as well.

1975-1999: The Microchip

Transistors did the work of dozens of vacuum tubes in a fraction of a vacuum tube's space. Microchips do the work of tens of thousands of transistors in a fraction of a transistor's space.

The microchip entered the market slowly, tentatively— not unlike the transistor. It was first seen on digital watches in 1970. In 1971 came the first small calculators. In 1972 the first video games. (Remember "Pong"?) Nineteen eighty saw the popular acceptance of personal computers (called "microcomputers" back then, in honor of their brain). By the time people learned what a microchip was, they were in everything — from video cassette players to lawn sprinklers to toasters.

Projection TV was introduced in 1973. VCR's dropped by in 1975. Camcorders (portable video camera recorders) in 1980. CD players in 1981. AM stereo (yawn) in 1982. Stereo TV (hooray), VHS-C and 8mm video in 1984. (A high-tech year, but not as bad as Mr. Orwell predicted.)

In 1987 we got Super-VHS, DAT (Digital Audio Tape) and, after a heated discussion with his publisher as to whether his name should be in the title or not (he thought no, they thought yes, they are the publisher, the name is in the title), Peter McWilliams, ever optimistic, brought out the 1988 edition of *Peter McWilliams Personal Electronics Book*.

Yes, 1987 was a great year for personal electronics, one of the best since, well, the invention of the light bulb.

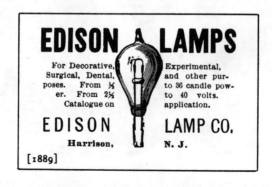

EDISON LAMPS
For Decorative, Surgical, Dental, poses. From ⅛ er. From 2½ Catalogue on
Experimental, and other purposes to 36 candle power to 40 volts. application.
EDISON LAMP CO.
Harrison, N. J.
[1889]

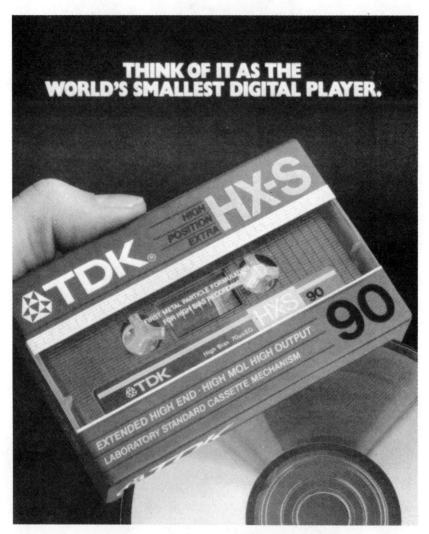

Think of it as deceptive advertising.

Chapter Two

What's All This Fuss About Digital and What Does It Have to Do with My Life?

he current craze for digital reminds me of the early days of computer software. Early computer software was hard to use. A few people then wrote programs easier to use. These were called, "user friendly." User friendly programs sold better than user unfriendly programs. Software manufacturers spent a fortune on little stickers saying "USER FRIENDLY" to stick all over their same old hostile software.

Well, the same thing seems to be going on with digital. Thanks to the success of CD players, "digital" sells. Whether it really is digital or not, everything today claims to be.

This book is digital. It got digitalized when I typed it into my computer, digitalized when sent to the typesetting computer, and digitalized again when run through the laser printer. (Ah, "laser" — another word that sells.) You are, in fact, reading a *triple-digital* book — three times better than the non-digital books by Hemingway, Faulkner and Twain.

See?

Understanding what digital is helps cut through the — What word shall I use? How graphic shall I get? — nonsense. Knowing a little about digital (and there's not that much to know) might also make living in the Brave New Digital World a little more comfortable.

Recorded sound began with Edison. The phonograph was a laboratory accident Thomas Alva had the wit to pursue.

Once invented, the premise seemed simple enough, almost obvious. Sound traveled down a metal horn and vibrated a needle. The needle transferred these vibrations to a rotating wax cylinder. The little wiggly line in the wax was a physical representation of the sound — it was directly *analogous* to the sound waves in the air — hence *analog* sound was born.

Sound continued to be recorded in just this way for the next hundred years. (Recording tape holds magnetic waves in invisible patterns that are analogous to sound waves.) All methods of reproducing sound that are not digital are called analog.

Digital is called digital because it reduces everything to *digits* — and only two digits, in fact, 0 and 1.

Digital recorders divide the spectrum of sound we can hear, 20 to 20,000 Hz (Hz stands for Hertz — one Hz is one cycle per second), into tens of thousands of little slices. In any given split-second, it assigns either a 0 or a 1 to each slice.

Let's say the 20-20,000 Hz spectrum is electronically divided into 40,000 equal slices. This would give us approximately one-half Hz per slice. In a given split-second, the digital processor "samples" the 40,000 slices and records a series of 0's (no sound at that one-half Hz) or 1 (yes, there is sound at this one-half Hz).

If the sound being sampled were, say, a small bell, the sampling at 20 through 10,000 Hz might be "no sound" (0's). Between 10,000 and 15,000 Hz might be various 0's and 1's, indicating the vibrations of the bell along the audible spectrum. From 15,000 to 20,000 Hz might be 0's again (silence).

This information is stored as a series of 0's and 1's. There is no real music on a digital tape or CD — just billions of 0's and 1's. When these sampled split-seconds are played back, one after another, we hear little bits of sound.

It's not complete music — our mind fills in the blanks. Our senses are easily fooled. When we go to a movie, we see 24 still pictures per second projected onto a screen. The screen is dark as often as it is illumined. It's picture-dark-picture-dark-picture-dark at a steady pace — 24 pictures and 24 darknesses per second. Even knowing this, we do not leave a two-hour movie saying, "Boy, I just spent an hour in the dark and an hour watching 172,800 still pictures!" even though that's exactly what we did.

The value of digital is that it records the music and *only* the music. Analog recordings are plagued by tape hiss or vinyl noise or scratches or dust or fingerprints or. . . Digital is pure sound, nothing but pure sound. The sands of time cannot scratch it.

The only true digital sound mediums today are CD's, DAT's (Digital Audio Tape), and the special PCM (Pulse Code Modulation) options of high-end VCR's and 8mm video decks (that's using the deck for sound only, no pictures). The only true digital video is LaserDiscs. There are no digital phonograph records. There is no digital video tape. There is no digital television.

So how can they call everything else *digital?* Anything that's run through a computer can be labeled "Digitally Processed," or "DIGITAL" for short (deceptively short, if you ask me).

Such as this *triple-digital* book.

THE PERSONAL ELECTRONICS BOOK

The term "electric" was to the 1880's what the term "digital" is to the 1980's. Products in no way connected with electricity were advertised as "electric." Here are a few samples:

CULTURED BOSTON PEOPLE USE
ELECTRIC LUSTRE STARCH.

It is the best Laundry Starch in the world. It is used by the best house-keepers for all laundry work. **Electric Lustre Starch** makes shirts, collars and cuffs look like **new**.

**BLUE PACKAGES, TEN CENTS EACH.
FOR SALE BY ALL GROCERS.**

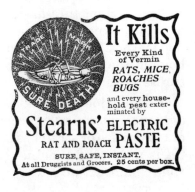

It Kills

Every Kind of Vermin *RATS, MICE, ROACHES BUGS*
and every house-hold pest exterminated by

Stearns' ELECTRIC
RAT AND ROACH **PASTE**

SURE, SAFE, INSTANT.
At all Druggists and Grocers. 25 cents per box.

Electric Insoles.

24242   Electric Insoles. Sure foot warmers. Recommended by many. State size of shoe worn. Has zinc and copper battery in each insole. Price, per pair.....................$0.75
Postage............................. .04

Electric Battery Plasters.

24243 The Lion Electric Battery Plaster has 2 silver disks on face of plaster, connected with a perfect copper and zinc battery on back, which guarantees a current of electricity. This current is diffused throughout the whole system. The battery can be charged with vinegar and used a number of times. Cures all aches and pains instantly. Each.................$0.45
Send for circular of Electric Belts and Specialties

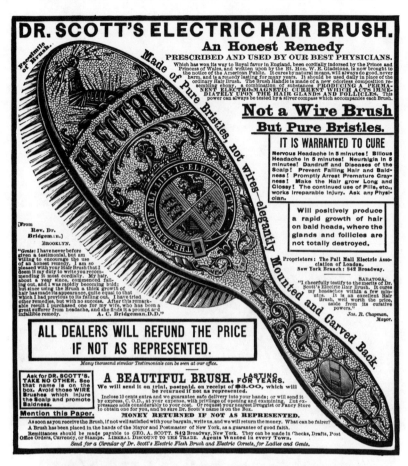

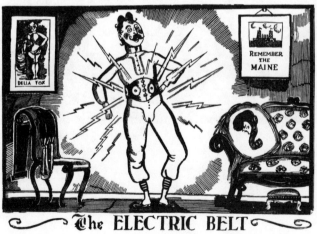

By the 1920's, John Held, Jr. was poking fun at the "Electric" craze of the 1880's.

33

Part One

Audio

et's divide people looking for an audio system into three categories — Lo-Fi's, Hi-Fi's and Audiophiles. (Audiophile is capitalized here because it is customary to capitalize major religions.)

I'm going to meander about the three and, as I do, see if you can find yourself among my arbitrary classifications. Please avoid the temptation to automatically assume you're an Audiophile because, after all, you *love* music, or a Hi-Fi because you hate organized religion, or a Lo-Fi because you don't have much money. You are what you are, and, as in all areas of personal electronics, if you buy equipment that suits your actual tastes, you'll be a lot happier.

In a nutshell, Lo-Fi's want *sound*, Hi-Fi's want *sensation*, and Audiophiles want *accuracy*.

Lo-Fi's want sound. Music is music to them. If the lyrics and the melody are intelligible and there's no noticeable distortion, that's all they need. Lo-Fi's seldom need to spend more than $300 on a complete system — $500 when they splurge.

Hi-Fi's want sensation. They don't just want to hear the low notes, they want to *feel* them. The bass drum and bass guitar should go thumping through their bodies. The low notes of a synthesizer should vibrate the living room; glassware on the kitchen shelves should tinkle. Hi-Fi's also want their highs to be dazzling — a cymbal crash an orgasmic experience; the upper register of a lead guitar should make the dog howl. Hi-Fi systems start at $500 and end around $5,000.

Audiophiles want accuracy; no, they *need* accuracy. They want the music to sound precisely the way it would if it were performed live. That is always the final criterion for an Audiophile. Theoretically, you should be able to close your eyes and not be able to tell if a real violin were playing in your living room or just a recording of a violin. ("Is it live or is it..."*) Audiophile systems begin around $2,500 and go into the stratosphere. (You can, without trying too hard or being thought silly, spend $30,000 on an Audiophile system.)

Audiophiles ask, "Does it sound real?" Hi-Fi's ask, "Does it sound good?" Lo-Fi's ask, "Is it sound?"

Audiophiles tend to listen to classical music and jazz. It's almost the only music nowadays that's still performed live without amplification. You can listen to a recording of an acoustic guitar and compare it with the memory of a "live" acoustic guitar, but who knows what an electric guitar is supposed to sound like? The sound of an electric guitar changes with each different guitar amplifier and speaker.

Hi-Fi's often like rock and pop. The world of rock and pop is populated with instruments for which there are no live performance reference standards — lead and bass guitar, synthesizer, electric piano, even voices. (When was the last time you heard an unamplified voice singing?) As there are no standards, there is no sense of right and wrong — it's subjective; whatever sounds best is best.

---

* It is ironic that Memorex should use the Audiophile's creed as their sales slogan. Memorex is owned by Radio Shack, Temple of Lo-Fi. But then Pillsbury owns Haagen Dazs and Campbell Soup owns Godiva Chocolates.

Audio

Lo-Fi's are happy if they can tell the difference between a banjo and a pipe organ and the difference between Frank Sinatra and Slim Pickens.

Audiophiles have reference standards. The devout make it a point to attend live concerts whenever possible, not just for the love of the music, but so that they have something to compare recordings to. A good recording is an *accurate* recording. A good system is one that recreates a live performance. You should be able to close your eyes and pick out individual instruments, precisely placed in space. ("Imaging" they call it.) A piccolo should be as loud as a piccolo truly is, a timpani as loud as a live timpani, and no louder.

Hi-Fi enthusiastics worship in rock concerts and discos. (I'm showing my age — they're called "clubs" now, aren't they?) Hi-Fi's want to *lean* into the sound. Sound should come from everywhere. It should be *loud.*

Lo-Fi's are happy if it's loud enough to hear.

One reason Audiophiles pursue their quest with religious fervor is because, in all likelihood, no matter how much they spend in terms of time, money and resources, they will not reach their goal of absolutely accurate reproduction in this lifetime. A recorded violin never quite sounds like a live violin. Perfection is just beyond one's grasp. The most one can hope for is excellence, and in the Church of the Divine Audiophile, excellence is defined as The State of the Art.

One of the high priests of Audiophilia, and a friend for the past fifteen-or-so years, is Robert Coyle. I met Robert when he ran the audio department of a shady camera store near the UCLA campus. Robert had two rooms for demonstrating equipment. One he called the dorm room. This was for selling high-profit Hi-Fi equipment to undiscriminating med students.

The other had no name, but we called it Robert's room. Here, if he liked you (and Robert likes everyone who likes good sound), Robert would set you up with a better system than the dorm-dwellers could ever appreciate — and usually for less money.

Not that Robert was a snob. I remember going in one day on my regular What's-New expedition and Robert pushed across the counter a small tape recorder with tiny headphones.

"Oh, come on," I said, dismissing at once that anything even remotely pleasant could come from such a small package.

"Try it," Robert coaxed. Only because I hate to be thought of as prejudiced, although I am, I put on the headphones. It was spectacular. Within an hour I was waltzing down the street with my first of many Walkmans.

Over the years I bought from Robert many things I didn't think I wanted, but I did.

A few years ago, Robert left the shady camera store and bought Shelley's Stereo, a shady stereo store in Santa Monica, California. He proceeded to revamp it into an unpretentious Audiophile Wayside Chapel.

His following followed him from the parameters of UCLA to the ocean, and soon Robert was able to open a veritable Temple of Audio in Canoga Park. Still cozy and cluttered (Robert is as much an absent-minded professor as priest), the Canoga Park Shelley's boasts not one, not two, not three, but *four* listening rooms. Each room features higher and higher end equipment. Those suffering from audio acrophobia feel a bit dizzy by the time they reach Room Four.

Robert gave me the tour, and then we went to lunch. The background music in the restaurant was sub-Lo-Fi. It was even sub-Muzak. (Lily Tomlin: "I worry about things. I worry that the man who invented Muzak is busy inventing something else.") The tape was worn and out of pitch. Terribly out of pitch. The sound was so bad that the people at the next table asked if it could be turned off.

The highlights of the lunch (in addition to the Italian sausage, which was wonderful) were:

★ There is a difference between Japanese design and North American design. Japanese design tends to be Hi-Fi. Canadian and United States design tend to be Audiophile. Here we're talking about design and not manufacturing because almost all manufacturing of electronics — Lo-Fi, Hi-Fi or Audiophile — happens outside North America.

★ Although the U.S. lost the manufacturing of electronics to the Japanese in the sixties, the manufacture of speakers is still an active endeavor in the Americas. This is especially true of Audiophile speakers, and it seems to happen primarily on the East Coast. (Advent, AR and Boston Acoustics.) This, Robert thinks, is because Europe — and especially the British Isles — tend to be Audiophiles, while the Japanese tend to be Hi-Files. England is closer to New England, hence the influence. The West Coast speaker manufacturers, influenced by Japan, tend to make Hi-Fi speakers. (Altec, JBL.)

★ Robert does not use the term Audiophile; he uses "musical," or sometimes "natural." The opposite of musical is "theatrical," what I'm calling "Hi-Fi." When he says, "That's a musical amplifier," he means, "This amplifier accurately reproduces the music." When he says, "That's a theatrical speaker," he means, "It's not accurate reproduction, but it puts on a good show."

★ Robert does not accept the idea that a Hi-Fi system is better for rock 'n' rollers. An audiophile system (or, "A very musical system," as he would put it) is best for *all* listening. Although there are no reference standards for what an amplified guitar should sound like, the producers of the *recording* decided it should sound a certain way when they mixed it. Robert claims that this original artistic intention is best recreated on an accurate system.

★ Digital sound has divided the Audiophiles right down the middle. This is the most important ecumenical split since the tube vs. transistor division of the 1960's, which was as significant, from an Audiophile point of view, as the Church of England splitting from the Church of Rome. Some say digital is not real music — they can *hear* and *feel* the difference. Others say digital sounds great, and sound is what it's all about. (*Every* Hi-Fier *loves* CD's). Robert believes analog recordings offer a more dimensional sound, with more depth and warmth, than CD's. He is not, however, anti-CD. He is aware that records are a delicate medium and without extraordinary care records sound worse and worse with each playing. CD's, with only reasonable care, will sound "new" forever.

★ Audiophiles are having more and more trouble getting good recordings. Audiophiles, you see, like to pretend they're in a concert hall, or an antechamber at Versailles. The *music* should come from the front and the *echoes* (Audiophiles prefer to call it "reverberation" or "ambience") should come from everywhere else. After all, in a concert hall, the music comes from the front, the reverberation from throughout the hall. This creates a concert hall ambience, all of which is part of accurate music. Recording engineers, it seems, like to use microphone-placement techniques that make this impossible to achieve. A piano is only, say, five feet wide. In solo piano recordings, engineers will often record the bass notes on the left channel, the treble notes on the right channel, and all the other notes spread out in between. This might give you the feeling that you're sitting at the piano, or even *inside* the piano, but it hardly gives you the feeling of listening to a piano sonata at Carnegie Hall. Poor audiophiles. They spend all this money on accuracy, and they are victimized by these damn Hi-Fi, sensation-hungry, theatrically-dominated engineers.

★ Contrary to popular belief, an audiophile system, according to Robert, need not cost any more than a good Hi-Fi system. Here the operative word is "good." A mediocre Hi-Fi system — in that Twilight Zone where Lo-Fi and Hi-Fi commingle — might only cost a few hundred dollars, and one would be hard-pressed putting together an Audiophile system for that. But when you go into the higher end of Hi-Fi, you're at the lower end of Aud-Fi. Based upon the principle that one pound of filet mignon is preferable to four pounds of hamburger, Robert recommends the less flashy, more accurate Audiophile system.

Dollar for dollar in Audiophile, you don't get as much to impress your friends. I remember going to Robert several years ago with $300 and the desire for a new amplifier. Back then $300 bought 75 watts per channel and lots of fancy features controlled by fancy controls that looked awfully impressive. Robert sold me a NAD with, as I recall, 20 watts per channel. The front panel was austere, bordering on monastic. But it sounded great. Musical, as Robert would say.

The same is true of turntables, speakers, tape decks, all the rest. You get more features and more raw power for your Hi-Fi dollar. You get more precise sound in a more subdued, less feature-hungry package with Audiophile.

hen deciding "Which Am I?" you need to ask yourself, "What do I really enjoy?" Is it important when you listen to the Beatles that you hear precisely what George Martin intended (Audiophile), or do you prefer to be dazzled by the highs and moved (or should I say vibrated) by the lows? (Hi-Fi.) Or do you just want to hear the songs and remember what you were doing back in the sixties? (Lo-Fi.)

Personally, I spend time in all camps. Sometimes I'm Lo-Fi. I just want music — a $50 radio-cassette player is all I need in the garage. Recordings of music from the twenties and thirties — of which I have a particular fondness — often sound better coming from a $100 boombox (or Personal Portable Stereo, as the manufacturers prefer). Its limitations seem to be the same limitations of the recordings of that era. On better systems, the scratches, clicks and surface noise of the original recordings are more prominent. Also keep in mind that for $300 today, you get a system that sounds better than Audiophiles spent thousands for back in the early 1950's — and that's thousands of 1950's dollars. Lo-Fi systems are also good for spoken word recordings.

Hi-Fi sound I find particularly enjoyable while watching television. When watching TV I am, after all, there to be entertained, and, if possible, dazzled. Hi-Fi equipment does this extraordinarily well. If you're a party kind of person, and want to dance, dance, dance, Hi-Fi is for you. I also like Hi-Fi in the car. I like my seat to vibrate with every drum beat.

For listening to music, I find Audiophile, although not as initially flashy as Hi-Fi, far less fatiguing. I can listen to my Audiophile system for hours. It doesn't tax me. In fact, it revives me. A few minutes of Bach or Haydn or Mozart — or even Judy Collins — and I'm a new human.

In the digital-analog debate, I urge you to listen to the same recording in both analog and digital and see if you can tell a difference. I can tell a difference. Whenever a difference can be perceived, some people will prefer one and some prefer another. I respect either choice.

But the first and last words of advice are *listen*. Can you hear a difference? Which difference do you prefer? And, honestly, is the difference worth more money?

Chapter Three

Audio Components

o-Fi's buy their audio components all in one lump. Hi-Fi's buy them in various configurations — sometimes all from the same manufacturer, sometimes not; at the very least, the exteriors match. Audiophiles buy their components in discrete units, one component seldom looking like any other, and certainly no two from the same manufacturer.

Preamplifier or **preamp.** This takes a weak audio signal and amplifies it sufficiently for the power amplifier to amplify it a lot more.

Power Amplifier or **power amp**. This, as advertised, amplifies the preamplified signal from the preamplifier and makes it real loud. Usually the preamp and the power amp are combined in one unit called an **integrated amplifier**. The output of an amplifier is measured in watts. For Hi-Fiers, the more watts, the better. For Audiophiles, the less distortion, the better.

Tuner. This tunes FM (and sometimes AM) radio broadcasts. When preamp, power amp and tuner are combined, it's known as a **receiver**.

Speakers or **loud-speakers.** From these come the sound. They are connected to the amplifier or receiver and usually come in pairs, one for each stereo channel.

Cartridge or **Phono Cartridge.** The cartridge holds the needle (in Lo-Fi systems) or the stylus (in Hi-Fi and Audiophile systems) and transfers the microscopic wiggles in the record groove into electrical impulses. (How many grooves are there on one side of a 33 1/3 rmp record with a playing time of 28 minutes? Answer below.)

Tonearm. The tonearm holds the cartridge and guides it across the record.

Turntable. The tonearm fits on the turntable. The turntable turns the records round and around.

Audio Components

Enough explanations. Let's sing! (To the tune of "Dem Bones.")

Oh, the stylus is connected to the cartridge.
The cartridge is connected to the tonearm.
The tonearm is connected to the turntable.
And the records go round and round.

The turntable is connected to the preamp.
The preamp is connected to the amplifier.
The amplifier is connected to the speakers.
And the music goes round and round.

Enough singing. Back to explanations. In addition to what might be considered a basic system (above), other popular components include:

Cassette Deck. Plays and records cassette tapes.

Compact Disc (CD) Player. No surprises here: it plays CD's.

Digital Audio Tape (DAT) Deck. A DAT tape is about half the size of a cassette and holds almost twice as much music as a CD. DAT decks allow you to record and playback digitally.

Subwoofers. The woofer in a speaker produces the low notes. (Maybe so named because when a dog goes "woof-woof" it's at the lower register of his or her bark.) A *sub*woofer produces *very* low notes — the bottom of the audible spectrum from 20 to 200 Hz (cycles per second). You don't so much *hear* these sounds as you *feel* them.

Headphones. These are little speakers. They sit on either side of your head. You can hear your music real loud, and everyone else around you doesn't.

(Answer to earlier question: All records have only *one* groove per side—one very long groove.)

Audio Components

Then there are the **Sound Processors.** These alter the sound in one way or another, the goal of which is to create more natural sound (for Audiophiles) or more spectacular sound (for Hi-Fiers). Among the popular sound processors are...

Reverberation. These are not the echo chambers of the sixties. When I was in high school, to have a reverb unit in your car was really cool. (To have a car was cool; to have a reverb unit was supercool.) The front speakers had the music, the rear speakers had the echo. It sounded like listening to an AM radio at the bottom of a deep well. Sometimes the delay was so great that the people in the front seat were listening to a different song than the people in the back. The delay in sound between the front speakers and the rear speakers is now measured in milliseconds, not minutes. The goal: to produce the ambience of a concert hall.

Equalizers. These divide the audible spectrum into a number of segments (usually from five to twenty) with a control for each segment. If the bass isn't enough, you can turn it up — and not just the bass, but precise segments of the bass. If it's too much, you can turn it down. You have the same command over the midrange and highs. Audiophiles use equalizers to compensate for various room inadequacies (the acoustically perfect living room has yet to be built). They use it to make the system sound as "natural" as possible. Hi-Fiers love the power, the control. "Listen to *this*!" they'll say while cranking up the bass.

Surround. These are variations of the Dolby theater sound system which extracts four channels from stereo's usual two. Three of the channels go to the front of the room (left, right and center) and the fourth channel is shared between two speakers in the rear. This is specifically designed for Dolby Stereo movies and TV shows (almost all major movies of the past seven years are in Dolby Stereo), but it also makes regular TV watching and music listening more enjoyable — in a dramatic, theatrical sense.

T he following chapters will explore each of these components in more detail, with the exception of Surround Sound and other sound processors, which I put in the Video section, (*Hi-Fi TV*, Chapter 14). Surround Sound is such a merging of sights and sounds, it's easier to discuss it in both audio and video terms.

Chapter Four

Amplifiers, Tuners, Receivers and Radios

nless you're a confirmed Audiophile, what you'll probably buy is a receiver — one unit incorporating preamplifier, amplifier and tuner. It's logical to combine these three, as they all work together and are likely to last about the same length of time (which, for most of today's electronics with no moving parts, is almost forever).

A preamplifier and amplifier in one unit is known as an integrated amplifier, but is usually just called an amplifier. (It's easy to tell an amplifier *without* a preamplifier — there are no controls on it, except maybe a master power switch. All the knobs and switches we associate with amplifiers are connected to the preamplified section of the unit.)

Here are some of the features available on integrated amplifiers . . .

Watts. The power of an amplifier is measured in watts — the more watts, the more volume the amplifier can produce. Actually, you can create ear-damaging volume levels with just a few watts, but the double- and even triple-

53

digit wattage ratings are sometimes necessary for peak power demands.

Let's say you're playing a violin solo. Your amplifier might be (depending on your speakers) consuming only four or five watts. Then, suddenly, the cymbals crash and the timpani booms. That demands a lot more power, and *fast*. The total wattage consumption might jump to thirty watts, or more. If you have, say, a twenty-watt amplifier, the violin will sound great, but at the peak of the timpani's power demand, you will hear distortion.

It's not just for the loud passages that people buy more watts than they "need." The closer an amplifier comes to its maximum power rating, the greater the harmonic distortion. If an amplifier is rated at, say, .05% harmonic distortion at 50 watts, it may only have .005% at 20 watts. If people overbuy their watts, they know everything they play — from the softest to the loudest — will be well below the amplifier's rated output, therefore the harmonic distortion will be even less than that touted in the amplifier's specifications.

For the most part, 25 to 35 watts per channel is plenty. If you plan to drive more than one set of speakers, if the speakers you drive are inefficient (the less power it takes to drive a speaker the more "efficient" it is said to be), or if you plan to drive an unamplified subwoofer (the low end of the audible spectrum consumes much more power than the midrange and high ends), you may need more.

Inputs. Most amplifiers have inputs for a turntable, a tape deck, a tuner and an aux. (In the old days you got forty acres and a mule. Now you get three inputs and an aux.) Aux stands for auxiliary, meaning you can plug whatever into it you want.

The more expensive amplifiers feature a second tape input (and provisions for copying between the two decks), a second phono input, and a CD input. Most people plug their CD players into the aux input, but a true CD input is different and is recommended for "serious" CD users. ("You mean in order to get a CD input I have to get a new amp?!" Welcome to the world of personal electronics.)

Speaker Outputs. All amplifiers, of course, have outputs for at least one pair of speakers. Some allow you to connect a second or even third pair; you can then select which pair or pairs are in use at any given time.

Headphone Output. Most amplifiers have these with the exception of some of the lowest low end and the highest high end. (Lo-Fi's and Audiophiles agree on one thing: minimalism. Less is best.)

Remote Control. Just what we need, another remote control unit. It does come in handy, however, when the phone rings, or when switching from, say, tape to CD. It's also remarkably useful when setting tone and volume controls. To make these adjustments from where you'll be *listening* to the music makes sense.

Tuners

T here's not much to think about when buying a tuner (or the tuner section of a receiver). Just a few years ago, when you had to turn a dial to get from one station to another, there were various meters to help you tune in the station you sought.

Now, thanks to digital tuning, we don't "fine tune" anymore. It's one of those phrases today's children will use but never know where it came from. (Digital time has destroyed the concept of "clockwise," for example.) Digital tuners lock precisely on the station. Now you dial the station like a TV channel, and that's it.

What puzzles me is why more tuners don't have numeric keypads so you can "touch in" the station you want. Scanning up and down the dial is dull. If you want 90.7, why not just touch "9" "0" "." and "7"? A freely offered Improvement Opportunity from Yours Truly to all tuner manufacturers.

Radio

What can I say about something as ubiquitous and inexpensive as radio? They're everywhere, in every size, shape and color. And they're cheap, $2.99 and up, except when they're on sale.

What can I say that everybody doesn't already know? We all know there are two kinds of broadcast radio, AM and FM. We all know FM is better quality but AM radios are cheaper. We all know you can get AM/FM in almost any portable configuration imaginable, or built into almost every other portable listening device (Walkman, CD player, TV, etc.).

Short of giving a history of radio — which would have absolutely nothing to do with buying a radio today — what can I say?

I can't think of a thing.

The town of Windham, Connecticut (population 21,000) has begun a new tradition: The Boombox Parade. It seems the high school couldn't afford to put together a band, and one embarrassing Memorial Day the Women's Auxiliary went marching down the street in total silence. To remedy the situation, for the 4th of July, the local radio station offered to play Sousa Marches and invited everyone with a portable radio to join in the parade. 1,500 citizens showed up, with everything from Walkmen to 1930's tube sets. It was dubbed The Boombox Parade, and has now become a semiannual tradition.

Amplifiers, Tuners, Receivers and Radios

NAD

For the past dozen or so years, NAD has been worshiped by people with Audiophile tastes and Panasonic budgets. Their $300 amp/preamp units have rivaled $1,500 amp/preamp separates in accuracy of sound. For Audiophiles, dollar for dollar, NAD is generally considered the best value in electronics.

Now NAD is challenging the higher-end Audiophile manufacturers with its Monitor Series. It includes the NAD 1300 preamp ($498), the NAD 2600 power amp ($748) and the NAD 4300 tuner ($548). (Also included in the Monitor Series is the NAD 6300 tape deck, reviewed in the chapter on cassettes.)

This comes to $1,794 for three pieces that equal a tuner; not quite, it seems, in the NAD tradition of low cost. But the operative word for NAD is value, not low cost. NAD claims, and many Audiophiles agree (well, *some* Audiophiles agree — the only thing *many* Audiophiles agree on is that most other Audiophiles don't know what they're talking about), the $1,794 Monitor Series equals many Audiophile components in the $5,000 range.

NAD equipment is designed in England, Mecca of Audiophile engineering, and manufactured in the Far East, home of cheap labor. This is the secret of NAD's value. It's a combination that's gotten them a lot of budget-conscious Audiophile fans, myself among them.

Nakamichi SR4-A Receiver

Nakamichi equipment is designed in the United States (subMecca of Audiophile engineering) and manufactured in Japan (home of quality electronics manufacturing). The combination is a good one.

The SR4-A receiver is a case in point. For $895 you get it all — preamp, amp, tuner — and a remote control to boot. The SR4-A has 60 watts of power per channel. For those with less money and/or power needs, Nakamichi makes two models that are virtually identical to the SR4-A except for power and price. The SR3-A has 45 watts per channel and costs $650. The SR2-A offers 30 watts per channel and retails for $449.

The remote controls volume, power, AM or FM reception, and allows selecting of ten preset stations, or tuning any other station by tuning up or down the dial. Unfortunately, the remote does not switch modes, so you cannot switch from, say, FM to CD or tape inputs without arising. An odd omission for such an otherwise well-designed and wonderful sounding receiver. (Audiophiles claim mode switching should not be done by remote. Maybe that explains the omission.)

dbx BX1 Power Amplifier

You say you like power, do you? How does 800 watts sound? Somehow I have images of turning this on, the lights dimming, and somebody saying in the darkness, "They just burned the kid."

The dbx BX1 can be configured for two-channel, three channel (two stereo channels and a subwoofer, typically), or four channel (Surround Sound, for example) environments. It's unfortunate it doesn't divide into six channels, which is optimum for Dolby Surround. (Left, right, center, left rear, right rear and subwoofer. Please see Chapter 14, *Hi-Fi TV*.) It seems to have plenty of power to power it all.

At $2,500 it's not cheap, but for Audiophiles and Hi-Fi's who want power and lots of it, the Maserati of amplifiers has arrived.

Chapter Five

Turntables, Tonearms and Cartridges

s you move up the Hi-Fi spectrum, the "record playing" portion of the system tends to become more and more specialized.

At the lower levels of Hi-Fi, the record player comes complete with turntable, tonearm and cartridge. If it has a provision for records to crash on top of one another in a moderately controlled fashion, this is called a **changer**.

The next level up, the turntable and tonearm continue together, but the cartridge is now an "extra added accessory." (The changer device often will continue to prevail.)

As the levels continue higher, the changer mechanism departs (and here the Audiophiles can open their eyes, for the very sight of a changer sets off waves of revulsion, horror and fear in an Audiophile's heart) and the need for a cartridge continues.

As one enters the DMZ between high-end Hi-Fi and Audiophile, the tonearm is separated from the turntable, and one must now make three selections.

In AudiophileLand, there is never a question. *Of course* one selects one's turntable, tonearm and cartridge separately — just as one buys underwear, pants and shirt separately — usually from three separate companies.

But, you may ask, why bother with a *good* record playing device? Aren't records on the way out? Aren't Digital Audio Tape and Compact Discs the wave of the future?

Yes, probably they are. Which, to my way of thinking, makes the selection of the record playing device all the more important — at least to us Baby Boomers who have record collections, and who want to listen to something not popular enough to be reissued on CD's.

Have you thought what it might cost to replace your record collection? Oh, sure, you paid $3.59 for a Mothers of Invention album back in the early seventies, you might have even gotten it at close-out in the mid-seventies for 99 cents — but do you know what that album is worth today, used? Somewhere between $50 and $75.

And that's not just Frank Zappa collectibles, either. *A lot* of albums have found their way out of print but not out of affection. Affection equals rapid inflation, and records have joined fine art and baseball cards as prized collectibles.

The better the turntable, tonearm and cartridge, the longer your (now valuable) records will last.

There is, of course, an upper limit. I'm sure a $2,000 turntable-tonearm-cartridge combination is as gentle on records as a $5,000 T-T-C (although certain Audiophiles would argue the point). But I'm also sure that a $2,000 T-T-C is easier on records than a $200 turntable, tonearm and cartridge.

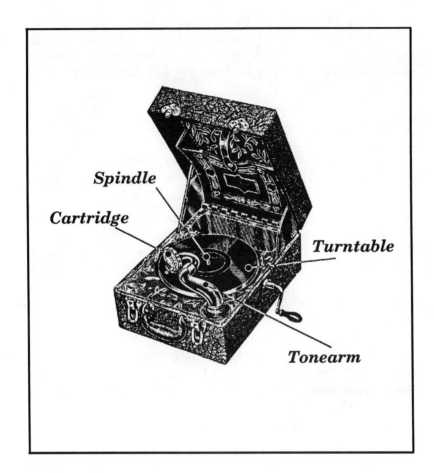

Spindle

Cartridge

Turntable

Tonearm

Buying a cartridge is a lot like buying speakers. Almost all cartridges today reproduce the audible range from 20 to 20,000 Hz. But each cartridge, like each speaker, has its own sound, and choosing which sound you prefer is your personal, subjective choice.

Keep in mind that the turntable and tonearm affects the way a cartridge sounds. If you listen to a $50 cartridge on a $2,000 turntable with a $2,000 tonearm, it's going to sound different (most would say better) than when played on a $200 changer.

If you consider your turntable-tonearm-cartridge purchase as *one unit*, you'll probably make a better choice. As you increase what you're willing to spend, spread the increase around between the units. Putting a $1,000 cartridge in a $200 changer is as foolish as putting a $20 cartridge in a $2,000 tonearm-turntable unit.

As your T-T-and-C is an important purchase, it might be worth investing some money in new records when you take various configurations for a test-listen. You'll be playing the same passages over and over (please see the suggestions on how to buy speakers on page 107) comparing one cartridge with another. Repeated playing tends to break down the record's vinyl.

Purists say you should play a record no more than once in 24 hours. This gives a chance for the vinyl to recombobulate itself. The purist's theory is that vinyl gets hot when the stylus comes tearing through the grooves, and this changes the shape of the groove walls. Repeated playings exacerbate this process, and the quality of sound diminishes with each playing.

With this in mind, it might be a good idea to buy, say, five copies of your favorite record and change copies during the test. When finished, you'll have the T-T-C of your dreams, plus five Christmas presents. ("This is my *favorite* album. I just *knew* you'd like it.")

I n all this talk of turntables, tonearms and cartridges, remember that the better the system, the more flaws it will reveal in your current record collection. It will reproduce the music more accurately, but it will also reproduce every scratch, dust molecule and fragment of tortilla dip on every record you own.

If you have been, shall we say, *casual* in your treatment of records (you know who you are), and almost all the new recordings you buy are tapes or CD's, getting a great turntable, tonearm and cartridge might prove an expensive curse.

You might want to bring along some of your ordinary, everyday records to the stereo store and see what they sound like on good equipment. You may wince and go home, happy with what you've got.

On the other hand, the salesperson may put a record you thought gone forever on a record cleaning machine and, when purged of its evil past by the laying on and vacuuming off of cleaning solvents, you may be surprised with the life in that old vinyl.

Thorens TD520 Turntable and Tonearm

Why, of all the turntables on God's earth, did I choose to review this one? Because it's one of the few that still plays 78's. My 78 collection is small but meaningful — *South Pacific*, signed by Mary Martin; Virgil Thomson's *Four Saints in Three Acts*, signed by the composer and Beatrice Wayne Godfrey, the original St. Teresa; *The Alexander Nevsky Suite*, signed by no one, but wonderful just the same; plus a handful of single 78's picked up at second hand stores over the years.

Not that the Thorens is *just* a 78 turntable. Far from it. It plays the modern slower speeds, too. (But not 16-2/3, darn it. I have this wonderful recording of Ben Franklin's autobiography that I haven't heard in fifteen years — the last time I had a 16-2/3 turntable.) $999.

The Thorens turntable and arm is a fully-qualified Audiophile turntable. (For an even more fully-qualified turntable, please see the SOTA STAR Sapphire review in Chapter 11.)

Shure Cartridges

When I was younger, so much younger than today, I thought Shure cartridges were as far as you could go in audio. Now I have discovered multi-thousand dollar cartridges, but a part of my heart still belongs to Shure.

Frankly, if you don't take the time to clean your records before each playing, you probably need a Shure. The brush in the front removes much of the dust records tend to collect just by being records. If you're going to mess with high-end Audiophile cartridges (see Chapter 11), *please* clean your records properly before each use. If you somehow know you're not going to do that, get a Shure.

Turntables, Tonearms and Cartridges

The top-of-the-line Shure is the V15 V-B. It costs $237.50, which seems like a fortune for those used to spending less than $237.50 on a whole *system*, but is the Bargain of the Century in Audiophile circles.

A bit lower down the Shure family tree, but a fine cartridge nonetheless, is the V15-HRP ($100). When outfitted with the N78E stylus ($34.95), it plays 78's — beautifully.

The N78E stylus is especially designed for 78's. The groove on a 78 record is several times wider than the groove of a regular LP. If you try to play a 78 with a regular stylus, (A) you run the risk of damaging the stylus, and (B) the stylus plays the information at the *bottom* of the 78 groove, which is usually dirt.

With the Shure N78E stylus, the stylus tracks the information on the *sides* of the groove, where all the information was put in the first place.

It's truly amazing how good 78's sound when played on the Thorens with the Shure cartridge — especially when cleaned on the Nitty Gritty Record Cleaner (see Chapter 18, *Audio and Video Accessories*.) I've begun to haunt second hand stores looking for 78's again. With the exception of recordings by major stars and some big hits, it's a lost era of American music.

WE ARE NOW PREPARED
TO SUPPLY THE

EDISON

TALKING

DOLL

EDISON'S
TALKING DOLL.

TO THE TRADE
ONLY.

For Wholesale Price and Terms, Address

EDISON PHONOGRAPH TOY MFG. CO.,

No. 138 FIFTH AVENUE,

NEW YORK.

[1890]

Doesn't look a <u>bit</u> like Edison to me.

Chapter Six

Cassettes

assette tapes are the most popular listening medium today. The humble cassette cuts across all lines — Lo-Fi's, Hi-Fi's and Audiophiles all use them and enjoy them. The higher-end Hi-Fi's and the digital's-fine-with-me Audiophiles are starting to use Compact Discs more and more, but Lo-Fi's shake their heads and wonder, "Why are they spending $14 for the same album they can get for $6.89?"

Cassette tape's ongoing popularity is easy to understand. They're small, portable, relatively inexpensive, almost indestructible, recordable, and any cassette will play on any cassette machine.

When shopping for a cassette player — be it a deck to add to your home stereo system, a portable "boombox," a Walkman or a player for the car — here are some of the terms you're likely to run across:

Dolby. Dolby is the noise reduction system that made cassettes popular for music reproduction. Prior to Dolby, most people thought the high-frequency hiss inherent in cassettes would forever limit the format to voice reproduction. The Dolby system reduced the hiss to such an extent that Hi-Fiers took to it immediately, and Audiophiles eventually.

Dolby is a patented process, so every machine you buy with the Dolby system will cost a bit more than without. It has become such a standard, however, that it may be difficult to find "without."

There are basically two Dolbys, "Dolby B" and "Dolby C." Dolby C does a better job of reducing hiss than Dolby B. Dolby B is the standard — when a cassette tape says "DOLBY" it means Dolby B. For most Hi-Fi uses, Dolby B is sufficient.

Dolby B is also more compatible with non-Dolby players than Dolby C. If you play a Dolby B tape on a non-Dolby player, you may hear an extenuated brightness at the high end, but that's about it. A Dolby C tape played on a non-Dolby player will sound more distorted than a Dolby B tape. If you use your tapes interchangeably — car, Walkman, home — and don't have Dolby C everywhere, Dolby B is the way to go.

Lo-Fi's could care less about Dolby: After the first few seconds, your ears adjust and you don't hear the hiss anyway — providing the machine used is capable of reproducing the upper end on which hiss is found. Hi-Fi's love Dolby — wouldn't play a tape without it. Audiophiles insist on Dolby C, and many like . . .

dbx. dbx (always lower case) is a superior system to either Dolby B or C, but it has two drawbacks. First, in the Battle of the Standards fought a few years ago between Dolby and dbx, Dolby won. Second, a dbx tape played on a non-dbx player sounds not-very-good. Lo-Fi's would never know the difference, but everybody else would.

These two limitations aside, dbx is great. You can add a dbx encoder/decoder to any home stereo system, and a few high-end car systems offer dbx as an option. If your music is car and home, and you're an Audiophile, dbx is certainly worth investigating.

Another problem for both Dolby and dbx is that, within a few years, *both* will be obsolete. Digital sound is so pure it doesn't require any noise reduction. Even the analog

Hi-Fi soundtrack of video recorders is so good, Dolby and dbx have not been invited along for the ride. Digital Audio Tapes (see page 99) will eventually replace cassettes, and our children will one day ask us, "What was Dolby?" Perhaps archaeologists will think the □□ Dolby symbol was the sign of a widespread but short-lived twentieth-century religion.

Metal. Metal refers to the type of microscopic particles that are glued onto the plastic tape inside the cassette. I have no idea where the term "metal" came from. In truth, *all* of the particles on *all* recording tape are metal. The metal is used to capture magnetic vibrations. The first was iron oxide, better known as rust. (Some tapes are rust-colored because they *are* rust.) Every few years, a new hot-shot alloy is found to replace good old iron and its chemical formulation is usually given. The favorite just before "metal" was chromium dioxide (CrO_2).

Each new formulation requires a special electronic compensation. Although a metal tape can be played back on a non-metal player, it sounds better on a metal-capable machine.

Lo-Fi's: don't even *think* about metal. Hi-Fi's: it'll impress your friends — go for it. Audiophiles: but, of course.

Automatic Tape Select. The machine decides which type of tape you are using (normal, CrO_2 or metal) and selects the appropriate setting automatically. If your cassette collection is like mine — spanning nearly twenty years, disorganized and haphazardly labeled — it's a good feature to have.

Automatic Reverse. I personally consider this essential. Why on earth, in this high-tech age, should we have to go to the tape machine every 45 minutes (20 minutes on prerecorded tapes) and turn over a tape? Some people, of course, consider this a necessary discipline. I've heard of one man who will only listen to 78 rpm recordings. This is not because he likes the sound of 78's, but because he feels getting up every five minutes to change the record keeps his mind focused on the music. (If he uses a wind-up Victrola I suppose he also feels he's *earned* his five minutes.)

Auto reverse does cost more, so it may not appeal to the low-budget Lo-Fi's, but the Hi-Fi's love it. Some Audiophiles think it screws up something called the azimuth. (The recording heads must be in perfect alignment, and the auto-reverse mechanism ever so slightly misaligns this alignment.) One Audiophile auto-reverse deck (Nakamichi) actually removes the tape from the player, turns it over, and puts it back, all within less than a second. This creates an irony: The most expensive and the least expensive decks don't offer auto reverse — all the others do. Once again, Lo-Fi and Audiophiles meet on the plain of minimalism.

Double Decks. This is the feature that drives the recording industry up a wall, over the edge and into depression. It's basically two transport mechanisms side by side that allow you to play one tape after another (the recording industry doesn't mind this) or record from one tape to another (the recording industry minds this very much).

Double-deck machines make copies of tapes faster because they record both sides of the cassette at the same time. In addition, many of them have a speedup feature. This speedup feature reduces quality a bit, but for Lo-Fi's (the most ardent users of double decks), who cares? Most Hi-Fi's would rather have a first generation copy (directly from a record or a CD), and Audiophiles wouldn't dream of listening to the quality (or lack thereof) of a tape dubbed from a tape on a double-deck recorder.

Walkmans

I do believe I invented the Walkman. I bought the first battery-operated stereo cassette player available. (This was in the late sixties.) Cassettes were then not considered a serious medium for recorded sound. They were for speech — talking books, dictation and the like. The unit had speakers, but no headphone jack. It was designed, I think, for executive dictation and playback. The stereo was just to make a vice president feel important. "I'm dictating in stereo." I removed the speakers and, with a little soldering, was able to attach headphones.

These were not your standard Walkman headphones. These were large, listen-at-home type headphones. Come to think of it, the cassette player was on the large side, too. Not bigger than a breadbox (did you know that Steve Allen coined that phrase, spontaneously, on *What's My Line? Remember What's My Line?* My age is showing. Back to my invention), but it would fit inside a breadbox without room for very many loaves of Wonder Bread.

I would walk down the street, carrying my attache case cassette player, wearing my large, black headphones. I looked like an executive Mouseketeer. And the *looks* I got from people. I mean, this is how Martians were represented on the *Late, Late Show*. But music was more important to me than fitting in. (Truth be told, not fitting in was more important to me than fitting in. I couldn't grow my hair as long as I wanted — it was curly and got tangled after a few months. I had to cut off the tangles, which made me look like a poodle who tried to mate with a power mower, so I'd cut it all off and start over. My headphones allowed me to not fit in without having to use conditioner every morning.)

The sound was not spectacular. The teeny amplifier on the deck was not designed to drive the massive headphones. And, as I mentioned, cassette tapes were not a Hi-Fi medium back then. But it was stereo, and it was portable, and I was the only one who had one.

Ten years later, everybody was doing it, thanks to the Walkman. For this advancement alone I think Sony should be awarded the Nobel Peace Prize. Remember, if you will, those dark and noisy days just prior to the introduction of the Walkman. The days of the Ghetto Blaster.

I lived then in New York on a one-way street going in a direction no one seemed to want to go. It was quiet there. Peaceful, by New York standards. But in early 1979, a war was in progress. At least once an hour, every hour, 24 hours a day, the tranquility of our block was shattered by CHUN-KA CHUN-KA CHUN-KA thrusting away at 128 beats per minute.

There were block meetings. There were contingencies sent to City Hall. There were demands for laws banning "oversized, portable sound reproduction devices." There

The first boombox — The Decca portable phonograph.

were incidents. There were police reports. There were lots and lots of nasty looks.

And then came the Walkman. It was cheaper than a Ghetto Blaster, more portable, and had better sound. Within six months, all was quiet again. A perfect high-tech solution to a war-like situation. If that isn't an accomplishment worthy of a Nobel Peace Prize, what is?

"Walkman" became generic faster than any word I can remember. Maybe "Hula Hoop" became generic faster, but I'm not old enough to remember. Regardless of manufacturer, everyone calls their portable-tape-player-with-headphones a Walkman. (Although the WalkClone makers refer to them in print as "Personal Stereo" or "Portable Stereo" or some such; in real life they call them Walkmans, too.)

And Sony doesn't seem to be fighting it. When companies fight against their trade names becoming generic, you see a slew of ads with the word "brand" in the headline, so we all know their name is a Brand Name. The "brand" is then followed by the generic name we're all supposed to really use but, of course, never do — Sanka Brand Decaffeinated Coffee, Scrabble Brand Crossword Game, Monopoly Brand Real Estate Trading Game. Thus far I haven't seen many ads imploring me to buy a Walkman Brand Portable Personal Stereo. So, I'll use the term Walkman in its generic sense. (And in the next edition of this book I'll print the letter sent to me by Sony's attorneys correcting me for my incorrect use of a Brand Name.)

Certainly, by now, everyone who has any use for a Walkman has one. I don't think anyone's waiting for the price to drop any further. (Ten dollars gets a no-name import at a no-name import shop.) Certainly it can't be lack of availability. (Every credit card payment envelope tries to sell me a portable personal stereo.) And didn't *Time Brand News Magazine* give them away free with a paid subscription? (A woman would appear on my TV screen at four in the morning, wearing a headset and a $200 hairdo, holding up something that looked a lot like a Walkman, saying, "Hi! I'm Amy! I'm your *Time* operator! I have a free gift for you! I'll be right back!" Well, I'm afraid I never made it through the song, which began, as I recall, *"Time flies, and you are there./Time cries and lets you care."* This song went on longer than *In-A-Gadda-Da-Vida*, and by the 27th chorus, I had an irresistible desire to see what Joe Franklin was up to.)

So, if you're replacing your Walkman, here's a list of features currently available . . .

Dolby. Dolby is, of course, the noise reduction circuit licensed by Dolby Labs of San Francisco. (Now *they* have taken *good care* of their Trade Name.) It reduces the hiss inherent in cassette tapes. There are two Dolbys, "Dolby B" and "Dolby C". Dolby C reduces noise more than Dolby B, but Dolby C costs more — particularly on personal portable stereos. Most cassette tapes you buy are recorded in Dolby B. (If it doesn't say "Dolby C" it's automatically Dolby B.) Dolby B is probably a good idea for a Walkman; Dolby C only if most of your tapes are already recorded in that format.

Auto-Reverse. This is a great one (that is, I like this a lot). Fiddling with and turning over the tape every 45 minutes or so (twenty minutes on a prerecorded cassette) is just plain Not Fun. Some people (Audiophiles) claim you lose your azimuth when you use auto-reverse. Well, I've lost my azimuth lots of times, and I'd rather lose that than my patience.

Metal Capability. Metal tape is currently the hotshot recording medium. (Two years ago it was Chromium Dioxide and a few years before that it was Ferric Oxide and before that. . .) If you do want the best sound, record on metal tapes, and if you record on metal tapes, get a Walkman that can properly play metal tapes.

Radios. What can I say?

AC/Battery. If you use your Walkman in one place, the ability to run it off AC current will save you a fortune. Don't pay more than $10 for this feature, however, as an inexpensive AC-to-DC battery replacement transformer costs about that much.

Rechargeable. I like rechargeable electronics. Over time they tend to pay for themselves, and finding just the right battery (AA or AAA?) at just the right time is a chore. Be careful, though, when buying a personal portable labeled "Rechargeable." I bought a Walkman (a genuine Sony Walkman — Model WM-F100II) and it came with a rechargeable battery. Literally. You had to charge the battery (which looked like a stick of chewing gum) in a separate charger and then install it in the Walkman. Why not an AC/DC adapter that plugged in the wall and let the Walkman run off house current while it charged the battery?

Line Out. I've yet to find a Walkman (or clone) with this simple feature, but I'm including it as a feature because I can't imagine the higher-end models not having this as a standard feature in the near future. Line out means you can connect the Walkman directly to your stereo amplifier at home and the Walkman acts as a tape deck. It's an easy thing to add, can't cost much, and I'm sure some people would use them. (The first manufacturer who includes a Line Out in a Walkman or WalkClone gets an automatic mention in my newsletter and column.)

Headphones. There are basically three types of headphones that come with Walkmans (Walkmen?):

★ The "original" headphones — the kind with two foam-covered circles connected by a band of wire; the wire goes over your head, the circles over your ears. Of the included-with-cost-of-purchase variety (see **Headphones**, page 119, for Walkman add ons), this kind is my favorite.

★ Then there's the kind that retain the metal band, but the circles are smaller, not covered with foam, and fit *in* your ears. I find these uncomfortable to wear, and they don't block out as much external noise as the foam over-the-ears ones. (I use a Walkman for blocking out external noise as often as I use it for a little traveling music.)

★ And then there's the kind that have no metal band at all and fit *in* your ears. These keep falling *out* of my ears. But then, who knows? I may have funny ears.

Some people must like the latter two kinds of headphones. Try them all on and see which one you like best.

When testing a Walkman, bring a tape you are familiar with to play. Not only is it your kind of music, it's also *your tape.* How your tapes are going to sound in your new Walkman is what's important.

Boomboxes

Once called Ghetto Blasters, boomboxes have gotten awfully suburban as the years have bopped on. They are strictly Lo-Fi, so buy one based upon (1) price, (2) looks, (3) price, (4) looks, (5) price (6) sound, and (7) price.

The idea of including a CD in a boombox (at a $200 increase in price) is, to me, absurd. The speakers in a boombox are incapable of reproducing the extended range of a CD. Most boombox speakers don't even reproduce the whole range of a cassette tape. Further, the jolts and jars boomboxes are heir to play havoc with CD players. Cassettes are a more durable, reliable and sensible sound source for boomboxes.

For about the same money as a CD boombox, you can buy a portable CD player and a good pair of headphones. Now, with the headphones, you *can* hear a difference between CD's and cassette tapes. When you need speakers, add a pair of amplified speakers designed for portable CD use, or plug it into your home stereo system. Either way, the sound you get will be better than a boombox.

Cassette Decks

A cassette deck plugs into a stereo system. The mere fact that you're considering a cassette deck as a separate entity automatically puts you in the Hi-Fi/Audiophile category — cassette players are built into Lo-Fi equipment, and the whole piece of equipment usually costs less than a cassette deck alone.

For Hi-Fiers, my suggestion is to get the cheapest deck that has all the features you want. For playing back through your Hi-Fi system, and for recording tapes for your car and Walkman, there's no need to spend more than, say, $200. (Unless you want a cassette changer.)

For those Audiophiles and high-end Hi-Fi's who are considering a cassette deck in the mucho-hundred-dollar range, allow me to offer these thoughts:

★ DAT (Digital Audio Tape) will soon take over high-end tape recording. You may have to invest more in a DAT deck than a top-of-the-line cassette deck, but the sound will be better and your place in the future of audio assured.

★ If you're considering the 8mm format for video (see page 197), some 8mm decks offer 24 *hours* of digital music on *one* 8mm tape. The digital quality is not quite as good as CD's or DAT's, but it's easily as good as most cassette decks. If you don't like digital sound, or if the price of DAT and 8mm is too dear, consider . . .

★ The audio track of Hi-Fi VCR (either Beta or VHS) is as good as, and perhaps better than, the best cassette decks. If your purpose is recording and playing back exceptional sound in your home (as opposed to making tapes for your car or Walkman), a Hi-Fi VCR might be the way to go. Consider the advantages:

1. The machine costs less. New VCR's with Hi-Fi start at around $400. It's impossible to find the sound-quality of a Hi-Fi VCR in a $400 cassette deck.

2. The tapes cost less. You can record up to five hours (Beta) or eight hours (VHS) on one $10 tape. (About one-

third the cost of five to eight hours of high-grade cassette tape.)

3. The music is uninterrupted — no changers and no auto-reverse to mess up your azimuth. (All the Beethoven Symphonies or all the Beatles' albums on one tape.)

4. You have a spare VCR — good for making copies or recording that second good show on at the same time as the first good show the night you have good theater tickets.

5. It's a good excuse to get a VCR — if you've been holding out, your excuse can be, "I bought it for the *sound*."

6. It's a good reason to get the other format. If you're in the VHS camp, but have occasionally wanted a Beta — or vice versa — this is the perfect excuse to get the other format. Your excuse can be, "I bought it for the *sound*."

7. It's a great excuse for getting a Super-VHS — use your old Hi-Fi VCR for your audio system and use the new Super-VHS for video.

Keep in mind that the only part of the Hi-Fi VCR that needs to work is the audio portion. The video heads seem to go first, and replacing them is a $300 repair bill. Rather than abandoning your VCR at that point, you can upgrade it to an audio deck par excellence. Or you can put an ad in the paper asking for someone else's pictureless Hi-Fi VCR. (I bet you can pick one up for $100.)

The video heads gave way on my Sony Beta Hi-Fi three years ago. This gave me the choice of (A) spending more repairing it than it was worth (SuperBeta had come along, and this was a regular Beta Hi-Fi), or (B) using it as a high-tech doorstop. It dawned on me that the audio track was almost digital quality (and, for Audiophiles who love analog, *better* than digital). I hooked it up to my stereo and have used that deck, constantly, ever since. It's especially nice for hours and hours of high-quality background music.

Mitsubishi DT160 Tape Changer

I love this machine. I love it because it incorporates a concept I need — and it *works*.

The concept is a cassette changer. Cassette changers seem to combine the best of both worlds: uninterrupted music with no damage to the music source, a reality decidedly *un*true of record changers.

I bought my first cassette changer, a Magnavox, many years ago. It never worked right. I kept taking it in for repairs, but eventually the model was discontinued and the repair people told me to stop bothering them with discontinued models.

A few years later, I bought a Sony. Good old, reliable Sony, right? Wrong. This never worked right either. It, too, was quickly discontinued, so getting repair was difficult. I finally had to ship it to the Sony Factory Repair Facility in New Jersey. They charged me $79.95 and, when the unit was returned, it *still* didn't work.

It was also dirtier than I remembered sending it. A check of the serial numbers confirmed my suspicions: it wasn't my player. (I know my machines, just as the owners of black cats know their individual cats.) Several calls to Sony (all long distance and all at my expense) sparked an investigation. My machine, it seemed, was sent to someone else who had opted not to pay the $79.95 for repair, and their broken unit was sent to me. I eventually got a refund, but they couldn't supply me with a new tape changer because they weren't being made anymore.

Finally, the Mitsubishi. Ah, the Mitsubishi. Sturdy, solid, and truly reliable. It's played all night, every night, for months, and it's working fine. I use it to play educational tapes — sort of sleep learning — but it works just as well for background music, or even hours and hours of foreground music.

And that's not all.

In addition to holding seven cassettes in the cassette changer, it has a separate single cassette player/recorder. This is good for playing single tapes, rewinding tapes, or, what it was designed for, making high-speed duplicates of tapes played in the changing mechanism.

And that's not all.

The Mitsubishi DT160 allows you to play the tapes one time through (auto-reversing each tape, of course); it also allows for continuous play (the seven tapes play all the way through, then start all over again, forever); and it can be programmed to play any tapes in any order.

And that's not all.

It can also be programmed to play any individual *track* on any tape in any order. Whew.

That's all, but that's enough. $385.

NAD 6300 Tape Deck

This is a tape deck for serious Audiophiles. It's part of the NAD Monitor Series discussed in Chapter 4. At $798, it lacks such basic amenities as auto reverse and auto tape select (metal, chromium dioxide and normal are selected manually).

It does, however, include two controls Audiophiles consider even more essential than the two omitted: play trim and bias fine-tune.

Play trim corrects the errors made by some cassette decks when recording using Dolby noise reduction circuitry. Sometimes this causes playback that is too bright (the sibilants hiss) or too dull. With the play trim knob, the correct balance between brightness and dullness can be adjusted to the user's taste.

The bias fine-tune is used to compensate for the differences in manufactured cassettes. It is used only during recording (play trim is used for playback). It takes ten steps (some complicated) to properly adjust the bias, which is a major inducement to (A) use the same brand and type of tape for all recordings, (B) give up Audiophileism, or (C) go digital.

Oddly, although the NAD 6300 doesn't feature the creature comfort of auto reverse, it does have a remote control. Go figure.

Nakamichi Dragon

What would it cost to get Audiophile cassette quality *and* auto reverse? Oh, about $2,000; $1,995 to be exact — the price of the Nakamichi Dragon.

The Nakamichi Dragon is one of those chicken-and-egg ponderings. Was it designed first, then someone said, "This looks like a dragon," or did someone think "Dragon" was a great name for an audio product and told the design department to create a black tape deck with scales? Whichever, the Dragon is both well designed and well named.

Except for those Audiophiles who flatly refuse to accept auto reverse under any circumstances, the Nakamichi Dragon is the Audiophile's choice. It has everything, and then some. (Except dbx and a remote.)

There's not much to say, other than this is as good as cassette decks get and, considering the advent of DAT, probably as good as cassette decks will ever get.

Chapter Seven

Compact Discs

ompact Discs (CD's) have revolutionized the way all Hi-Fi's and many
Audiophiles listen to music. The Lo-Fi's
just can't understand what's going on.

"They last virtually forever!" the
enthusiastic Hi-Fi will say to the Lo-Fi.

"So do cassettes," the Lo-Fi will
answer.

"You don't have to clean them," the
Hi-Fi will counter.

"You don't have to clean cassettes."

"But you have to clean records."

"You do?"

"CD's have no background noise, just music."

"That's what I want music for: background noise."

Not since the Nixon-Khrushchev Kitchen Debates
have there been such fundamental disagreements about a
small appliance.

CD's are, of course, those five-inch circles of silver-
colored plastic with rainbow patterns. These rainbows are
caused by the diffusion of light glancing off the billions of
pits on the CD's surface. (Actually, the surface is clear plastic. The pits are just beneath that surface.) Each pit (or lack

of pit) represents one bit of information. A laser beam reads tens of thousands of these per second and creates the illusion of sound. (See page 29 for a fuller explanation of digital sound.)

CD's are not as indestructible as we were first led to believe. Initial reports were that you could tap dance on a CD, use it for a Frisbee, throw it in the Cuisinart, toss it in the dishwasher and, when the Hotpoint had done its duty, play a Beethoven sonata.

Not so. The protective plastic is, to my way of thinking, not very protective. It scratches *easy*. Granted, a minor scratch doesn't destroy a CD's sound the way it does on a record, but a major scratch will have Pavarotti sounding like Max Headroom. ("A-A-Ave Mari-i-i-a-a-a-a-a...")

CD's certainly don't require the care ordinary records do. A little respect — handle them by the edges, put them back in their little plastic holders when through — and they'll sound great for a long time. (There are rumors that CD's *do* deteriorate over time, but I won't trouble you with those.)

Compact Discs

Here are some of the features you'll find on CD players . . .

Repeat. This repeats the same disk over and over.

Programmable Play. This allows you to select the selections you would like to hear, in any order. The player will automatically play them in that order.

Shuffle or **Random Play** or **Juke Box.** This selects and plays selections on the disc at random. It may sound silly, but it's a great feature. It adds new life to an album you've *almost* heard too many times. It's also fun for driving your classical friends nuts. Just play the movements of a concerto in random order. (They may not notice.)

Disc Changer. The player holds from five to ten discs and plays them automatically. With a changer, you can have hours of non-stop music, programmed by you or selected by the player.

Compact disc players are available for the home, car or walkabout.

CD players cost anywhere from $150 to $2,800. My suggestion to Hi-Fiers: Buy the least expensive model that has the features you want. The only real test: Bring in a beat-up CD and see which of the models you're considering will track it with the least errors. If it sounds good, too, buy that one.

Audiophiles: You may not want a CD, but if you do, you will no doubt be able to hear differences between one player and another. Select carefully, in the same way you selected your turntable, tonearm and cartridge.

Nakamichi OMS-7AII CD Player

Shall we start at the top? At $1,850, the Nakamichi OMS-7AII is not the most expensive CD player on the market, but it ain't the cheapest either.

Is there a difference between the sound of this CD player and a CD player costing, say, $350? Yes. Does it sound better? Yes. What do I mean by better? It sounds more, as Robert would say, musical. Would most people notice the difference? If you played one and then played the other in an A/B test, yes. If you played the same CD on both players a week apart, probably not. Would everyone prefer the Nakamichi? Not necessarily. (Some prefer the brighter, hotter sound of less expensive CD players.) For those who can tell the difference and prefer the sound of the Nakamichi, is it worth the $1,500 difference? To very, very few.

Those few are, of course, called Audiophiles. For Audiophiles — who are not that sure about digital anyway — the Nakamichi has a natural enough sound to convince more than a few to Go CD. This, in many cases, was no small achievement.

In careful A/B testing between a $1,000 turntable-tonearm-cartridge combination and a $750 CD player, it was hard to tell the difference between a record (analog) and a CD (digital). When the same test was performed between the $750 CD player and a $5,000 turntable-tonearm-cartridge, the records sounded better than the CD every time. But, between the $1,850 Nakamichi and the $5,000 T–T–C, Audiophiles thought the CD sounded as good as the analog about 25% of the time.

Compact Discs

This isn't what you would call a screaming victory for digital, although, in fact, it is. If money were the issue, the $1,895 Nakamichi compared with the $5,000 turntable-tonearm-cartridge combination is a real bargain. If time and fuss were the issue, it's much easier to plop a CD into the Nakamichi than it is to do the necessary cleaning and treating of a record and the stylus prior to an Audiophile playing.

For Hi-Fi's, the Nakamichi represents enormous over-spending. To an Audiophile, it's downright cheap.

My only reservation is in quality control. The first Nakamichi I owned developed tracking problems within six months. The second unit, sent for review, arrived in a semi-operable state. I trust that this is just the unluck of my draw and not representative of Nakamichi CD players in general.

Technics SL-XP5 Portable CD Player

You may not consider the difference in price between a Walkman (oh, $75 for a semi-deluxe model) and a portable CD player (this one is $375) worth it for your occasional traveling needs.

Walkmen win over portable CD players in more than just price. Walkmen are smaller, lighter and not subject to skipping when jarred. Also, cassette tapes require far less special attention than CD's. (You can throw a pile of loose cassettes in your overnight bag — try doing that with your CD's. No, *don't* try doing that.)

But CD's win the contest in one important area: sound. No matter how good your Walkman sounds, after five minutes of listening to a portable CD player, you'll find the Walkman hopelessly and forever muddy. (Don't even listen to a portable CD player unless you are ready to make the switch.)

Some people think the cost of a portable CD player is not worth it, and some may still think the cost of a home CD player is not worth it — but what if you could have *both*, would that be worth it?

That's what portable CD players really are. They're not just portable, they're *convertible*. You can hook them up to your home stereo, use them happily there, and when you travel you have a musical traveling companion. (In two-person households, Who-gets-the-portable-CD? has replaced the Who-gets-the-car? altercations of old.)

Portable CD players for the home have at least one other advantage: size. Some people just don't have room for another large component in, on, or around their stereo system. A portable CD can fit almost anywhere.

The Panasonic CD is an especially nice one. Unlike many portable CD players (most of the Sonys, for example), the Panasonic's buttons are not as subject to accidental pushing. Some manufacturers think putting "feather touch" buttons on portable CD's is a great idea. I find it one of the most foolish design flaws in personal electronics. Some portable CD players cannot be picked up or moved without the danger of unintentionally stopping the player.

The Panasonic's most vulnerable button is on top: the play/pause button. Hitting that accidentally will, at worst, put the player in the pause mode. Another press of the button puts it back the way it was. If the stop button is pushed, as it so easily can be on some players, you have to start at the beginning again. After a few restarts, you begin wondering, "Who designed this thing?"

A particularly nice feature on the Panasonic is the battery level indicator. It lets you know at a glance how much power remains and whether a recharge is in order. The only lack of features I could find was a shuffle play which, alas, is one of my favorites.

When buying a portable CD, plan on buying headphones separate. The little Walkman-style headphones

Compact Discs

provided with most portable players are not sufficient for the broader dynamic range of CD players. The smaller headphones work, of course, but if you're going to all the trouble and expense of CD's, there's no point in limiting the sound just before it enters your ears. Plan on another $50 to $100 for headphones. (See Chapter 10, *Headphones.*)

Sony CDPC10 CD Changer and CDPC5F Carousel CD Changer

Why would Sony market two units at about the same price that do the same thing, except that one holds ten CD's and the other holds five?

The CD changer ($504) holds ten CD's in a removable cartridge, the Carousel CD changer ($450) holds five CD's in a lazy Susan type arrangement.

Could it be that the rumors one hears about the many repair problems of the cartridge-based CD player are true? Could it be Sony knew about this going in and wanted a backup unit on the shelves ("This one holds less CD's — but it doesn't use a changer. Costs less, too."), just in case the rumors spread?

Even if none of this is true, the Carousel concept is, for most people, better than the cartridge. To replace a single disc in the cartridge changer requires removing the cartridge, removing the disc, replacing the disc, and replacing the cartridge. Replacing a single disc in the Carousel requires simply opening the drawer and replacing it.

Further, finding which disc is which in the changer is a chore. With the Carousel the drawer slides open and displays the available CD's, one after another.

The Carousel especially shines if you mostly play one disc at a time. Loading a single disc in the Carousel is as easy as loading a disc in any CD player. Loading a single disc into the cartridge system requires removing the cartridge, inserting the disc, then replacing the cartridge.

The 10-CD player is, however, more programmable. You can play any track on any CD in the stack, one after another, unattended. You can be the DJ and the host of your own party all at once. If you do a lot of this, the cartridge player may be for you.

Both players include shuffle, and will randomly play the contents of one disc before moving onto the next. Neither, however, will randomly select a track from one CD, then randomly select a track from another, then randomly select a track from another. All the tracks on one CD are randomly played, then it moves onto the next CD.

Both come with remotes, the cartridge remote being more elaborate than the Carousel.

Do you suppose Sony will get in trouble with Kodak over the use of the word Carousel? When "Carousel" is mentioned in personal electronics, most people think of the Kodak Carousel slide projector. Think we'll have some nasty legal letters and maybe even a lawsuit to look forward to?

Sony, as they say, has it coming to them. They sued a poor woman, whose name happened to be Sony, and made her remove the name "Sony" from her restaurant. (As though one associates Sony, the electronics company, with foot-long hot dogs.) Sony, of Sony's Restaurant, couldn't afford to defend her own name against a meganational corporation — but Kodak, that's another story. Film, er, slides at eleven.

Compact Discs

Onkyo DX-C600 CD Changer

For those who prefer a more Audiophile (or at least higher Hi-Fi) approach to CD changers, I beg to put before you the Onkyo.

The Onkyo uses the cartridge concept, the cartridge holding six CD's. It is fully programmable, has a remote, and costs $600. Fewer CD's and greater cost? Why not get the Sony? Many Audiophiles think the Onkyo sounds better.

IMPROVED
~ at Lowered Cost!

A NEW vacuum tube has made it possible. Radiola V and Radiola RC have been topping them all in popularity for dependability and long range—receiving over thrilling distances—up to 1,500 miles and more. Now both are converted to dry battery operation. This means greatly lowered cost —gives the far-away farmer the same good service it gives the city man. Complete now at a combination price remarkably low.

Radiola V or Radiola RC Complete $142.50

The New Way: Complete for dry battery operation, including three new type WD-12 Radiotron vacuum tubes; pair of head telephones; "A" battery consisting of three dry cells; "B" battery consisting of three 22½ volt units. $142.50.

The Old Way: The price of Radiola V or Radiola RC, when equipped for storage battery operation, formerly came to $207.50.

This symbol of quality is your protection

RADIOLA V
as illustrated

A long distance receiver built for a life time—ruggedly—solidly. A sensitive detector, with two stages of amplification.   Mahogany finished—attractive — and simple to operate.

★

Radiola RC—included in the new adjustment—similar in quality and performance.

Radiola
REG. U.S. PAT. OFF.
Radio Corporation of America

Chapter Eight

Digital Audio Tape

This is a tale that will have you believing the stories of Standard Oil buying and suppressing a machine that turns water into gasoline for three cents a gallon. (Variations on the story have GM sitting on the plans for a car that would last forever and cost $29, and General Foods withholding a pill that would provide all our nutritional needs for twelve cents a day.)

There are two parts to this story, but first, here's what the story is about.

The story is about DAT — Digital Audio Tape. A Digital Audio Tape is half the size of an audio cassette with twice the playing time of a CD. And, unlike a CD, you can record on it. The portable ones will be about the size of a cigarette package. And, unlike CD's, you can jog with them.

Sound like the perfect recording medium? Uh-huh. A little too perfect, it seems.

Flashback three years. Digital Audio Tape and Compact Discs are in final stages of development. Philips, developer of the CD, goes to Sony and other DAT developers, and says, in essence: "If we come out with two, competing digital formats in a market that doesn't even know what digital is, we may both lose. So let's put them out one at a time, and let everybody buy one of each.

"If we put DAT out first," the argument continued, "Nobody will buy CD's, because the small advantage CD's have over DAT (rapid random access of material) isn't enough to make people buy CD players. *But*, if CD's come out first, by the time DAT's come out, everybody will buy *both!*"

The argument, along with some undisclosed sharing of the CD wealth on Philips' part, prevailed. DAT was put on the back burner, CD players introduced, and the rest is digital history.

And now for part two of our story.

CD's have become outrageously successful — even more successful than the manufacturers ever dreamed. The electronics folk are prepared (nay, eager) to release DAT machines, but now guess who's rearing its greedy little head?

The recording industry. The recording industry are the people who, you will recall, complained about cassette tape, saying it would drive them out of business, and now they make more money selling prerecorded cassette tapes than they do selling records. These are the same general group of people who sued Sony for introducing home video recording, claiming it would end their profits on old movies, and who are now making more money from the sale and rental of video tapes than from paid admissions to movie theaters.

They've tried for years to get a special fee put on blank tape (yes, they want some of your money every time you buy a blank tape — so when you send a recording of the baby's first words to grandma, CBS and Warner and all those other record companies would get a cut). Now they want to destroy DAT.

The recording industry lobbied hard and long and have had bills introduced in the House and Senate requiring that all DAT machines contain a special microchip. This chip would prevent the recording of any music encoded with the CBS encoding system.

And you can bet that, sooner or later, *everything* will be encoded — CD's, records, cassettes, radio, TV. You can further bet the chip won't stop at DAT machines. Next they'll be required in regular cassette recorders, then video machines, then . . .

There are many ramifications of all this, but three stand out.

First, DAT is being withheld from us because the manufacturers are afraid the law might pass. If it does, they'll have to recall all the DAT machines.

Second, it removes our right to make copies of tapes, records, etc., for our own use. (The Supreme Court decided in the "Sony vs. Basically These Same People" case we had that right.)

Third, the CBS encoding process actually degrades the quality of sound. It works by removing a notch of the music, well within the audible range. All music will sound not-so-well if these bills pass.

What to do? Call, write, telegram your elected officials in Washington. To find out who your elected officials are, or more about this issue, call 1-800-282-TAPE. It's a toll-free call to the Home Recording Rights Coalition.

And, in a final irony, guess who's behind the Home Recording Rights Coalition? The very electronics manufacturers who held back the DAT technology for the past three years.

Small world, huh?

JVC XD-Z1100 DAT Deck

Working with the JVC DAT deck confirmed every suspicion I had about Digital Audio Tape — it's great. Unless the recording industry succeeds in destroying DAT (while blowing off its own foot in the process), Digital Audio Tape is the recording medium of the future.

The JVC DAT deck looks and operates as any cassette deck, except for the sound. It's pure, digital sound which, to my ears, sounds even better than CD's. (It's smoother somehow.) Another difference between a DAT deck and a cassette deck is the predominance of numbers. Each track on a DAT tape — either prerecorded or home-recorded — is assigned a number. Tracks can be found and played by simply pushing its number on the remote. I found the JVC DAT's track-finding ability faultless.

The primary advantage of CD's over DAT is random track selection. CD's can go from track to track almost instantly. DAT's cannot. But DAT's are not as bad as one might expect, especially one who is used to working with regular cassette tape. The worst case I could create, using a prerecorded tape, was just under twenty seconds to go from the end of the last track to the beginning of the first. A full rewind of a two-hour tape takes 35 seconds.

JVC has been marketing DAT decks in Japan for some time. They have the experience and size to make the first generation units offered for sale in America the equivalent of the second generation units from some manufacturers.

As accustomed as I am to the miracles of personal electronics, it still amazes me to put a little tape into a player and have two hours of incredible sound come out.

Actual size of a DAT tape

Actual size of a quarter

Actual size of a square inch of gold

Actual size of a juju-bee

Actual size of a page number in this book

Chapter Nine

Speakers

peakers are the most subjective part of audio. Everybody's got a different opinion about which is best, and there seems to be a speaker for every opinion. Like True Love, once you find yours you will be happy (for at least six months), providing the search doesn't kill you.

And the search is not an easy one. Unlike other areas of audio, very little you can read will direct you to your Perfect Pair. It's an experience you're looking for, a very personal experience, and it's going to take a lot of listening (to speakers) and a lot of non-listening (to salespeople).

Ideally, when selecting speakers, you should hear them in the same room, playing the same music, from the same source, through the same amplifier. Further, you should be able to switch instantly from one pair of speakers to another. This, like most ideals, is difficult to achieve. It's a physical impossibility to have all manufactured speakers in the same room at the same time, unless that room is at San Simeon, in which case the speakers wouldn't sound as they would in your home anyway.

And even this ideal is a compromise ideal. *Ideally*, you should select speakers in your own room using your own equipment.

In selecting speakers, here are the problems one must overcome:

1. There are lots and lots and *lots* of speakers. There are more speaker manufacturers than almost any other category of electronics, and each manufacturer features three, six, ten, forty different models.

2. Speakers sound different in different environments. The size of a room, the shape of the room, the furnishings in the room, all contribute to the sound that eventually reaches your ears — and it's the sound as it reaches your ears that's important.

3. Speakers sound different in different locations within the same room. A little higher, a little lower, a little closer to the wall, a little farther from the wall, a little farther apart, a little closer together, a little angled in, a little angled out — all of these, and many more, affect the way the same speakers sound within the same room.

4. Speakers sound different with different amplifiers. Amplifiers are far from neutral. One amplifier can make a given pair of speakers sound great, another amplifier can make the same pair of speakers sound awful. The same is true, although to a lesser degree, of turntables, CD players, tape decks, and all the other components in a system.

5. Speakers sound different with different music. Speakers that sound great playing rock might not hold up playing classical (unless it's the *1812 Overture*). Some speakers sound great with music but not so great with vocals.

6. Speakers sound different at different volume levels. Some speakers thrive at high volume, others self-destruct. Some sound wonderful at "normal" listening levels (yet another subjective term), but become uneven when played softly or loudly.

7. It's hard to remember sound. Sure, we can remember the difference between a transistor radio and those monolithic speakers the size of a small Winnebago at Stereo

City, but remembering the subtleties from speaker to speaker is difficult. For most people, the memory of sound is far less accurate than the memory of, say, sight or taste.

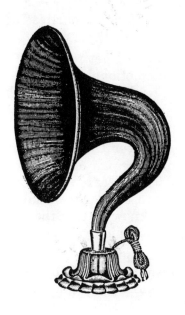

Sound impossible? (Was that a pun? If so, I apologize.) Well, what's a problem to one is a challenge to another. In addition to the general audio/video buying advice in Chapter 28, here are some ways of rising to the challenge of finding your perfect speakers.

1. There is no such thing as the *one* perfect pair for you. To use the relationship example, I know we (as a culture) believe in the concept of a single, solo, solitary star-crossed lover waiting for us somewhere "out there," and when we find him/her/it everything will be perfect. All our other relationships are just marking time until The One arrives.

Those of us who have been in love more than once, however, know the reality behind the myth. (Of course, falling in love means you sincerely believe that all those others were not really love at all, but *this one* is. It's harder to remember love than sound.) In fact, out of the five billion people on this planet, there's probably two or three thousand you could fall utterly in love with, settle down with, and raise whatever you dream of raising. (Children, vegetables and consciousness seem to be very popular among my friends these days.)

But before I get too far off on a controversial point people will emotionally defend to the death, allow me to simply make the point that of the, oh, five hundred different speakers out there, twenty or thirty will meet your audio needs just fine.

If you enter the Audio Jungle with the attitude, "There's only *one* pair of speakers out there for me and I've *got* to find it," the search is likely to be an ordeal. If you approach it with the same casualness as a trip to the video rental store, knowing that there are any number of movies you'll probably enjoy, you'll have more fun.

2. Know your budget. Set a reasonable upper limit for what you want to spend on speakers. Reduce this by 25%, and use this reduced figure as the "absolute upper limit" you tell the salesperson you want to spend. You will then be shown speakers in your price range. You could also start at half your projected amount. You may find something you love. No need to spend more than you have to.

3. Know your category. Are you a Hi-Fi or Audiophile? (Lo-Fi's aren't reading this chapter. "You mean you have to buy speakers *separate*?" they ask. "Everything I've ever bought had speakers *built in*.")

Dollar for dollar, the Hi-Fi's will get larger cabinets and louder volumes than Audiophiles. Audiophiles, in the more modest spending ranges, will wind up with speakers that are smaller and less dramatic — but more accurate — than their Hi-Fi counterparts.

Audiophiles should listen to speakers in Audiophile stores. Don't be surprised if you say, "I can spend $1,000 on speakers," thinking that should really buy you something, only to be shown a speaker the size of a breadbox. "The Hi-Fi's get bigger cabinets in the $200 range," you think. You timidly smile at the salesperson, "*These* are $1,000 a pair?"

you ask, hoping you were misheard and those larger ones over there are what you *should* be looking at. "No," the salesperson says, touching the smaller ones, "These are $1,000 *each*."

Hi-Fi's can shop anywhere. Listen to them all, and buy the ones you find most, well, sensational. Keep one thing in mind, however: If you like your music loud, be sure the speakers can take *loud*. The peak passages on CD's have blown more speakers than, well, you invent your own analogy.

4. Know your listening space. Some speakers can take over a room. They must be so many feet from this wall and so many feet from that wall and so many inches off the floor and so many inches from the ceiling and, and, and.

If you're an Audiophile you may have to acquiesce to these demands, but most Hi-Fi's want their living rooms for living. (Audiophiles will point out that Music is Life, hence the living room should be arranged around Music. Hi-Fi's want the living room arranged around the couch.)

Look around whatever room the speakers are going to inhabit and decide how much room they may or may not have. Keep this in mind when shopping. Ask the salesperson, "Where does this go in a room?" "Will it fit on a bookshelf?" (Not so much "Will it fit?" but "Will it sound OK on a bookshelf?") "How many feet does this need to be from walls, floors, ceilings, etc.?" If you find an honest salesperson, you may find your choices narrowing.

Then, listen to speakers in that environment. If you're going to put yours up against the wall, put them up against a wall in the listening room. If you're going to use them for coffee tables, put them on the floor. It'll avoid disappointment later.

Be able to tell the salesperson the dimensions of your listening room, as well as its acoustic characteristics. Is it a "live," "bright" room (hardwood floors, lots of windows, little furniture), a "dead," "dull" room (wall-to-wall carpeting, heavy draperies, lots of overstuffed furniture) or somewhere in between?

5. Bring your own music and, if possible, music source. At the very least, bring your own CD's and records. Let it represent the range of music you listen to. Try to bring along your turntable and/or CD player. And, if possible, bring along your amplifier, too.

Many stores will allow this if you make arrangements ahead and come during quieter times. (Weekday mornings are usually best.)

If you're buying new equipment, pick your components first and save speaker selection for last. Then have the store set up your configuration for speaker selection. You may at that point change components, but it gives you a starting point.

6. Start by listening to the same selection on every speaker in and around your price range (including inexpensive speakers). Pick your favorites. As you narrow them down, start listening to other selections. Continue narrowing your choices, then begin A/B testing.

A/B testing is designating one pair of speakers as A and another pair of speakers as B. Set the right A speaker near the right B speaker and the left A speaker near the left B speaker, about the same distance apart as they would be in your listening area at home. Then sit about as far away as you would sit at home and switch back and forth between the A and the B speakers.

A winner will eventually emerge (let's say it's B), and a new challenger assumes the position of A. If you reach a point where both A and B sound great and you can't decide, put one of them aside for the Grand Finals, and continue eliminating other contenders with the A/B method.

When making subtle selections, more accurate decisions are made when comparing A to B, rather than A to B to C, or, worse, A to B to C to D.

Also, when comparing speakers in an A/B test, keep in mind that some speakers will be louder than others, and, when comparing, the louder speaker will generally sound better. A superb audio store will be able to compensate for these differences in speakers and set the volume of the two pairs of speakers to match each other. Many stores will not be able to do this, and a salesperson will have to fiddle with the volume each time you switch. It's awkward, but hearing one noticeably louder than the other will misrepresent the quieter speaker.

7. Time for the Grand Finals. This can take place in only one place — your place. Yes, your listening room. If the speaker salespeople have put up with your nonsense thus far, they'll go a bit further to make the sale. The bit further is your place.

Take the top two or three pairs of speakers home for the Big Showdown. (Some stores will allow this if you (A) take them at the end of the business day, (B) return them by the start of the next business day, and (C) sign credit card slips for all three just in case you never return.)

You may need the help of a friend, first to transport the speakers, to help you lift them to their new proposed locations, and to turn the little A/B switch on your amplifier while you listen. (Most amplifiers can accommodate two sets of speakers and switch between the two. If not, you may have to "borrow" a switching box from your dear friends at the audio store.)

Then spend the evening with the speakers. In your listening environment, one may emerge as the clear and immediate winner, or it may continue to be a tie. In that case, buy the cheapest pair — and a bottle of Scotch for your now-frazzled salesperson.

Subwoofers

There is a category of speakers — or maybe I should say speaker enhancement — gaining quick and well-deserved popularity over the past few years: subwoofers. Subwoofers produce the sound below 200 Hz, sound we don't so much hear as *feel* — the low notes of an organ, the boom of the bass (either guitar or drum), the ominous vibrations of a synthesizer.

Subwoofers are the darlings of Hi-Fi's and Audiophiles alike. Yes, they actually agree on something, but, of course, for different reasons.

Hi-Fi's like subwoofers because you can *feel* them, I mean *really feel* them. I mean, it's *almost* like being in a disco! Too much is just enough.

Audiophiles like subwoofers because it helps capture the dynamic overtones of all instruments. Many instruments have harmonics in the lower registers of sound, and the subwoofer adds a subtle third dimension to the music, a more accurate, natural quality. In addition to these harmonic overtones, the subwoofer helps directly duplicate the sound of timpani, organ, tuba and some of the larger string instruments.

Speakers

Your system will generally have just one subwoofer. Sound below 200 Hz is non-directional (you can't tell where it's coming from) so there's no point in a subwoofer for each stereo channel.

Subwoofers also sit comfortably on the floor, so many of them can double for an end table. In fact, most of them look more like tables than speakers.

When watching TV, especially movies (see Chapter 14, *Hi-Fi TV*) in Dolby Stereo, subwoofers are almost essential. The boom, bang and crash of the sound effects — not to mention the enhanced quality of the music — makes the movie come alive.

I am a great fan of subwoofers. Once added to a system, it will be much blessed by both Audiophile and Hi-Fi alike.

The two most popular self-powered subwoofers among Audiophiles are the *Audio Pro* ($1,424.50 — although you can usually get one marked down to $1,424) and the *Velodyne UDL-15* ($1,350). The current leaning, it seems, is toward the Velodyne.

If the four-figure prices frighten you, consider the *Mitek PSW-200* subwoofer. This doesn't have the power of either the Velodyne or the Audio Pro, but it still sounds good, and costs $699.95, which sounds even better. (Why don't they just add a nickel and make it $700?)

To my Plebeian ears, it's a tossup between the Audio Pro and the Velodyne. The Audio Pro looks the best, especially in natural wood. If looks are as important as sound, the Audio Pro may be the way to go. Audiophiles, however, tend to lean toward the Velodyne. And, if money is as important as sight or sound, look carefully at the Mitek price while listening to its sound.

Audio Pro

Velodyne

Mitek

Speakers

Assorted Speakers

It's silly to even attempt to review speakers. Anything as subjective as speakers does not lend itself well to review. Oh, sure, you can describe and rhapsodize, but what possible good does that do the reader? My opinion of which speaker is best is about as valuable as my opinion of which work of art is best: the Mona Lisa or the Sistine Chapel? It's a choice you'll have to make for yourself.

(When making your choice, avoid what Art Buchwald calls The Five Minute Louvre: On your way to the airport, have the cab stop by the Louvre. Run upstairs and see the Mona Lisa; run downstairs and see the Venus de Milo; on the stairway, take a quick look at the Winged Victory; run back to your cab — The Five Minute Louvre.)

Here are some speakers that I've enjoyed and a few comments about them. Listen to these and a lot of others.

Bose Roommates and
Acoustic Research Powered Partners

These are two of the best of a relatively new category called powered speakers — they have amplifiers built into the same case as the speakers. They're especially popular as loudspeakers for portable CD players or Walkmen, or as rear speakers for a Surround Sound system.

The Bose lists for $229 a pair, the Acoustic Research (AR) Powered Partners $379.95 a pair. The AR has volume and tone controls the Bose lacks.

Both sound remarkably good, especially when attached to a portable CD player. The sound is so good, in fact, one might be tempted to buy a portable CD player with a built-in FM radio, a pair of these speakers, and that would be that. This is especially true for smaller rooms or apartments.

The AR's are larger and heavier than the Bose. The tone controls do come in handy, as most CD players and Walkmen don't have them. The volume controls are necessary for some Surround Sound processors.

The Bose are smaller, small enough, in fact, to pack in a suitcase for traveling. They're each the size of this book and about five inches deep. When you pack, you can choose between twelve copies of my book or a pair of Bose. (I'd take the Bose.)

Altec Lansing 301

Robert would call these "theatrical" speakers, and no wonder: Altec Lansing has been supplying Voice of the Theater speakers to movie theaters for decades. In walnut, these are $750 a pair, in black lacquer, $900. I'll take walnut, thanks. (What is the passion these days for black paint? And why does it cost more than natural wood? The puzzlements of personal electronics.)

Speakers

dbx Soundfield 100

dbx claims to have found a way to make stereo imaging accurate from points other than a single point equidistant between both speakers. Some think this is great, some say it can't be done, others say if it can be done it shouldn't be done because it destroys the possibility of accurate imaging from *anywhere* in the room. Ah, the great debates in audio. dbx is a company devoted to good sound, so this is no mere gimmick. Listen for yourself and decide. $899 a pair.

Energy Refcon

These are speakers from our friends in the Great White North (unless you're reading this book in Canada, in which case, "Hi!"). I like the sound of all of them, especially the larger ($1,800 a pair) models.

(For more speakers, please see Chapter 11, *Audio Systems*.)

Chapter Ten

Headphones

hy are these things called headphones and not headspeakers? That's what they are — little speakers that fit on either side of your head.

The reason, of course, is that headphones were around before speakers. "Phone" means "voice" or "sound" (from the Greek). Telephone is voice or sound from a distance. Megaphone is sound made louder. In the early days of radio ("wireless"), one listened through headphones. Speakers (short for "loudspeaker") came later. (The speakers on early phonographs were called "horns.")

In the twenties, headphones meant you couldn't afford a loudspeaker. Headphones all but disappeared for musical listening in the thirties, forties and fifties, only to resurface in the late fifties with the advent of stereo.

The Walkman, of course, put a headphone on everyone's head. Some adventurous types plugged their Walkman headphones into their home stereos and liked the result.

Headphones come in basically three types: *in* the ear, *over* the ear, and *around* the ear.

119

In-the-ear headphones come with ultra-small radios and tape players. A little circle of plastic fits in each ear and is supposed to stay there. I have no idea whose ears these were designed for, but they weren't mine. If I put them in one way they hurt, if I put them in another they fall out. God bless those whose ears are the right size for these, and God especially bless the rest of us whose ears are not.

Over-the-ear headphones have two foam rubber pads about the size of quarters with a metal band holding them together (or apart, depending on how you look at things). These are the "classic" Walkman headphones.

Around-the-ear headphones surround the ear with cushioned plastic and look, depending on the manufacturer, like earmuffs or Mickey Mouse ears. These are generally the more expensive variety. (Remember the Mickey Mouse Club? I mean the *original* Mickey Mouse Club. Have you seen the *contemporary* Mickey Mouse Club? They have one Mouseketeer of every racial, geographical, religious and socioeconomic type. It looks like a little United Nations with ears. I remember when Annette was as ethnic as they got.)

People in the market for headphones include . . .

A. People who want to upgrade the sound of their Walkmen.

B. People who purchased portable CD players and realize their included-free-with-Walkman-purchase headphones just don't make it.

C. People who like to play their music loud and have noticed that a Neighborhood Improvement Committee has been formed; the sole improvement this committee seeks is the removal of the music lover from the neighborhood.

D. People who want the very best sound, but cannot yet afford the very best speakers, but can afford the very best headphones.

E. People who want yet another toy to show off with The Audio System. (After a few selections — which invariably includes the first five minutes of Beethoven's Fifth, the last five minutes of *Bolero*, and something by

Jackson Browne — they will casually hand you a pair of exceptional headphones and say, "Listen to these.")

F. People who want to play their old Rusty Warren records but don't want to wait until the kids have grown up and moved away.

Buying headphones is just like buying speakers, only easier, because you don't have to worry about room acoustics. All the other suggestions on buying speakers in the last chapter should see you well and happily into a new pair of headphones.

YOU TURN THE KNOB

Radak
Trade Mark Reg. U. S. Pat. Off.

DOES THE REST

NO "lessons"—no training—no mechanics necessary to receive radio music, news, entertainment with a Radak Receiving Set. One little knob to turn and the sound comes in strong and clear. Ask your electrical or radio dealer. Radio catalog, 6c.

CLAPP-EASTHAM COMPANY
America's Oldest Exclusive Radio Set Makers
141 Main St., Cambridge, Mass.

[1922]

AKG Headphones

AKG makes great headphones. Their AKG K2 ($40) makes an excellent inexpensive replacement (improvement) for Walkmen and CD players.

The AKG K240 DF ($135) is a wonderful at-home headphone, and the AKG K340 ($215) almost the ultimate. (The ultimate concludes this chapter, but the ultimate, as you might have guessed, costs la bundola.)

Sony MDRV6

Here's my favorite headphone for portables. It has cushions that fit around the ear, so hours of isolated, comfortable listening are possible. It folds up, almost fitting into a large pocket; certainly fitting into an attache case or carry-on bag. Best of all, it sounds wonderful — designed especially, it seems, for portable CD players. $129.

Koss JCK-200 Wireless Headphones

Here's a great idea, but, like cordless telephones, the technology does not seem to be quite there yet. The Koss has a transmitter that sits somewhere by your stereo (the higher up the better, I discovered). The headphones have a receiver on top and pick up the transmitted music. Well and good, except they also tend to pick up random electrical noises and buzzes, and, if anything comes between the headphones and the transmitter, phase out. Still, it's fun, and Hi-Fi's will think it's worth $159.95 just to hand a wireless pair of headphones to their friends in an otherwise silent room and say, "Try it on."

Stax Lambda SR Pro

The ultimate. Well, not quite: Stax also makes more expensive ultimates, but this ($799) is so close to the ultimate I'm nearly giddy.

The Lambda SR Pro comes with its own amplifier, about the size of a three-pack of VHS tapes. The amplifier operates on batteries or AC power. The amplifier plugs into the headphone output or a tape output on your preamp; the Lambda headphones plug into the amplifier. Its portability makes it the Audiophile's Choice for use with portable CD players or cassette decks while traveling. It's also, by the way, the Audiophile's Choice for at-home listening.

Although the price seems high, it is a bargain for Audiophiles-in-training: all they need is a source (CD player or cassette deck) and they're in business for around $1,000 — dirt cheap by Audiophile standards. Granted they won't have any sound in the room, but what is music for, listening or disturbing your neighbors?

The difference between this and the Sony MDRV6 for portable CD's? Small. The difference between this and the AKG K340's for the home? Smaller still. But, as the Audiophiles in France say, *vive le difference.*

*I couldn't find a graphic to illustrate "Systems."
I tried to find the R. Crumb cartoon with the caption,
"Dis is a system?!" and failed. So I present an ad from
Billboard, 1933.*

Chapter Eleven

Audio Systems

here is a marvelous Stephen Sondheim song called *Putting it Together*, the last line of which is, "And *that* is the state of the art." When questing after the state of the art, or even the state of the very good, you'll be faced with the challenge of putting it together.

When you put it together, it's called a system. This chapter is about audio systems.

When buying an audio system from scratch, you are faced with one fundamental decision: Should you do it yourself (with a little help from friends, salespeople, magazines, and maybe even a book or two), or should you let a Big Electronics Manufacturer do it for you?

As usual, the answer to that question lies in the answer to this question: How involved do you want to get?

In general, you will end up with a better system if you put it together yourself. Not only will the system be better, dollar for dollar, but, more importantly, it will be better suited for you. You will be making all the choices all the way down the line, component by component. Your tastes and preferences will prevail.

When a large company assembles an all-in-one "entertainment center," they may choose the best of their products, but the best of their best is seldom the best that's available (for the money) in all component categories. Furthermore, they make their choices based upon whatever criteria they have, criteria you may not share.

These prepackaged electronic monoliths do have certain advantages: you're buying from one company, so if something goes wrong, there's only one finger to point in one direction; a single remote controls everything; it's sometimes more aesthetic and usually comes with some kind of display rack. Also, it's a single purchase. You can compare systems and make your selection within a week. Shopping for individual components often takes longer.

Any one of these reasons may be compelling enough for you to get a manufacturer-selected system, but, "with a little time and perseverance, plus a little luck along the way," (as Sondheim said in *Putting it Together*), you can put together a system of your own that is truly your own.

"My" Audiophile System

I put quotation marks around "my" because the system I'm about to discuss really isn't mine (it belongs to the manufacturers who may be clamoring for it any day now), but it is probably close to one I would put together if I were to go more Audiophile than I already thought I was. But that's part of the story. . .

Audio Systems

To people accustomed to buying "phonographs," buying the turntable, tonearm and cartridge separate from the amplifier and speakers is an unfathomable mystery. When you tell them that the turntable, tonearm and cartridge themselves were all purchased separately, they shake their heads. When you tell them the turntable alone — just the part that turns the records round and round — costs more than most whole stereo systems (hell, costs more than some used two-bedroom house trailers) they change the subject in the way people tend to change the subject when a bag lady starts talking about her latest trip to Mars.

No one better understands the amusement and bemusement of the general public toward Audiophiles, and Audiophile turntables in particular, than Rodney Herman, designer of the **SOTA STAR Sapphire Turntable.**

SOTA stands for State Of The Art, which is one of the better-named companies in audio. They make what is generally considered the best turntable in audio. (Their only real competition for the high-end Audiophile dollar is Lynn.)

When I talked with Rodney on the phone about my project (this book), he insisted on flying from San Francisco to L.A. to install it for me personally. It was, as they say, an offer I could not refuse.

In consort with Rodney and Robert Coyle, we selected the **SME Series V Tone Arm** and **SME Virtuoso DTI cartridge**. ("We" selected. *They* selected. I just nodded a lot.)

The SOTA STAR Sapphire turntable is $1,600. The SME Series V Tone Arm, $2,025. The Virtuoso DTI cartridge, $1,200. As Rodney rattled off these prices over the phone, I added them in my head. My head has never been known for its mathematical achievements, and since the advent of the pocket calculator, whole segments of the brain formerly set aside for remembering times tables have completely atrophied. Nonetheless, I realized this turntable-tonearm-cartridge was going to cost somewhere in the neighborhood of $5,000. I immediately began referring to it as, "The $5,000 Turntable."

Later that week, Rodney arrived with The $5,000 Turntable. As he began setting it up, I sensed he was uneasy about something. Eventually he asked, "What electronics and speakers do you plan to use with the turntable?" It was his diplomatic way of saying, "Your current system sucks."

"You don't think this system would properly showcase your turntable?" I asked, suppressing an urge to say, "And so what's wrong with my system, anyway?"

"It would be like putting a Ferrari engine in a Pinto," he said. Audiophiles have a way with words.

Rodney put the Ferrari engine in my Pinto, and my Pinto sounded better. I already had what I considered to be no slouch of a turntable. The turntable-tonearm-cartridge combination was about $1,000, $600 of which was spent on the cartridge. I considered this extravagant at the time, but I was persuaded by my own argument of the irreplaceable nature of my record collection. (Anybody remember The Incredible String Band? How about Maffit/Davies? I'm not just old, I'm obscure.)

I didn't really expect the $5,000 turntable to sound much better than the $1,000 turntable, but it did. It didn't sound five times better, mind you. It didn't even sound twice as good. But it did sound better, and, in Audiophile, each step towards better gets smaller and smaller and more and more expensive.

Rodney allowed, after listening to it, that my system wasn't all that bad after all. It was a system Robert had put together for me six or seven years earlier during more austere times, and although I added to it over the years (Robert builds expansibility into his systems), I saw no reason to replace it.

It seemed a good idea, however, to put together a genuine Audiophile system, of "reasonable cost" (all things being relative), and review it for the book.

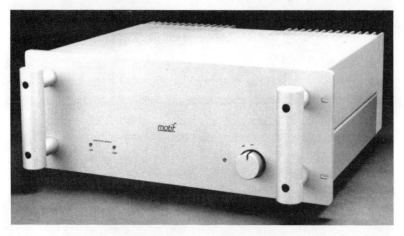

After more conferences with Rodney and Robert, "we" chose the **Conrad Johnson Motif MC8 Preamp** and **MS100 Power Amp** ($2,250 and $3,250, respectively). Conrad Johnson is an interesting company. Their speciality is tube amplifiers for audiophiles who believe tubes give a better sound. The Motif series is a bold departure for the company: they're transistorized. The Conrad Johnson people believe they've found a way of making transistors sound as good as tubes.

Then came speaker selection. "We" picked the **Celestion SL600 Speakers** and the **Celestion System 6000 Subwoofers.** The SL600's list for $899 each, or $1,799 a pair. Somehow you end up paying a dollar more for the privilege of buying a pair. The System 6000 is $2,999.

I also listened to the new **SOTA Time Domain Series Panorama Speakers.** They start at $1,295 for a pair in cherry wood. (More in other woods.) They sounded every bit as good as the SL600's. These were not included as part of the final system, however, as Rodney thought — generously, I think — there should not be too much equipment from any one manufacturer.

So here I had "my" Audiophile system (no tape deck, tuner, CD player or DAT recorder yet, mind you). It came to $15,123 (or $15,122 if you buy two separate Celestion speakers instead of a pair). But the Subwoofer system, it seems, requires a separate power amplifier. This can be a "low cost" amplifier, say, oh, $750. Add a few hundred for special cables to hook it all together (and that's the cheap way of doing it — some Audiophiles spend thousands on the speaker cable alone), and I wound up, without trying hard at all, with a $16,000 system.

As you might expect, it sounds wonderful. Sixteen thousand dollars wonderful? For an Audiophile, sure. This equipment makes some people very, very happy, and I'm happy happiness is available for them.

Keep in mind that Audiophile systems require special care, and, as they are called upon to reproduce more delicate shadings of music, the machinery tends to become more delicate itself. Also, every imperfection in your records will be reproduced along with every subtle nuance. (One Audiophile casually, but seriously, recommended I not play any Columbia records — they, apparently, have notoriously bad pressings.)

The stylus is delicate, and, in Audiophile, is part of the cartridge. (It doesn't slide out for easy replacement.) One slip while placing the tonearm on the record and goodbye stylus.

The amplifier could drive only one set of speakers. (I was accustomed to putting speakers all over the house.) One never, it seems, attaches more than one pair of speakers to a good amplifier. What happens if you want more speakers? Easy: Connect another amplifier to the preamplifier and run the speakers from the new amplifier.

The Celestion subwoofers, while accurate, are also delicate. They tended to distort at lower volume levels than did other subwoofers I've reviewed. Again, Audiophiles tend to listen to music at lower listening levels than Hi-Fi's.

All of this, of course, should not be surprising: One does not expect a Stradivarius to be rugged just because it's expensive. The price of Audiophile is more than just dollars, and those who pay the price feel it's worth the cost.

"Feeling" is the operative word here. Audiophiles, more than anything else, want the emotional impact of the original performance. All the money, care and rearrangements of their lives are not just to add a few cycles per second above or below the audible spectrum. It's to open a little wider the channel of communication between themselves and the great recording artists of all time.

Rearrangement of lives? Well, rearrangement of rooms at the very least. I, for example, have a redecorated living room. The speakers could not, of course, sit on top of bookshelves where mine had happily sat for years. Audiophile speakers are instruments. They radiate sound in 360-degree spheres. They must have room around them, on all sides, to develop their true potential. They had to come out, into the room. This meant the end of the couch was too close to one of the speakers. Solution: Move the speaker? No! Move the couch. And that was only the beginning.

All of this is known in audio as WAF, or Wife Acceptance Factor. It's a term I find hopelessly outdated: There's no reason why the husband wouldn't have to tolerate his wife's Audiophileism. I thought of SAF, Spouse Acceptance Factor, but then the people who complain about audio taking over the living room and still not being able to run a pair of extension speakers into the kitchen might not be spouses. So I coined RAF, Roommate Acceptance Factor.

But, even with their inherent cost and delicacy, more people, I think, should at least listen to Audiophile systems. Those who are naturally drawn to them—and that's maybe one in ten — might find themselves with a new hobby that will provide them with extraordinary pleasure.

Me? I appreciate it, but I'm not as attached to it as I am to, say, 35-inch TV screens or Surround Sound. I'm enjoying it while it's here, and when it goes back to from where it came, I will enjoy again the $3,000 system Robert put together for me years ago.

Bang and Olufsen Beocenter 9000
and Penta Speakers

Bang and Olufsen, in terms of sound, has always been somewhere between Hi-Fi and Audiophile (depending on which Audiophile you talk to), but in terms of design, it has always had the highest RAF (Roommate Acceptance Factor) around. The Beocenter 9000 and Penta Speakers system is no exception.

It sounds great, but it looks spectacular, and as the roommate of an Audiophile once said, "It's not how it *sounds* but how it *looks* that's important, and, darling, this looks *marvelous*."

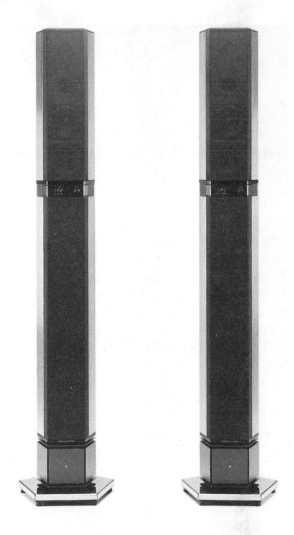

The preamp, amplifier, tuner, tape deck and CD player are all contained within a sleek wedge of stainless steel. (That "sleek wedge of stainless steel" line I stole from a car magazine's description of the DeLorean. Remember the DeLorean?) There's not a knob, switch or orifice in sight. It could be a piece of modern sculpture. (Various Bang and Olufsen pieces are part of the permanent collection of the Museum of Modern Art.)

This control center is called the Beocenter 9000. (I keep wanting to call it the *Bio*center — too much South California living, I suppose.) By touching the right spot on the Beocenter, a stainless steel panel glides out of the way to reveal the CD player. Touch the opposite side of the Beocenter, and a panel glides aside to reveal the tape deck. Touching other points along the 9000 control on, off, volume, tone, radio, CD track, tape track, and all the other necessary functions of an audio system.

It can also be controlled by the sleekest remote control you have ever seen, and the sexiest one you've ever held.

(All the Freudians are now mumbling to themselves and shaking their heads. Remember Freud?)

The Penta speakers will also have the Freudians raising their eyebrows and pulling on their beards. They are pentagons, eight inches across, that rise five feet into the air. (Come on, gang: as Freud himself once said, "Sometimes a cigar is just a cigar.") It looks like having a scale model of the twin towers of the World Trade Center in your living room.

The speakers sound good, but, to my ears, sound infinitely better with the addition of a subwoofer. (Any of the ones reviewed in Chapter 9, *Speakers*, would work fine — Bang and Olufsen does not make a subwoofer, although one wonders what it might look like if they did.) The addition of a subwoofer usually ranks high in RAF rating: they tend to look like end tables and can, in fact, be used for just that.

The price: $2,995 for the Beocenter 9000, $2,995 for a pair of Penta speakers. (This is Hi-Fi pricing. Audiophiles are more straightforward: $6,000 takes it all.)

Yes, of course, you could get better sound for the money, but, remember: you're not just buying electronics, you're buying *art* — and acceptance.

Chapter Twelve

Car Stereo

et's face it — cars are a Hi-Fi/Lo-Fi medium. Automobiles are just too small and too noisy to be taken seriously as an Audiophile listening environment.

Not that car stereo people don't try, and not that there isn't lots of perfectly splendid-sounding equipment available, but put it in a moving car and it all becomes high-end Hi-Fi.

It's impossible to produce proper bass notes in a car. It's too small. Low-frequency waves need lots of uninterrupted *space* to properly develop. Most living rooms are too small for most Audiophiles; a car, well, there's just no *room*.

Without proper low notes you don't have accurate sound. Any Audiophile will tell you that without woofers and subwoofers churning out the bass, music will never sound real. And the low frequencies are not just for kettle drums and tubas — the harmonics of many instruments require the lower register of sound.

The high end is masked by the white noise of a car going down the road. The hum of the engine, the friction of the tires, the whooshing of the wind create a white noise that neutralizes the high end.

Without a high end, how can you have natural sound? Further, without *silence* how can you have natural sound? (I think the Audiophile religion is an offshoot of Zen.)

In addition, a car is simply too brutal an environment for audiophile equipment — speakers in particular. The interior temperature of a car can go from 40 below to 160 above. Equipment also tends to be jolted, dusted and jarred. Audiophile equipment subjected to this torture wouldn't sound Audiophile for long.

As much trouble as cars provide Audiophiles, they are a Hi-Fier's heaven for the same reasons. Because the space is small, the bass notes can really *vibrate* the car. Because the car's white noise neutralizes highs, the hiss of cassette tape is less noticeable. And in a car you can play it *loud*.

Lo-Fi's are more than happy with the single-speaker AM radio that came with the car. AM/FM radio? Heaven on earth, joy on wheels. (Most Lo-Fi's listen to call-in talk shows in the car anyway.)

I love car stereo. I spend more time critically listening to music in my car than anywhere else. At home I'll listen for a few minutes, then start reading liner notes or absent-mindedly pick up a magazine or just drift down that inner mental waterway. I'll often get so interested in what I'm reading (or thinking) I'll turn the music down. An hour later it will dawn on me, "Wait a minute. I sat down to listen to music." And the process begins again.

In a car there is just enough going on to keep my attention focused on the moment — what with all the watching and steering and pedaling (brake pedaling and gas pedaling that is) — I'm just enough involved to have precisely the amount of unused mental energy it takes to listen to music.

It's also a Hi-Fi-free zone. If I want to turn the sub-woofers up so they vibrate my seat with every beat, I can do so without guilt. In a car you can *really* shake, rattle and roll.

S electing car stereo is difficult. What a system sounds like in an auto-stereo store is different from what it will sound like in a car, and what it sounds like in a car is different from what it will sound like in *your* car. And, of course, you can't have four or five systems installed in your car so that you can make a well-informed choice. (Well, you *can* do that, but it's not practical.)

Certainly, listen to stereo in a car (as opposed to a showroom). Also notice how much of the trunk is used for stereo equipment — you may not be willing to sacrifice that

Radios entered cars in 1927.
Romance had entered some time earlier

much space. (I sat in one car, and the sound was amazing — especially the bass. I mean, talk about the earth moving. On investigating further, it seems that the entire back seat *and* trunk was filled with speakers, amplifiers, wires and subwoofers.)

And, if you haven't bought car stereo in a while, don't be surprised by the prices. If you grew up when I did, you'll probably remember entire systems being installed for $39 — $59 with tape deck. Except for low-end Lo-Fi's, those days have passed. These days, well, I saw a $15,000 Toyota outfitted with $17,000 worth of stereo equipment.

What you select has a lot to do with your car. One manufacturer's speaker may be too large for your door, another's may be just right. One tape deck may fit in the hole provided by the auto maker, another may require major dashboard surgery. A good auto-stereo store will try to live up to the car stereo slogan: "All the sound that fits."

Car Stereo

Alpine and Kenwood Systems

This is just writing, ok? There are so many variables in choosing a car stereo — the acoustics of your car and the quality of the installation, for example — it's impossible to review in any marginally useful way car stereos. I don't want to pretend that any of this will be helpful to you at all. But maybe, just maybe, if we're both lucky, a line or two might help.

If I were to buy a car stereo — a good car stereo, $1,500 or more — I would do this: I'd find a good car stereo store, one that specializes in custom installation. I'd ask to hear stereos *in cars*. That may take several trips, because the cars you're apt to hear stereos in are usually customers' cars just before they're picked up.

When I found one I liked, I'd say, "I like this sound. Give me this sound in my car." That will give the installer an idea of what you like. Then you can talk equipment and prices.

In asking around about car stereo, two names alternated at the top of almost everybody's list: Alpine and Kenwood. Alpine I was familiar with — I'd had Alpine equipment in my car for the past four years.

Kenwood was something of a surprise. The name Kenwood I had associated with lower-middle-of-the-road home Hi-Fi of the late 1960's. (I think I might have owned a Kenwood receiver. I forget. It was a forgettable element of an unforgettable era.) Apparently, in the early 1980's, Kenwood decided to be the leader in auto stereo, and, some think, they have succeeded.

The point being this: If you're confused about which electronics to buy, you can't go wrong with Alpine or Kenwood. You can go right with a lot of other brands, but Alpine and Kenwood are a good place to start, even for lower-priced installations.

But what is it like to get a car stereo installed today? What would an ultimate car stereo sound like? I called Alpine and called Kenwood and said to each of them, "I'll give you a car; make it sound great."

Kenwood sent me to SNA Auto Sound in Reseda (The Valley), California. There Neil Adams, who owns and runs the place with his wife Sue (SNA: Sue & Neil Adams), took a look at the car. Within ten minutes, he knew what he wanted to do.

Then came the big question in auto sound installations: "How big can we make The Box?" The Box, in auto stereo, is where the subwoofers need to be put. Subwoofers, it seems, need a box (the air within the box, actually) to develop their full potential. Cars with trunks can sometimes use the trunk for the box (the subwoofers are mounted on the rear deck), but fastbacks and sports cars need The Box.

The bigger The Box the better, but the bigger The Box, the less car you have left. It's a choice: space vs. sound. For the Kenwood system I was using a colleague's car, a person whose taste in sound and size of car nearly parallels my own. It was his choice how big the box could be. He basically said, "Do what you need to do, but leave me enough room for my skis."

A week later, they had done what they needed to do, and it sounded wonderful. Too wonderful. My Alpine system, by comparison, sounded terrible.

The Alpine system — installed in my new car by the person who installed the Alpine system in my old car four years before — was, before listening to the Kenwood system, disappointing. After listening to the Kenwood system, it was depressing.

I called Alpine. I suggested that my suggestion of who should install the Alpine system was probably a bad one. I asked them for a better suggestion. They sent me to Radio-Active Sound in Los Angeles. This car stereo store is owned by another husband and wife team, John and Cathy Stolkin. (The men's room is labeled "John," the women's room is labeled, "Cathy.")

They have a super installer, Jeff. Jeff thought my system sounded awful. (I thought it was merely bad.) He popped off one of the grills, and he found that the prior installer had *left in the original speakers which came with the car*. This is the equivalent of paying a doctor to remove your appendix and another doctor finding your appendix intact. La scandal.

Cathy, John and Jeff took my car unto their fold (after asking me how big a Box I could live with), and a week later my car sounded as good as the Kenwood car.

Which is better? No way of knowing. Both sound remarkable (and feel remarkable, too, what with all those subwoofers vibrating away in their Boxes). For a while my friend thought mine sounded better, but then he found out that his installation cost more, so he now thinks his sounds better. I'd be happy to have either system in my car. Hell, I'd be happy with either system in my *home*.

The cost? Plenty. The pleasure? Plenty. The joy? Lots. What price fun?

Alpine 7385 Tuner/tape deck	$ 550.00
Alpine 5902 Compact Disc Player	600.00
Alpine 3337 Graphic Equalizer	370.00
Alpine 3530 4-Channel Power Amp.	430.00
Alpine 3528 4-Channel Power Amp.	330.00
Alpine 3652 Electronic Crossover	70.00
Alpine 6170 7" Subwoofer (1 pr.)	100.00/pr
Alpine 6040 Midrange (2 pr.)	90.00/pr
Alpine 6010 Dome Tweeter (2 pr.)	130.00/pr
Custom Speaker Enclosure (The Box)	200.00
	$3090.00
Custom installation	800.00
TOTAL	*$3890.00*

Kenwood KRC-939 Cassette Tuner	899.00
Kenwood KDC-9R CD Player	849.00
Kenwood KGC-4400 Graphic Equalizer	149.00
Kenwood KEC-1100 Electronic Crossover	149.00
Kenwood KAC-9020 Power Amplifier	429.00
Kenwood KAC-8020 Main Amplifier	329.00
Kenwood KAC-7020 Main Amplifier	229.00
Kenwood KFC-2020 8" subwoofers	159.00/pr
Kenwood KFC-5050 midrange/woofer	119.00/pr
Kenwood KFC-1010 1" dome tweeter	99.00/pr
Custom Subwoofer Enclosure (The Box)	200.00
	$3610.00
Installation	1000.00
TOTAL	*$4610.00*

Part Two

Video

ust as listeners can be seen as three basic groups — Lo-Fi, Hi- Fi and Audiophiles — allow me to divide the watchers into three categories: Videophiles, TV Viewers and Couch Potatoes.

Couch Potatoes *love* television. If it's on TV, it's worth watching. After all, the station paid somebody good money to decide what would and would not be on TV. Who is a Couch Potato to argue with someone good enough to get paid by a TV station?

TV Viewers are selective. They subscribe to *TV Guide*. They review options, choose carefully, and watch with pleasure.

Videophiles consider *time* to be among the most precious commodities on earth. Whatever time they spend in front of a TV screen must be time well spent. They don't just select programs, they research them. They care enough to watch *only* the very best.

Potatoes enjoy commercials as much as programs. After all, they saw on *60 Minutes* once that commercials cost something like ten times more per minute to produce than TV shows, and if it costs more, it has to be better.

Viewers watch commercials selectively. The sight of George C. Scott selling Renaults, for example, is enough reason to watch a commercial.

Videophiles never watch commercials. It's a matter of principle. They also never open junk mail. Same principle.

Potatoes have no need for Video Cassette Recorders. What's the point? Why record something *now* and watch it *later*? Why not just watch it now? Besides, later there'll be something else on.

Viewers will often videotape something. This is especially true if they go out for the evening or if two programs of value are on at the same time.

Videophiles tape everything. They like the control. If something is dull they can fast forward. If there's a commercial, they can fast forward. If there are titles, chase scenes, establishing shots, musical interludes or Eddie Murphy, they can fast forward.

Other than a TV (color, please), the only other piece of video equipment a Couch Potato considers essential is a remote control. It doesn't have to be wireless, it doesn't have to control the sound — a cable box over by the couch is just fine, thank you. Potatoes without remote controls are not helpless creatures — they simply pick one station and watch that. Once a week they get up to change stations. The only program a couch potato might get up to change is an exercise show.

Viewers think the new larger screen stereo TV's are great and they are Seriously Considering one. A second VCR is also on the list, and maybe one of those portable camera-recorder things. And the all-in-one Entertainment Centers with CD's and speakers? Well, that would be nice — maybe when Jim retires.

Videophiles left two-channel stereo long ago. They've had Dolby four-channel Surround Sound for some time. With five speakers and a subwoofer, minimum. And three amplifiers. And a 35-inch monitor. And . . .

Couch Potatoes never rent video tapes. Why rent? There are lots of movies on TV all the time — for free. A movie's just another TV program, anyway. But what about non-movie videos? Say, *Jane Fonda's Low Impact Aerobic Challenge*? Asking a Couch Potato this is like asking a Couch Potato, "Why is Cheez Whiz in an aerosol can better than Cheez Whiz in a jar?" Some things are just, well, self-evident.

TV Viewers will occasionally rent a video, if they know they'll have time to watch it within the 24-hour rental period, and providing it will not be on cable within the next six months.

Videophiles never rent videos. If possible they *buy* LaserDiscs. If not, they'll buy videos. They don't want their state-of-the- art VCR's crudded up with the gook left on the tape by the previous God-knows-how-many renters of the video. It's like taking a bath in someone else's water.

So where do you fit in? I'm something of a Videophile myself, probably more of a Videophile than I am an Audiophile. I'd rather not watch a movie that's available in Dolby Stereo unless I can watch it on a Surround Sound system. (Regular stereo just isn't enough, sorry.)

I'm a Viewer in that I will watch a commercial every now and then. (George C. Scott selling cars?! John Denver selling cereal!?)

And I confess to an occasional night of Couch Potato-ing, flipping from channel to channel, movie to preacher to rerun, all night long with no goal in sight other than the hope I will be able to gather enough will power to turn the thing off and go to sleep.

The first television image: Felix the Cat, 1930 (NBC).

Chapter Thirteen

Television

emember when the only technical decision you had to make when buying a TV was "Black & white or color?"

The *big* decisions involved the *cabinet*. When I was growing up, I remember whole living rooms being redecorated to match the style of the new console. ("Well, George and I had always wanted French Provençal, and, well, when we saw this new Magnavox, it was, 'Goodbye Early American!'")

Now you have about as many technical choices as channels to watch, providing you get a cable-ready set, which is one of your choices.

In some cases they're not even called TV's anymore. A large box arrived the other day from Pioneer. It was labeled "Component Display." We couldn't figure out from the box if this was a display screen for a TV, or a piece of furniture on which the TV sat for proper displaying in one's living room.

It was, in fact, a TV. Not a monitor, but a whole TV, in one unit — speakers, tuner and all. It's what *I* would call a TV, but it's Pioneer's TV, so I guess they can call it whatever they want. The only real problem comes when people start

149

calling Component Displays "CD's." We already have CD's in audio and CD's at the bank. We don't need another CD. Maybe we'll call it Pioneer's Component Display, or PCD. No, that sounds like an insecticide. I think I'll let Pioneer figure it out.

Here's what's available in television today...

Black & White or Color. Believe it or not, almost 4,000,000 black & white TV's were sold in the United States last year. (By comparison, 18,000,000 color sets were sold.) Half of these black & white TV's were the little portable pocket-sized units. The rest were for the home. Two million people chose black & white over color. Many of these two million bought black & white for economic reasons, but one has to assume that a good number bought black & white because they *prefer* black & white. Black & white is a choice that one out of five TV buyers chose last year.

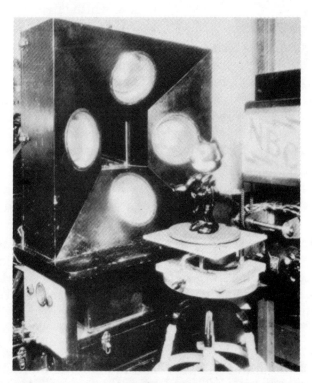

Felix offered no chromatic challenges — he had only two colors to start with: black and white.

Television

Black & white is no longer called black & white by the Electronics Industries Association. Black & white is now monochrome. Well, not in my book. (And this *is* my book, isn't it? I guess the one you're holding is *your* book. Let's just call it "our" book. Can we agree that black & white should remain black & white, and refer to it accordingly in our book? Thanks. It's fun sharing a book with you.) I doubt if one of those four million people walked into an electronics store and said, "I would like a monochrome TV." Try asking for a monochrome TV at Discount Emporium. They will think you're out of your mind.

Remote Control. Why jump up to change the channel, or adjust the volume, or turn the whole thing off? Granted, some people avoid remote controls for health reasons — changing their minds and changing channels is the only exercise they get. For the rest of us in peak athletic condition — or who have abandoned all hope — remote controls are a gift from Recline, the god of laziness.

And if you're going to get a remote, go all the way and get a *wireless* remote. A wired remote creates almost as many problems as it solves. Imagine one more thing to become tangled with the phone cord. Imagine one more thing to trip over on those 120-second dashes from the TV to the kitchen to the bathroom and back. Imagine vacuuming over the wire and having nothing sticking out the end of your Hoover Upright but a remote box and a TV. As they used to say in the early days of radio, "Get a wireless."

Cable Ready. All TV's must (by law) tune the full VHF and UHF band. Cable operates on a different band. A TV that can tune in cable channels without a cable converter box is known as cable ready. Naturally, we pay extra for this. Some people don't need it. A cable box with a remote often works just as well, although the cable companies usually charge an extra monthly fee for it. Buying a cable-ready TV eliminates the converter box rental. To get the movie stations on many cable services, however, requires a converter anyway. (The movie stations are often scrambled.) TV dealers in your area usually know if a converter is required even with a cable-ready set. I consider cable ready a necessary feature on a VCR, but an optional one on a TV.

High Resolution. Television pictures are made up of a series of horizontal lines. From a distance, these lines merge to form a picture. Broadcast TV (the networks, local stations, cable, etc.) sends out 330 lines of horizontal resolution. Most sets today are capable of displaying the full 330 lines.

Getting the Horizontal Resolution just right.

Some of the super sets, however, have a higher resolution. They display more than 450 lines. If broadcast TV is sending only 330 lines, why bother with a 450-plus-line set?

A few reasons. First, some people don't trust manufacturers' specifications. I know it's hard to believe, but some people are actually *leery* of big business. I don't know why. Big businesses got big by being reputable, kind and honest, right? We all know that. But there are some out there who, inexplicably, think some manufacturers' claims of 330 lines is, well, stretching it a bit. No, I never sat down and counted horizontal lines, but I guess some people have, and they don't always come up with 330. The point being, I guess, that if they *advertise* 450 lines, you'll probably end up with *at least* 330.

Second, some people use their TV screen as a computer monitor. For sharp display of text and graphics, computer monitors require more resolution than color TV's.

Third, LaserDisc players and Super-VHS provide more lines of resolution than broadcast TV's 330. If you watch a movie on LaserDisc or a home video made with a Super-VHS camcorder, you'll see a picture better than NBC's broadcasting that night — providing you're watching on a high-resolution TV.

High resolution is more expensive, but it's also the future. How often do you buy a TV, anyway? Spread out over the useful life of the set, a high-resolution TV might not be much more expensive after all.

Picture within a Picture. This is a small picture within the main picture on the screen. You can watch one station (or video) while keeping tabs on another. It's useful when you want to, say, keep up with the score of a baseball game without watching the game (put the game on the picture within a picture), or to find out when the commercials are over on the program you're watching while you wander around the dial. Some TV's permit more than one picture within a picture at the same time.

Stereo, MTS (Multichannel Television Sound) and Surround Sound. Irresistible and recommended. Please see the next chapter.

Components

Yes, TV is falling apart. You can now buy a TV in pieces — sort of an audio-visual Erector Set. Here are what the parts are called and what they once did when TV's came all in one piece.

Monitor. What we once called the screen. Now it's in a box all by itself with the classy moniker monitor.

Tuner. This tunes in the TV signal. It used to be called the channel selector. Needs to be hooked up to a monitor, amplifier and speakers.

Amplifier. Amplifies the sound from the tuner. It has what we used to call the volume control.

Receiver. A receiver is a tuner with an amplifier built in.

Speakers. Yes, the lowly speaker has retained its name. It was called a speaker in the forties and it's called a speaker in the eighties.

Of these components, the amplifier and speakers can double as your audio amplifier and speakers. Some receivers can handle everything — phono, CD, tape decks, DAT decks, LaserDisc players, VCR's and, oh yes, TV.

Projection vs. Direct-View TV

The TV's we grew up with are direct-view televisions — you directly view the picture on a picture tube. The big ones you see in bars and dormitory lounges are projection TV's — the picture is projected either on the rear of a plastic panel or projected onto a screen across a crowded room.

Here your choice is a simple one, sharpness vs. size.

Some people like the sheer magnitude of projection TV's. They like to move their heads from side to side when watching two characters conversing, as though they were at Wimbledon.

Those some are not overwhelming numbers. Only 300,000 projection TV's were sold in the U.S. last year. (Compared with 18,000,000 direct-view color sets.)

"Not a very good picture."

"We can make a fortune on this."

"Not such a bad picture after all."

Others prefer sharpness. They notice that even an inexpensive color set is sharper and more detailed than the most expensive projection set. (A smart retailer will display the projection TV's on one side of the store and the direct-view TV's on the other. It avoids unwelcome inadvertent comparisons.)

Before you are dazzled by the size of a projection TV, consider the following: It is not the actual *size* of the screen that's important, it's the *percentage of total eye area filled* that counts.

For example, a drive-in movie screen is larger than a five-inch portable TV screen, but if the drive-in screen is 100 yards away, and the TV is ten inches from your face, the

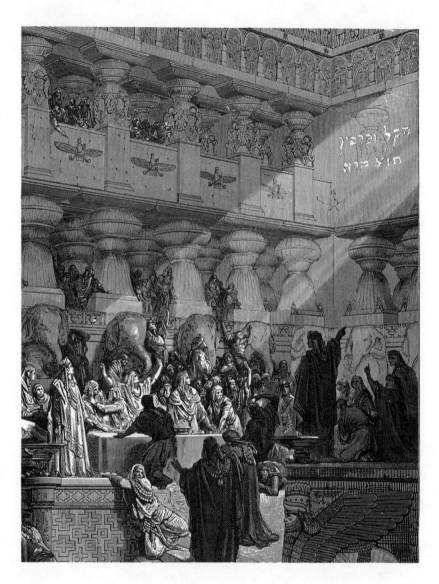

Early projection TV.

TV screen will appear to be larger. Children have been playing this game for years: They hold their thumb up to the moon and, because their thumb looks bigger than the moon, they can tell their friends, "My thumb is bigger than the moon" — and prove it.

So, if you sit closer to a 27-inch or 35-inch direct-view TV, the same amount of eye area is occupied as watching a 60-inch projection TV from farther away, and you'll have a sharper picture.

Some people buy projection TV's thinking "the whole family can watch." A problem with projection TV, though, is what they call the field of vision. If you sit directly in front of a projection TV, at just the right height, you get the maximum brightness (which, at its best, is still not as bright as the dullest direct-view screens). If you move left, right, up or down, this brightness decreases, usually quickly and dramatically. Everyone watching gravitates toward the center of the field of vision. The family who buys a projection TV might find themselves with more togetherness than they actually bargained for.

Besides, how often has your entire family wanted to watch the same thing at the same time? For the price of your average projection TV, you could buy a family of five a 19-inch color set and an inexpensive VCR — *each*. Now, tell me what family wouldn't be happier with that solution?

I think projection TV's are a wonderful idea whose technological time has not yet come. The trade-offs in sharpness and brightness are far too great. When a truly sharp wall-size screen becomes available, I'll be the first in line.

Selecting a TV

Only a couple years ago, this would have been the shortest section in the book. "Buy a Sony," it would have read, and we all could move on to more important matters.

In the past two years, however, almost every other TV manufacturer has made dramatic strides forward and Sony has not. Some manufacturers, many feel, have not just caught up to Sony, but have surpassed it.

It now seems to be open season on Sony, once the undisputed king of quality television. I can't tell you how often I've heard, from expert and novice alike, "I was going to get a Sony, but then I saw the _____ and I liked it so much better." Even the Premier of Japan pronounces his name "Knock-A-Sony."

It's not that Sony has gotten *worse*, you understand; it's that so many other companies have gotten, if not better, at least *real good*. After years of turning out mediocre TV's, these manufacturers took a look at Sony's commitment to excellence and Sony's impressive sales figures (Sony would often outsell the competition, even though a Sony sometimes cost twice as much) and decided, "There's gold in them thar high-end TV's."

The result is more and better televisions on the market. The *choice* is not as easy, but *your* choice will probably be easier to live with.

Watching TV at the 1939 World's Fair.

Like audio speakers, the purchase of a TV is a subjective one. The new sets have a variety of design philosophies that produce a variety of visual results. It's not a matter of better results or worse results, just *different* results. Ignore microblack this and fine-dot-pitch that — the one you prefer is the one you should buy. Just as you shop for speakers by listening, shop for television by viewing.

Here are some suggestions on selecting a TV. . .

1. Decide which features you want — high resolution, stereo, approximate screen size, etc. This may take a trip to a well-equipped video store to have all these demonstrated. Then go home and decide which options you (A) need, (B) lust after, (C) desire, (D) want, (E) wouldn't throw out of your bedroom, and (F) can do without. Overlay your budget on this list and see how far down the alphabet you can go.

2. Return to the store (it's probably best not to decide on features *and* picture on the same visit) and ask to see televisions with the features you want. Knowing the features will narrow the number of sets to look at.

3. Watch a live broadcast if possible. Local news shows are usually a good bet (the anchorperson part). Also prime-time network sitcoms. The idea is to get the best original signal possible. (Good and bad sets look about the same with *I Dream of Jeannie* reruns.) The better the broadcast signal, the better the good TV's will look. *Never* compare TV's using a regular VHS video.

If you plan to buy a high-resolution TV, ask to see some high-resolution programming on it — a LaserDisc or prerecorded Super-VHS tape.

4. Look at various sets and begin picking your favorites. Make notes. Even if you can remember every-

thing, make notes. You look like a *serious* shopper when you make notes.

5. If you don't like something about the picture, ask the salesperson to adjust the set, or do it yourself. Most TV's have a lot of leeway in how they can be adjusted. Adjusting color, contrast and sharpness can make quite a difference.

Whoever adjusted the set before you might have been (A) another educated consumer (such as yourself) with pictorial tastes different from yours; (B) a Martian who has not yet accustomed itself to Earth colors; (C) someone on drugs; (D) a fan of MTV; (E) all of the above.

6. As you narrow your choices, begin A/B testing. Watch the same program on two TV's next to (or relatively close to) one other. Don't try to remember what each picture looks like; compare one against another while both are in front of you. Adjust each so they're at their best. Pick your favorite. Then compare your favorite against the next contender.

7. If you come down to two or three that look about the same (all wonderful, one hopes), make your final choice based on cabinet style, price, brand name recognition, or whatever other variables you find important. But pick the picture first. You'll be looking at that long after the cabinet has become just another part of your living room.

RADIO & TELEVISION

Leaning Tower of Babel

Television's proud edifice, though still unfinished, is already showing cracked plaster and faulty brickwork. Last week, the architects were blaming everything from the other fellow to the unseasonable weather.

Hardest hit were the networks, which have poured the most money into TV and reaped the least profit. This year CBS has made $500,000 less than it did in the first half of 1948. Du Mont's books have a reddish tinge and ABC, which can least afford it, is losing most of all. NBC does not release a balance sheet, but it is no exception. Of 76 TV stations in the U.S., only six claimed to be breaking even or making money. Manhattan's WPIX, owned by the New York *Daily News*, dropped $1,000,000 in 1948.

Although more than 100 manufacturers were making TV sets, 90% of the sales still went to the industry's Big Eight (Admiral, Crosley, Du Mont, Emerson, General Electric, Motorola, Philco and RCA). Last winter both big & small manufacturers were booming confidently ahead in the expectation that 1949 was going to be a 2,500,000-set year. This spring they crashed into a roadblock of buyer resistance. By last week, many of the smaller companies were hanging on by their fingernails.

Despite the surface evidence that television had built too quickly and recklessly, the industry was keeping its fingers crossed and hoping that it would be snug and shipshape by the first winds of winter.

Time *magazine's slightly clouded crystal ball.*

Ah, television! Childhood memory #1.

THE PERSONAL ELECTRONICS BOOK

Three Televisions

I am not *Consumer Reports*. God bless them, and everyone interested in personal electronics (and canned tuna) should certainly have a subscription, but I'm not them. I do not buy one of everything on the market and attach it to an automatic kicking machine that simulates 27 years' worth of wear in four hours.

When it came time to review televisions, I did not get one of all five hundred models on the market. I got three (plus two 35-inch TV's, which I'll get to in a moment). Not what you'd call exhaustive. I was mostly curious to see if, in television receivers, money equaled quality.

I got one each in three price categories: the Hitachi 22-inch CT2260, $599.95; the Pioneer 26-inch SD2600 Component Display (TV), $1,000; and the Toshiba 25-inch CZ2697, $1,499.

Right off, Pioneer won on the price. None of this $999.95 business; $1,000, straight shot.

In appearance, the Toshiba was the immediate winner: sleek lines, slim profile, component black; nice. The Pioneer came in second: black, solid; ok. Externally, the Hitachi was the clear looser: some sort of plastic coating, desperately attempting — but failing — to look like inexpensive wood veneer.

Then the sound test. Here, again, it was Toshiba first, Pioneer second, Hitachi dead last. Both the Toshiba and Pioneer have stereo speakers built-in. The Hitachi has a single mono speaker. To get stereo TV with the Hitachi, you have to buy a special adapter.

Then the big test: picture. I decided the fairest test was to connect the TV's to the same source through the antenna input. This is how most people watch TV — through cable or antenna. (The alternative was direct connection through one of the AUX inputs, but this would have bypassed the tuners.)

The three were connected to a LaserDisc player, so an excellent original signal was generated.

Television

Toshiba

Pioneer

Hitachi

The room was darkened, and the test began. Guess what? The Hitachi won! It was clearly the best picture: sharp, true colors, and a three-dimensional quality to the images. There seemed to be a layer of white gauze between the TV image and the viewer on both the Toshiba and the Pioneer. The Hitachi was like watching images through a clean window.

Well, naturally no one believed this. We knew the Hitachi was a slightly smaller tube, and smaller tubes tend to look sharper than larger tubes, but, even taking that into account, it was still a better picture. We thought maybe the Toshiba and Pioneer needed adjustment, so we adjusted. In vain. The Hitachi still looked best.

(One reviewer spent quite a bit of time frantically adjusting and readjusting the Toshiba: he had fallen in love with its design and was planning to get one, but couldn't justify the purchase unless he got the picture at least as good as the Hitachi's — he never did.)

All this, unintentionally, proved a point I'd made all along: in personal electronics, the external appearance or trade name or cost has little, if anything, to do with how it performs. (Which is one of the things I like best about *Consumer Reports*: the $50 Ordinary Walkman often beats out the $300 Ultra Super Deluxe Walkman.)

Lest I bore you with repetition, I'll make the conclusion brief: in shopping for a TV, don't select by specification, brand name, cost or design. Buy with your eyes.

Mitsubishi

35-inch Tube Televisions

For the Videophile, or a Viewer who has just won the lottery, there is no real choice in television screens: 35-inch tube televisions are in a classification unto themselves.

The two most popular 35-inch tube (as opposed to projection) TV's are Mitsubishi and Sharp. Both use the same picture tube. It was developed by Mitsubishi at a cost of $50,000,000. (Or, as they say in personal electronics, $49,999,999.95.) It seems the larger the tube, the more the expense and difficulty in making the tube increase. (A set with a 41-inch tube is on the market in Japan. The cost? A mere $12,000, uh, $11,999.95. All right. That's the last of the 999.95 jokes. Honest.)

To get their money back sometime in this century, Mitsubishi sells the tube to other manufacturers, including Sharp.

Sharp has two models — $2,795 and $2,995 — the higher priced model having better speakers. Mitsubishi has a variety of models, beginning with a $2,500 table model (for *large* tables) and escalating to $3,300 for deluxe consoles.

Both provide excellent pictures. The Mitsubishi remote is more elaborate than the Sharp. The Sharp, on the other hand, has outputs for surround speakers (although not genuine Dolby Surround) whereas the Mitsubishi does not.

The newer Mitsubishi 35-inch TV's have a direct Y/C input. This is important when using the set with high resolution sources, Super-VHS, for example. The older Mitsubishi's had "over 400" lines of horizontal resolution; the new ones, 560. You may find some of the older ones on sale. How to tell the difference? See if it has a Y/C connector input in the back. (You don't have to crawl behind the set; it's listed in the instruction manual.)

Yes, 35-inch TV's are expensive, but, if you're anything like me, after living with one for a while, you'll never want to look at anything else — until those 41-inch sets, at dramatically reduced prices, hit our shores.

"Sounds like it's coming from everywhere, doesn't it?"

Chapter Fourteen

Hi-Fi TV

he most important thing in decades to happen to tele*vision* is *sound.*

Since its invention and until a few years ago, the sound portion of TV has been all but ignored. I mean, *radio* was the sound portion of television, and radio was already invented. By the mid-fifties when television got into full swing, the sound from most TV's was worse than most radios — the speakers were smaller, and the amount of money spent on amplifying the sound portion of the TV signal insignificant.

There were a few experiments, not so much to improve the quality of sound, but more its direction. In the late 1950's, ABC, the perennial third-place network, experimented with stereo TV. (Anything for a rating point, right?) An AM radio was placed to the right of the TV and was tuned to a radio station broadcasting the right channel. The left channel came from the TV. I remember watching a couple of Lawrence Welk shows this way.

The drawbacks of the system were obvious — both the radio listener and the TV viewer got only part of the soundtrack; there were no left and right channels, just center and right; and the differences between the sound of one's AM radio and the sound of one's television became painfully evident.

It was a failed experiment, but, if somebody has copies of those old Lawrence Welk programs, it might be interesting to see them released on a stereo video tape, just for old time's sake.

The first thing I did with my first TV (I must have been about fifteen — my grandmother gave me a barely working black & white set from her basement) was add an external speaker. This improved the sound markedly. The next thing I did was figure out how to bypass the el cheapo internal TV amplifier. A convenient *Popular Science* article told me how. I attached the TV to my fledgling stereo (one channel was a mono portable phonograph, the other channel the aux input from an AM radio) and, lo, it worked.

I invited my parents down (I had moved into the basement by then) to demonstrate my latest invention: Multi-Speaker-Almost-High-Fidelity television. After what I thought was a thrilling demonstration, my mother said, wincing, "It's a little loud," and my father added, looking at the wires and haphazard electrical connections and shaking his head, "You'll burn the place down yet." Ah, well. I guess even Edison was not much respected in his youth.

From that point on, my TV, such as it was, was always attached to my stereo, such as it was. In the early 1970's, when I was writing for a music magazine, I visited A&M Records. They had a video tape of one of their groups. I can't remember the group, but I remember the sound. It was on a 3/4-inch tape with a full stereo soundtrack and connected to top-of-the-line equipment. I remember watching the screen and listening to all that sound and thinking, "Someday I'm going to have a TV with sound like this."

Someday, for all of us (with a little ready cash), has arrived.

A few years ago, somebody noticed that the band used to broadcast TV signals was as good a carrier of sound as FM, and that FM had had high fidelity stereo sound for years. PBS, in fact, broadcast the audio portion of various broadcasts over FM, much to the enjoyment of opera and classical lovers everywhere.

These people wondered, "Why can't we upgrade the quality of the TV signal to FM-radio standards, and while we're at it, why not add stereo, too?"

I must warn you that the people who sit around wondering things like this are usually employed by TV manufacturers. Their job is not so much to advance the state of the art as it is to find a reason for you to buy a new TV. (Remember the "Halo of Light" surrounding the picture tube? Too young for that? Then remember the speaker-phone built into the TV? Come on, that was only a few years ago.) Such "improvements" are not necessarily great leaps of technological progress. But in the case of stereo TV, it is.

Like FM, the two stereo channels are "multiplexed" (combined) when broadcasting. A conventional TV receives a monaural signal, but a stereo TV separates the signal into the original stereo pair.

This is also known as Multichannel Television Sound or MTS. A variation of this is called Separate Audio Channel (SAP). SAP allows for simultaneous transmission of two audio tracks at once — one in English and one in Spanish, for example.

You've probably noticed that you see more stereo programming on NBC than on ABC and CBS combined. If you ask NBC, they will tell you it's because they enjoy being the technological pioneer, they pioneered network radio (ABC was once the Red Network — or was it the Blue Network? — of NBC), they pioneered color TV and . . .

The real reason, of course, is that NBC is owned by RCA and RCA is owned by GE and RCA and GE make and sell televisions. (RCA also made and sold radios — Radio Corporation of America, you know — and made and sold color TV's.) Now it's stereo TV. *

ABC and CBS are, well, dragging their corporate feet. Both of them broadcast, occasionally, in stereo, but neither has converted its owned and operated local stations for stereo broadcast. This is silly because, although stereo TV is a small percentage of the total TV population, the people buying stereo TV's are more educated, more cultured, more intelligent, more, well, wonderful — people just like us, in fact — than ordinary TV viewers. We're the very people advertisers want to reach. The fact that we all own VCR's and fast forward through commercials is beside the point. While we're fast forwarding, we're getting the message subliminally. We'll say no subliminally, too, but that, too, is beside the point.

---

*In late 1987, GE sold its consumer electronics divison (including RCA) to Thomson, but GE retained ownership of NBC. Now that the ties between NBC and the manufacturing of radios and televisions has been severed after, lo, these many years, it will be curious to see if NBC pioneers any more technological advancements.

It's not just the few programs broadcast in stereo that sound better. Almost *all* TV sound sounds better these days. Here are some of the reasons:

1. In the old days, network television had to be sent around the country over telephone lines. These were special high-quality lines, but they had to limit the frequency response of the sound portion. No one cared, because no one (except maybe me) had a TV on which you could tell the difference. This led to an interesting situation: Locally produced inexpensive TV programs sounded better than expensively produced network shows. Communication satellites — the current method of network distribution — have no restrictions on the quality of sound.

2. When the soundtracks for television shows were mixed, the engineers intentionally narrowed the frequency response for clarity. If a full range recording is put through a five-inch speaker, the bottom end might rattle the speaker and the top end might sound shrill. If you cut off the bottom and the top, however, and boost the frequencies associated with the human voice, then it will sound better over a five-inch TV speaker — but awful through a hi-fi system. (Notice how flat some of the old TV shows sound today.) Shows are now mixed with stereo, or at least full-range hi-fi, in mind.

3. In years past, the primary form of preserving and playing back TV shows was film. Video tape, which took over as the standard about fifteen years ago, has a much broader spectrum of sound than a 16mm film soundtrack.

4. When the rumblings of stereo TV began six or seven years ago, most TV stations, both network and local, began upgrading their audio equipment. This process is, for the most part, complete. Even programs not broadcast in stereo usually have high-fidelity-quality sound.

hen buying a stereo TV, pay no attention to the sound of the TV itself. Plan from the outset to bypass the speakers and amplifier that are built into the TV. Although I'm impressed with the quality of stereo TV, I'm not impressed with any of the speakers-built-into-the-cabinet stereo TV's I've listened to, even the expensive ones. They never quite get the bass notes (some don't even try) and the stereo separation is not very good. (Left should be over *there* and right should be over *there*.)

Ideally, you already have an audio system and you plan to put the TV in the same room. This is not always true, but it's an ideal. All you'd have to do, then, is plug the output from your TV into the input of your stereo system and — magic.

If you watch TV in a room separate from your audio system, it's still worth buying a separate amplifier and speakers for your stereo TV. Unless you're a videophile, there's no need to spend a lot for these. Because the vision part of television will dominate your awareness (80% of our brain is used to process visual images), the sound for TV doesn't have to be as good as the sound for an audio system.

If you don't have an audio system, what a wonderful excuse, er, opportunity to get one. There are receivers available that pick up TV and FM *and* have inputs for everything else, from phono to CD. And then there are those complete Home Entertainment Systems. Hmmmm. Tempting. In the old days you shopped for a TV and wound up buying a living room full of furniture. Today you shop for a TV and wind up buying an audio-visual paradise.

Surround Sound

If you think stereo TV sounds exciting, wait until you hear about Surround Sound — or, should I say, wait until you *hear* Surround Sound.

It all began about the time of the first *Star Wars* movie. Dolby Laboratories, the people who invented the Dolby noise reduction system for cassette tapes, came up with a way of combining four stereo channels into the standard two stereo channels of 35mm movie film.

This was not the old four channel ("quad") sound. Because it was designed for movies, three of the channels were placed in the front — left, center (for dialogue) and right — and the fourth channel was spread across the back of the theater — the Surround channel.

The Dolby system caught on, and almost every major film of the past six or seven years (and many films before it, including all the George Lucas/Steven Spielberg epics) are in Dolby Stereo.

What does this mean to you, Mr. and Ms. TV Viewer? Well, with a bit of money (quite a bit of money, in some cases) you, too, can have four channels of stereo surrounding you while you watch TV.

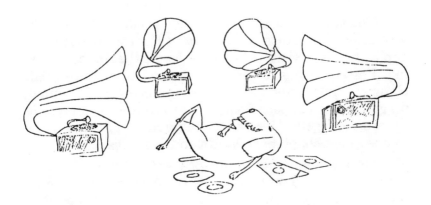

Like stereo itself, the technology to divide the two Dolby-encoded stereo channels into four is not expensive. Many high-end TV's and video receivers have Surround Sound built in — just add a pair of inexpensive speakers to the rear of your room and you're in business.

Surround Sound adds to the enjoyment of all TV, especially stereo broadcasts. (When watching *The Tonight Show*, for example, Johnny comes from the center, Ed from the left, Doc from the right and the audience from the two speakers in the rear. It sounds as though you're watching from the audience.) When you rent a Dolby-encoded movie, your living room comes alive — spaceships soar over your head, the monster sneaks up from behind, the background noise in a diner rattles from all around.

And, like stereo itself, you can get Surround Sound for around a hundred, or you can spend yet uncounted thousands, pursuing the ever-elusive State of the Art.

The state of the art in audio is reproducing a live performance. The state of the art in Surround Sound is duplicating a movie theater. (Please note that in the following, I'm not going to consider the *source* of the sound. Naturally, no matter how much you process a poor sound, it's going to sound poor. Sometimes the more you process it, the worse it gets. More about the quality of the original source in the chapters on VCR's and LaserDiscs.)

Once you have your four speakers — two in the front (for left, right and center) and two in the back (for the Surround channel) — the next step in improving your Surround Sound system is adding a subwoofer. Dolby Surround movies are infatuated with the subwoofer. They use it constantly. The bad guy enters, they vibrate you with ominous low notes. A car door slams, your living room shakes. A bomb explodes, your windows crack.

Subwoofers add a lot to CD's, tapes, records and other audio sources, but subwoofers are almost essential for proper Dolby Surround Sound.

After a subwoofer, the next step up is making sure all your speakers have enough power — I'm talking raw watts, here. Dolby-encoded movies seem to enjoy what I call The Loud Surprise. It's used in suspense, drama, comedy, you name it. Everything is quiet and peaceful on the soundtrack, you're almost straining to listen, when suddenly CRASH! BOOM! BAM! — The Loud Surprise. Sometimes this is the audio equivalent of shooting a cannon into the audience in early 3-D movies — but I'm not here to discuss the artistic use of The Big Surprise, I'm here to talk equipment.

Loud noises consume a lot of power. If the sound demands more watts than your amplifier can put out and/or your speakers can accommodate, the result is distortion. You don't want the sound of that buzzing chain saw to be distorted, do you? Of course not. So, if necessary, get more watts.

The next level up has to do with the center channel. On most sound processors, the center channel is produced in the same way the center channel is produced in audio. The left and right speakers send out the same information, which gives the illusion of Sinatra singing between the two speakers. This is sometimes called the "phantom channel."

If your audio system has good imaging (placement of voices and instruments at precise locations within the field of sound), the center channel should be quite pronounced. If you sit at a spot equidistant between the two speakers ("the sweet spot" it's called — I hate that phrase; I don't think I'll use it any more), you will hear dialogue coming from the phantom center speaker, which, of course, should be the location of your television screen.

If there's only one or two people watching TV, sitting at the equidistant location is not difficult. If, however, several people (or two people who don't much like each other) try to watch, the people a few feet from either side of the equidistant point will not have the illusion of the center channel coming from the TV screen.

If you have crowds watching TV, you may want to get a Surround processor with a separate center-channel output. The center channel sits just above or just below the screen and guarantees that dialogue will sound as though it's coming from the screen no matter where a person sits.

Now if you want a discrete center channel, we must explore some more technical details, learn the difference between *passive* and *active* Dolby decoders, and also learn about *steering*.

When you set out to make the phantom center channel less ectoplasmic, you come across certain difficulties. The problem is: how to get the sound, which once came out of the left and right channels, to no longer come out of the left and right channels but to come out of the center. This means removing *some* but not *all* of the sound from the left and right channels. (Music or sound effects must still come from left and right, but dialogue from the center.)

The proper directing of sounds is called *steering* — the correct sound is steered from the left and right channels into the center. A man named Peter Schieber invented the best way of doing this, and, up until recently, to make a proper Dolby Surround decoder with a center channel meant licensing the Dolby Surround circuitry from Dolby and the steering circuitry from Mr. Schieber. Only Shure and Fosgate cared enough to license both.

In early 1987, however, Dolby licensed from Mr. Schieber the right to incorporate his steering circuitry in a new generation of Dolby Surround processors. This new generation is known as Dolby Pro Logic Surround. Some machines will say:

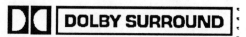

and others (perhaps in the stores by the time you read this) will say:

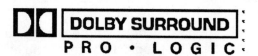

The Pro Logic units have circuitry for a "properly steered" center channel. These are known as *active* decoders. The regular Dolby Surround units are called *passive* decoders.

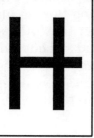

ere are some random observations I have on Surround Sound.

★ I love it. Watching a good movie, in the comfort of my own home, with sound coming from absolutely everywhere (including me when I gasp at some of the audio effects) is, second only to great seats for a great play, my favorite form of entertainment. I defy you to watch the first ten minutes of *Indiana Jones and the Temple of Doom* on a properly set up Dolby system without lust for Surround Sound overtaking your heart. You've got music, you've got singing, you've got dancing, you've got dialogue, you've got fighting, you've got special effects — everything you've always wanted to see in a Surround Sound demonstration, and more.

★ Surround Sound tends to make good movies better and bad movies worse. Each audio surprise increased the joy of *Ruthless People,* while each heavy handed sound effect only added to the already leaden humor of *Ferris Bueller's Day Off.* (And if you liked *Ferris Bueller*, you would have liked it even more with Surround Sound, and if you hated *Ruthless People*, you would have, etc.)

★ While stereo TV shows, and a number of non-stereo TV shows, tend to sound great in Surround Sound, commercials, for the most part, do not. Apparently ad agencies are processing the heck out of their old mono

177

soundtracks to give the illusion of stereo on a two-channel system. This may sound better on two-channel, but it sounds awful on four-channel. Yet another reason to fast forward through commercials.

★ If only two people regularly watch movies, and they don't mind sitting equidistant between the two speakers, there is really no need for the center channel. Even on those rare occasions when all the relatives come in and they actually stop talking and eating long enough to watch a movie, they'll be so impressed by the *quality* of the sound nobody will notice that the dialogue isn't coming from the precise center. Besides, people tend to compensate — when they hear dialogue and see an actor's lips moving, they tend to *think* they're hearing the words come from the screen.

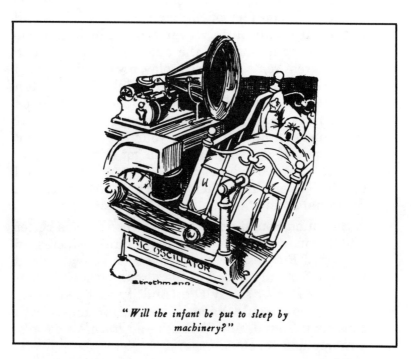

"Will the infant be put to sleep by machinery?"

Although John Philip Sousa was making a fortune on his recordings, he was never a fan of technology. This is an illustration from his 1906 article "The Menace of Mechanical Music." Sempre Fidelis, John?

See
it
Better

Hear
it
Better

STROMBERG-CARLSON
TELEVISION

Shure HTS 5000, Fosgate DSM-3602 and dbx CX1 Sound Processors

Shure and Fosgate are the most devoted manufacturers of the Surround Sound. Their aim is to reproduce the Dolby theatrical experience in the home. They were the first manufacturers of Dolby Surround decoders to incorporate steering technology. For a while they were the only two with true center channels.

dbx is the first to use the official Dolby steering circuitry, Dolby Pro Logic Surround. (Here's an irony: dbx and Dolby battled it out for the standard in tape noise reduction. Now dbx is the first to license Dolby's Pro Logic Surround.)

Shure is fanatical about Surround. They produce a center channel, right channel, left channel, surround channels and a subwoofer output. Period. All they want to do is duplicate the Dolby theater decoder as closely as possible.

Fosgate plays around a bit more. They provide outputs for all the above, but they add *side* speakers. Dolby doesn't call for side speakers, but Fosgate figured side speakers would help spread the sound around.

In the "Regular" mode on the Fosgate, the side speakers play the surround information, the noises and music that usually come from the rear speakers only. This is very close to pristine Dolby Surround. In the "Medium" mode, the side speakers begin to process some of the right and left channel information. In the "Wide" mode, the right and left channels spread even wider, creating a broader range of sound across the front and sides of the room. The rear speakers, of course, continue to process the surround information.

In choosing between Shure and Fosgate, one is faced with the Audiophile vs. Hi-Fi criterion: do you want accuracy or do you want theatricality? The Shure is closer to the Dolby standards. When Stephen Spielberg mixes a film in four-channel Dolby, the results he hears will be closer to the results produced by the Shure unit. Accurate. The Fosgate, however, has more speakers and more processing and more places for more sounds to come from. Theatrical.

The dbx unit follows Dolby's Pro Logic specifications closely. But the unit is more than just a Surround decoder. It is an audio/video preamplifier with inputs for nine components, including a turntable.

Which is best? It's a personal choice. And the first choice is what you want to spend for Dolby decoding. None of these units is cheap. The Shure 5000 is $749; the Fosgate DSM-3602, $1,195. The Fosgate has more inputs, a wireless remote (the Shure is wired) and two 40-watt rear speaker amplifiers. The dbx does the most, and it costs the most, $1,500. It has no remote of any kind.

If you use your current stereo as front amplifier and speakers, you'll still need at least one stereo amp for the rear speakers (which you will also need) and a mono amp for the center speaker (which you will also need). I am assuming your current stereo also has a self-powered subwoofer. If not, add that. A Dolby Surround system without a subwoofer is like a day without orange juice.

And, keep in mind that all three units may be too purist for your own enjoyment. There are at least two areas I wish they had been a bit less pure.

First, neither the Shure nor the Fosgate have a decent mode for listening to regular, non-Dolby-stereo TV programs. Some regular stereo TV sounds good in Dolby, some doesn't. (Commercials tend to sound terrible.) They both have "Mono" modes, but these send all the information to the front speakers. Personally, I'd like a little impure processed reverb coming from the rear. dbx has three digitally processed modes, all of which sound good with regular stereo or mono TV.

Second, the remote control units do not allow for the selection of mode. Some non-Dolby-stereo programs sound good in Dolby, some sound better in regular Stereo (on the Shure), or the Regular, Medium or Wide mode (on the Fosgate). None of these can be controlled from across the room, which is where you need to be to hear which sounds best. It's also a pain when you're just roaming around the dial, going from stereo program to mono program to Dolby-encoded movie channel. You have to get up every time to switch modes. With the dbx, alas, you have to get up to do *everything*.

This is because, from a purist point of view, remote controlled switches are not as good as physical switches. Ah, the price of perfection. You'll have to ask yourself if it's a price you're willing to pay.

Yamaha DSP-1 Sound Processor and M35B Amplifier

Yes, the Yamaha DSP-1 has Dolby Surround, but it also has Carnegie Hall, Munster Cathedral and thirteen other listening environments.

When you listen to a concert in a concert hall, everything you hear doesn't hit your ears at the same time. Echoes of the original sound arrive milliseconds later than the original sound. This echo lets you know, for example, whether you are in a large hall or a small room. The reverberation is something we usually sense more than hear, but it is essential to the presence and feeling of any room. This is why the "acoustics" of some concert halls are praised over the acoustics of others.

In an effort to recreate this in the home, the Yamaha engineers went to various musical places around the world and recorded the precise ambiance of each location.

They went to three concert halls (Carnegie among them), a chamber music room, Munster Cathedral, a church, a jazz club, a rock concert hall, a disco, a pavilion, a stadium and a warehouse loft. They also added two surround modes in addition to Dolby's, and something called "Presence," which seems to be a synthesized four-channel effect, and (Audiophiles forgive me) which I find awfully enjoyable.

The DSP-1 requires a set of speakers (known as subspeakers) at the rear of the listening room. For full appreciation, Yamaha recommends a second pair of subspeakers in the front corners of the room as well. These four speakers should be placed high in the room. The primary music comes from the regular main speakers, the ambiance from the two or four subspeakers.

Each pair of subspeakers requires a separate amplifier. Any could be used, but the Yamaha M35B was designed especially for this purpose. It's a no-nonsense preamp and amplifier with 40 watts per channel for two channels or 20 watts per channel for four channels. Because the subspeakers generally require less power than the main speakers (echoes aren't as loud as the primary music), 20 watts per channel is plenty. The M35B and the DSP-1 complement each other perfectly. The M35B is $249.

The results are fantastic. The listening room becomes alive. The walls disappear. If you closed your eyes, you would think you were *in* the environment described. Don't like that one? Push a button on the remote. You are transported from a stadium to an intimate jazz club to a disco instantly.

Want to hear Stevie Wonder singing in a pavilion? Push a button. Horowitz playing in a warehouse loft? Push a button. Twisted Sister performing in a church? Push.

All this may sound hopelessly Hi-Fi, and it is: Hi-Fi's love this manipulation of music. But, for entirely different reasons, any number of Audiophiles do too.

Yamaha designed the DSP-1 to Audiophile specifications. You may or may not know this, but Yamaha is the largest manufacturer of musical instruments in the world. A number of years ago, the story has it, Yamaha bought several Steinway pianos, took them to Japan, took them apart, and figured out a *better* way to make a Steinway. They did, and many now think the Yamaha grand pianos are on a par with Steinway grands, at a much lower price.

In other words, Yamaha is more than just a motorcycle company.

Audiophiles, you will recall, desire recreation of live music. Judiciously used, the DSP-1 can help create the illusion of a live performance as well as any component in the Audiophile arsenal.

Nonjudiciously used, it's lots of fun. You can *watch* Cosby on TV, but *hear* Cosby at Carnegie Hall. Sporting events can be watched in the ambience of the stadium (or a chamber music room). Sunday morning sermons can be heard as though preached at Munster Cathedral (or a disco).

And then there's Dolby. The Dolby button produces genuine, authorized Dolby Surround Sound. This includes no information coming from the two front subspeakers, as Dolby has no provision for two front subspeakers. But Yamaha does. Surround 1 and Surround 2 take the Dolby Surround signal and play with it a bit. With two extra front speakers, they have more to play with. You might like the results.

The DSP-1 can also alter the acoustics of any of the programmed listening spaces, using 16 different parameters, or you can create your own. Your recreated parameters are stored in memory. So, if you don't *quite* like the way Carnegie Hall sounds, change it.

My only complaint — quite the reverse of my complaint about the Shure, Fosgate and dbx — is that almost *everything* has to be done by remote. The front of the unit is spartan. If you misplace your remote, you've pretty much misplaced your DSP-1.

But that's a small quibble. On the whole, the Yamaha DSP-1 is an ambitious concept, brilliantly executed. $899.

NEC AV-250, AV-350E and AVD-700E

Ok, so you want Dolby Surround, but you want it on a budget. How does $299, complete with rear amplifier and remote, sound? Just use your current stereo for the front, add a pair of speakers for the rear, and you're in business, or should I say Dolby?

The AV-250 also has Hall and Matrix modes. These synthesize non-Dolby stereo and mono signals for four-speaker listening. If you don't like these, you can press the By-Pass button on the remote, and it's as though the AV-250 wasn't there.

The NEC AV-350E is a four-channel audio amplifier as well as sound processor. It powers both front and rear speakers at 30 watts per channel, or two front speakers at 60 watts per channel. It has four video inputs, a CD input, and an audio tape input and output. Alas, it lacks a phono preamplifier. Attaching a turntable would require a phono preamp and the use of the audio portion of one of the video inputs.

It has a full remote, and can be considered the heart of a complete audio/video center. $579.

The AVD-700E is the top of NEC's sound processing line. At $729 it has *no* amplifiers, but it has practically everything else. The "D" in the "AVD" stands for Digital. It is a deluxe digital sound processor along the lines of the Yamaha DSP-1.

Unlike the DSP-1, the AVD-700E does not reproduce the listening environments of various halls, churches, etc. That seems unique to Yamaha. The NEC, however, in its Creation mode, does allow for some spectacular delay effects.

In the Dolby Surround mode, the AVD-700E permits two pairs of surround channels in addition to the left and right front channels. The delay on each pair can be adjusted, so your Surround can truly surround you.

This is a sophisticated piece of equipment that deserves a better instruction manual. It omits a great deal, especially about using the Creation mode, but includes such essential information as, "We recommend that you not install the ADV-700E on a surface likely to damage the unit."

"Congratulations on your new VCR."

Chapter Fifteen

Video Cassette Recorders

hen I was young, I remember watching a program on The Future. One of the luxuries promised was a TV that recorded programs for later viewing. A young boy, about my age, was called to dinner by his mother.

"Not, now, Mom! I'm in the middle of a program!" he whines.

"Now, young man!" the mother yells, "Right now."

The boy begrudgingly turns off the TV and drags himself to dinner. (Which, back in the fifties, was probably pressure-cooker pot roast.)

The New Improved version of the future had the mother calling the boy to dinner, the boy saying, "Yes, mother, right away," and turning a knob on the TV.

This, the announcer told us, activated the Watch It Later feature on the TV of the Future. The boy skips into the kitchen, says, "My, dinner certainly does smell good, mother!" and the family has a happy, loving meal — together again thanks to technology.

I can't tell you any more about the program because at about that point I had to turn off the TV and go eat dinner.

THE PERSONAL ELECTRONICS BOOK

The way we think of home entertainment has been completely changed by a simple machine. (I should probably not call it simple — from a mechanical point of view the VCR is the most complicated piece of personal electronics around.) The VCR has, among other things, eliminated worry.

We no longer worry about missing programs due to dinners, plays, dates, PTA meetings or just run of the mill sloth. Just set the VCR — as much as a year ahead on some models — and forget it.

We no longer worry about two great programs on at the same time. We now just record one and watch the other.

We no longer worry about not getting all the elements aligned to catch the latest movie on its last go 'round. Within a few months it will be out on video, and we'll just stop by the store and rent the tape.

We no longer worry about watching something wonderful and that our friends might never get to see it. We just record it and play it back for them, or send them the tape.

We no longer consider commercials a National Menace. We just fast forward through them. ("Zapping," some people call it.)

In a little over twelve years, the words "VCR," "video," (as in "I'm going to rent a video") and "tape" (as in "Please tape it for me") have entered the language.

We worry less and enjoy television more, all thanks to one machine, the video cassette recorder.

Video Cassette Recorders

n 1975, I decided I had missed quite enough television. I was going to get one of those Future Machines promised to me, by television, in my childhood.

I knew about professional 3/4-inch video recorders. I called a professional video supply house and asked the price. They told me and I was ready to order one when the salesperson said, rather casually, "We just got in this half-inch recorder from Sony. That might do you just as well."

The half-inch recorder was the first BetaMax. It recorded for a maximum of one hour. There was no timer built in. To record a future event I had to buy a separate timer that turned the machine on and off, once. The timer would go on and off a maximum of 24 hours ahead. One day, one on, one off, one hour.

Despite its limitations, I was in love. I began a habit I have yet to break: recording shows rather than watching them. I'd tell myself I would watch it later. For many of those shows, later has never come. Over the years, I've accumulated thousands of hours of carefully selected programs I have yet to watch. I still have some unwatched shows from that first BetaMax. Even shows I love, such as *St. Elsewhere,* I'm six months behind on.

I may never see some of these shows, but I'm not worried. They're there, ready and waiting to be watched. Freedom from certain worries is one of the nicest gifts a VCR brings.

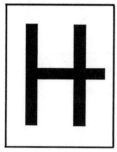

ere are some of the features available on VCR's. . .

Timer. Most VCR's have a timer that permits recording, say, four programs on different channels over fourteen days. The more elaborate timers allow a dozen or so programs over the course of a year. Why anyone would want to set a timer for something a year ahead is beyond me, but it's there if you need it.

Remote Control. A must for VCR's. One of the joys of a VCR is fast forwarding through the dull parts. Who wants to get up every time there's a boring or irritating moment on TV? You'd be in great physical shape at the end of a month, but it's better to get a remote. With a remote you don't *need* to be in great shape.

Cable Ready. This allows you to tune cable stations directly, without the use of the cable company's converter box. It's essential if you have cable and want to record programs on different stations unattended. To record using a converter box, you have to set the channel on the box, and that becomes the only station you can record until you physically change the channel on the converter. Although I consider cable readiness an option for TV's, it's almost essential for VCR's.

Freeze Frame. This freezes a frame on the screen. Most units have freeze frame (sometimes it's called "pause"), but the quality of the frozen frame varies from machine to machine.

Heads. Generally speaking, the more heads, the better the VCR. Just as generally speaking, the more heads, the more you pay. If all you do is record and playback, you can get along fine with two heads. If you like a steady still frame and fast scanning with a fairly stable picture, get four heads. If you like editing, try five.

Hi-Fi. Not just a small step, but a giant leap in recorded sound. (Neil Armstrong has been helping me with the more difficult passages of this book.) With the introduction of Beta Hi-Fi, the sound track of VCR's went from fair to phenomenal. Beta called it "Hi-Fi" and not "Stereo" because VHS already had a not-very-good stereo on its non-Hi-Fi tracks. (The non-Hi-Fi track is called the *linear* track.) Eventually VHS introduced Hi-Fi as well. If you like good sound, a Hi-Fi VCR is a must.

Dolby Stereo. Alas, the Dolby name here indicates an inferior form of sound. It's from the pre-Hi-Fi days, and many inexpensive VHS machines have it. Beware the seller who demonstrates a Hi-Fi VHS machine and then says of a cheaper model, "This one has stereo, too." Yes, it has stereo. No, it does not have Hi-Fi. It's a big difference. The way the boundaries between the two are intentionally blurred in advertising and selling VHS VCR's is, from my point of view, a scandal. I guess it's buyer beware. So, beware.

Stereo (MTS) tuner. Here's yet another form of stereo, and this one's a good one. This allows the VCR to record stereo television broadcasts. If you have a TV that's not stereo but is still a good TV, you might want to get a VCR with a stereo tuner. You hook up the audio portion of the VCR to your stereo and the video portion to your TV. Also, any programs you record on the VCR will automatically be recorded in stereo.

Picture Effects. These include as many as nine pictures within a picture. A picture within a picture allows you to watch one program source while another program source is in a little box on the screen. With multiple windows you can view selected still frames of a tape at the same time (to analyze, for example, a golf swing, tennis backhand or romantic maneuver).

HQ. HQ is supposed to stand for High Quality. If you ask me, it stands for High Confusion. It's really four different picture enhancements for VHS machines. Four picture improvements for regular VHS are not just well and good but desperately needed. The confusion comes from the fact that, in order to advertise the machine as HQ, a manufacturer need only add *two* of the improvements. Two HQ is better than no HQ, but all HQ is better than two HQ. The more expensive the VHS, as a rule, the more HQ it's got.

Trying to find out which two (or three) of the four a manufacturer has added might take the detective skills of Sam Spade. On each HQ machine you consider, you'll just have to ask, ask, ask. Your salesperson is not likely to know offhand, so you have to insist, insist, insist. I hope they'll come up with a way of differentiating between the HQ's so that buying an HQ VHS doesn't stand for Hard Questions.

Maybe <u>he</u> can explain HQ to us.

Video Cassette Recorders

Super-VHS

VHS is the standard for home video recording. Ninety percent of all VCR's sold in the United States are VHS. It's a twelve-year-old system that's beginning to show its age. Two years ago, VHS-Hi-Fi dramatically brought the notoriously bad VHS sound up to state-of-the-art levels. Now Super-VHS takes care of the picture. It's a great picture, and Super-VHS-Hi-Fi should set the VCR standards for the next dozen years.

As I mentioned in the last chapter, television is made up of a series of horizontal lines. (You can see them if you look closely at a TV screen.) The number of lines is known as "horizontal resolution." Broadcast television (TV stations and cable) send out 330 lines of resolution. Regular VHS has 230 lines, which is why regular VHS pictures never look as sharp as broadcast television.

Super-VHS has more than 400 lines of horizontal resolution. The improvement is remarkable. The images are sharp, clear; the color defined, precise. It's hard to tell the difference between a broadcast TV show and a Super-VHS tape of the show.

The 400-plus lines (it's 430 at the fast recording speed, just over 400 at the slow speed) open up a new world of higher-resolution TV. Already high-end TV's can display more than 450 lines — although regular television continues to broadcast at 330 lines. When a commercially prerecorded Super-VHS tape is played on a high-resolution TV, the results are astonishing. A Super-VHS prerecorded movie, for example, will be almost twice as sharp as a movie on regular VHS.

Also, there are camcorders with Super-VHS resolution. This means the tape you make of Junior's baseball game, grandma's birthday party or mother's latest marriage will be sharper than the programs broadcast by NBC, CBS or ABC.

Unfortunately, Super-VHS tapes cannot be played on regular VHS machines — although you can use a Super-VHS machine to record and playback regular VHS tapes. This incompatibility between regular and Super-VHS means video stores will have to stock a double inventory of tapes. It may take a while before the movie you really want to see is available on Super-VHS. (And once you see a Super-VHS movie, you'll be spoiled. "Luxury comes as a guest and soon becomes the master" —Hindu proverb.)

The recordings you make off the air, however, more than justify getting a Super-VHS as soon as your budget allows. This is especially true if you keep a library of tapes for future viewing. I've had a SuperBeta machine for three years and, frankly, I find it hard to watch the thousand or so regular Beta tapes I recorded before the advent of Super-Beta. And the difference between regular VHS and Super-VHS is even more pronounced than the difference between regular Beta and SuperBeta.

The cost of Super-VHS is apt to be high for most of 1988, and blank tapes (Super-VHS requires a special tape — same size and shape as regular VHS, but special inside) will cost more as well.

If you've been considering a new VCR, Super-VHS is probably worth the price. It can play all current VHS tapes, and be able to play all future VHS tapes. It's a wise investment that's not apt to become obsolete.

Super-VHS is one of those great solutions I like to write about. Until now, when choosing a VCR format, one had to decide between a better picture (SuperBeta) or compatibility with everyone else's VCR (VHS). Most people chose compatibility, although, after comparing SuperBeta with regular VHS, many did so with a heavy heart.

Now, if you're willing to pay more than SuperBeta, you can have it all. Within a year or so the prices of Super-VHS machines should be comparable with SuperBeta.

Meanwhile, Sony, the originator of Beta, has not exactly thrown in the towel. They've announced Extended Definition Beta (ED-Beta) which will boast 500 lines of horizontal resolution. Although no marketing plans have been set, they should probably be available sometime in 1988. If the Beta format lasts that long.

Video Cassette Recorders

Beta vs. VHS

Although the dominance of Super-VHS in the future is all but assured, if you plan to buy a second VCR during 1988, you *might* want to consider a Beta. The one and only reason for this is the price of SuperBeta Hi-Fi machines compared with that of Super-VHS Hi-Fi machines.

SuperBeta's been around for a while, whereas Super-VHS is new. As with all new products, the first generation is more costly and the price goes down over time. The Super-VHS machines will therefore cost more than Super-Beta.

Let's say you're in the market *now* for a second VCR. You already have a VHS. You want better picture quality than the VHS can deliver. The automatic response is, of course, "Get a Super-VHS."

But let's consider this scenario. A Super-VHS machine costs, say, $1,000. A SuperBeta machine, say, $500. For recording and playing back TV programs, the SuperBeta will give almost as good a picture as the Super-VHS. (Broadcast TV is limited to 330 lines, you'll recall.) You keep the SuperBeta for a year or so, and then buy a second or third generation Super-VHS for, oh, say, $500.

You will then have (A) a used (very used by now) regular VHS, (B) a year-or-so old Beta, and (C) a brand new Super-VHS. Note that the money you spent on the last two ($500 twice) is the same as spending $1,000 once on the first-generation Super-VHS. In a way, it's like getting the SuperBeta machine free.

This idea has certain advantages and disadvantages, other than the ones stated above. The advantages:

1. You will have a Beta VCR, which means when you walk into the video store and say, "Do you have [fill in movie title here]?" and they say, "Sorry, we only have it in Beta," you can say, "Fine."

2. You can play any tapes from any of your friends, including those die-hards who have been sticking to Beta all these years.

3. The SuperBeta is proven, whereas Super-VHS is a new technology. As with most new technologies, the improvements between the first and second generation are nice — and sometimes necessary — to have.

4. The Super-VHS tape is apt to be expensive for the first year. SuperBeta takes any Beta tape, and these tapes are cheap.

The disadvantages:

1. Whatever new movies are released on Super-VHS during your SuperBeta year you will not be able to enjoy in all their glory. The bulk of prerecorded Super-VHS tapes, however, are not likely to hit the market until 1989 or later.

2. If you use a camcorder and want the best, it's probably best to go with Super-VHS from the start. (See *Camcorders*, Chapter 17.)

3. If you tend to keep tapes you record off TV, in years to come you might come to regret your Beta collection. Your VHS tapes will always have a player, but if your SuperBeta permanently conks in, say, five years, do you really want to have to buy a new Beta for the Beta tapes you have? (Providing, of course, there are any Beta machines to buy in five years.) If you just record off TV, watch what you've recorded, and record over the same tape again, this shouldn't be a problem.

4. Your friends will not be as impressed with a Super-Beta machine as a Super-VHS one.

This SuperBeta idea is just a thought — making the best of options during transitional times.

JVC Super-VHS

8mm

Once upon a time, 8mm referred to home movies. Now it again refers to home movies, except this time the "movies" are video.

The 8mm format has certain advantages as a camcorder format (please see *Camcorders*, Chapter 17). As a VCR deck, it has one serious liability: it's a format that hasn't caught on and, with Super-VHS around, will probably never catch on.

Most people who use 8mm use it for camcorders. More and more 8mm camcorders have playback built into them. People with 8mm home decks use them for playing back 8mm videos taken with a camcorder or for copying an 8mm camcorder tape to another format (VHS or Beta) so they can send a video to friends and relatives.

The use of an 8mm deck as a VCR (recording and playing back television shows) is relatively rare. The use of an 8mm deck for playing prerecorded movies is even rarer — there aren't many 8mm movies around.

There are certain advantages to 8mm decks. These include. . .

1. The tapes are small, about the size of an audio cassette. On a deck, each tape holds four hours of video. (Only two hours on an 8mm camcorder.)

2. The sound quality is excellent. In the normal mode it rivals Beta and VHS Hi-Fi, and . . .

3. Many of the 8mm decks can be used as audio tape decks. When used for audio only, the decks record and playback in PCM (Pulse Code Modulation), which is a form of digital sound. It's not as good as CD's or DAT's, but it's good — and you can record 24 hours of PCM sound on *one* 8mm cassette.

Somehow these advantages have not been strong enough for people to run screaming to their electronics stores demanding 8mm VCR decks. The future of 8mm camcorders is uncertain. The future of 8mm video decks is grim.

Goldstar KMV-9002 Viewmax VHS VCR/TV

Here's a not very good idea. They've welded a VCR to a television. Now, televisions last, what, fifteen years? VCR's are lucky to limp into five. So, for the remaining ten years of the TV's life, it has grafted to its bottom an unworking reminder of the happier days of its youth. Not a very nice thing to do to a TV.

I guess there are practical applications for this — retail showrooms, hotel rooms and the like. My artist friend Maurice Grosser said, "The only thing essential in hotel art is that the pictures be bigger than a suitcase." In this same theft-prevention-through-size mode, I guess the TV will keep any number of VCR's in otherwise vulnerable situations from being stolen. $650.

In defense of Goldstar, however, they do make good low-cost VCR's.

Samsung VR2610 VHS VCR

Like its fellow Korean, Goldstar, Samsung has made its name in low-cost VCR's. This is but one of them. This one retails for $379.95, which means you can buy it for much, much less.

Mitsubishi HS422-UR VHS Hi-Fi VCR

Ah, Hi-Fi. Ah, Mitsubishi. Two happy names in VCR's, together again. This one's $900. Great picture (as great as regular VHS can get), great sound, great features. But, if you're spending that much, wouldn't you really rather have a *Super* VHS?

JVC HR-S700U Super-VHS Hi-Fi VCR

The first of the Super-VHS machines. Super-VHS seems to add about $300 to the price of a comparable non-Super-VHS machine. To these eyes, the extra money is well worth it.

All the good things you've heard about Super-VHS are true. The picture is sharp, clear, steady, etc., etc. Look at a

Super-VHS tape played back on a high-resolution television and you're looking at the future. It's a bright future, and the good news is that it's here now.

JVC invented VHS and Super-VHS and has an excellent reputation for reliable manufacturing. For a first generation of a new product, it's often best to go with the people who know the most about it, and nobody knows more about Super-VHS than JVC.

NEC DX-5000 Digital VHS Hi-Fi VCR

It's sad to review a unit like this. So much time and skill and engineering and, yes, love went into this product; it's a shame it's all in vain. It reminds me of the 78 players that came out at the dawn of the LP. All museum or attic pieces somewhere.

Now, really, would you rather buy this regular VHS for $1,349, or a Super-VHS for $1,200? Yes, that's what most people will decide. There is a whole range of top-of-the-line VCR's — at least one model from every VCR manufacturer — that have just become obsolete. Such is the price of progress.

Sony SLHF 1000 SuperBeta Hi-Fi VCR

Beta's last hurrah. Sony's sending it out in style. Sony is now the only manufacturer of Beta. If you want Beta, you've got to buy Sony. Not that that many people want Beta, mind you.

We Videophiles have been Beta loyalists for years because the picture has always been better than VHS, but we're going Super-VHS in droves. We still, I suppose, need replacement Beta machines for our libraries of Beta tapes, and the SLHF is a fine VCR. It's a wonderful VCR. It's a fabulous VCR. There are only two problems: It's Beta and it's $1,700. Oy.

MISS BOURKE-WHITE's outstanding photographs have earned her a world-wide reputation. She is an exacting judge of picture quality. "Finest I've seen!" she says of RCA Victor's Eye Witness projection television pictures. "In projection television, *brilliance is the thing* and this RCA Victor receiver gives you the most I've ever seen."

This beautiful RCA Victor projection console shows you pictures fifteen by twenty inches big, almost the size of a full newspaper page. They're the *largest* home-size Eye Witness television pictures ... and they give the sharpest black-and-white contrast in projection television.

The Eye Witness Picture Synchronizer, an RCA Victor development, corrects the timing of the picture signal, *locks the picture in tune* with sending stations. With FM sound through the famous "Golden Throat," you *see and hear* as though you were an eye witness right at the scene!

Remote Control!

You can adjust picture brilliance from your easy chair with this 3-inch by 4-inch remote control unit, furnished with Model 9PC41 and finished to match the cabinet of your choice.

Viewing screen folds into cabinet which is finished in matched and hand-rubbed mahogany, walnut or, for slightly more, blond. Authentic 18th Century design. *RCA Victor 9PC11. AC.*

$795*

plus Federal tax and installation

Chapter Sixteen

LaserDiscs

aserDiscs entered the market at precisely the wrong time. They deserved a better break.

When first introduced, LaserDiscs were up against not only VCR's, which could record as well as playback, but also a competitive disc format from RCA.

RCA's disc format was truly inferior to LaserDiscs, but RCA, being RCA, decided, "We're RCA. People will buy what we tell them to buy." So they spent half-a-billion (that's "billion" with a "B" as Dan Rather would say) dollars on marketing their disc player.

Well, truly bad eventually lost, but not until tens of thousands of people invested hundreds of dollars each in a dead-end technology. RCA casually announced one day they weren't making any more players, they weren't making any more discs, and that, as they say, was that.

RCA played a similar trick on us in the early fifties. They refused to accept the superiority of the lp record and spent years selling consumers the idea of albums made up of 45's. (Remember those 45 changers? Your grandmother probably has one in her basement. Mine does.) And remember 8-track tapes? Guess who pushed 8-track tapes when the clearly superior format was cassettes? Yep.

So RCA confused the video disc issue, and people who should have and would have bought LaserDisc players instead bought expensive doorstops.

So, LaserDisc players got off to a slow start. Of course, calling it DiscoVision for a while didn't help, nor did the 30-minutes-per-side limitation of the original discs.

But LaserDiscs survived, entirely because of the heroic sustaining efforts of Pioneer. A company with less guts would have pulled the plug long ago. Pioneer has stuck it out.

LaserDiscs

It's unfortunate, from a let's-admire-their-courage point of view, because their efforts will no doubt be in vain. The reason? Super-VHS.

Until Super-VHS, LaserDiscs had the best picture and sound around. Super-VHS's picture is as good, and the VHS Hi-Fi sound is almost as good. Considering the disadvantages of LaserDiscs when compared to video tape, this will probably mean the end of home LaserDiscs. (The industrial and educational use of LaserDiscs is still growing.)

What are these disadvantages?

1. You can't record on a LaserDisc. This, ultimately, is why people chose the poorer VCR picture — they wanted to record TV programs, not just rent movies.

2. No still frame. In the extended play mode (the mode that almost all LaserDisc movies come in, with the exception of a few X-rated titles, on which the still frame is considered essential) you can pause, but the screen goes blank. When you pause on a VCR, a still picture remains on the screen.

3. You have to turn the disc over every hour. This may not seem like much, but it's a nuisance sometimes. And there is something psychological about turning over that disc. Everybody wants to use the time to get something to eat or go to the bathroom or call the babysitter or, or, or. The Turning of the Disc often becomes an unscheduled thirty-minute intermission. Sometimes the disc never gets turned.

4. There are very few video stores selling LaserDiscs. There are even fewer stores renting them. Finding the disc you want, especially in a small town, can be a problem.

The advantages of LaserDiscs?

1. Until video tape makers release their catalogs in Super-VHS, LaserDiscs offer the best picture for prerecorded movies, concerts, etc. Although new movies are likely to be released in Super-VHS, it will probably not be until 1990 before the Super-VHS catalog equals the current LaserDisc catalog.

2. The new laser players and discs offer true digital sound. It's the best video sound available anywhere. The

sound in your living room can be better than the best movie theater. (Providing you invest *una fortuna* in audio equipment as well.) The Hi-Fi track on both Beta and VHS rivals digital sound, and most people can't tell the difference — but LaserDiscs offer the only digital soundtrack for movies today (and in the foreseeable future).

3. LaserDiscs are generally "safer" to rent than video tapes. Every inch of video tape must come into intimate contact with the playback heads of your machine. If some cretin with a $200 bargain VCR wrinkled, bent or in some way damaged the tape, the damaged tape can cause damage to your video playback heads. This doesn't happen often, but it's possible. (This is why some Videophiles buy new tapes at video stores with trade-in policies.) With LaserDiscs, nothing comes into contact with the disc. Even if someone tap dances on the disc, it will not damage your player.

4. It's easy to locate a specific scene on a LaserDisc. Most discs are divided into "chapters" and each chapter has a title or an explanation of its contents. If you like watching certain scenes from movies, or watching Jane do a specific exercise, what would take minutes to locate on a video tape takes only seconds to locate on a LaserDisc.

5. Laser players have the best still frames. This is why they're so popular in education and industry. If the disc has still-frame capability (most movie discs don't, most educational discs do), the still picture is rock-steady and crystal clear. And, unlike VCR's, the frame can remain on screen for hours with no harm to either the player or the disc.

6. They're rare. You'll probably be the only kid on the block to have one. If you think CD's are pretty with their moray rainbow patterns, take a look at a LaserDisc. Awesome, as my friends from The Valley would say. There's something impressive about loading a LaserDisc, listening to it whir to speed, and watching the LaserVision symbol sweep onto the screen rattling your subwoofer. You know you're in for an audio-visual treat.

R eturning to my arbitrary categories given at the start of this section, LaserDiscs are essential for all Videophiles and desirable to TV Viewers in certain special situations (living next door to a LaserDisc rental store, for example). It's a dying format, but for the next year or two it will continue to be the video state of the art.

S ome LaserDisc players have a CD player built in. This usually adds several hundred dollars to the price of the LaserDisc player. Considering the cost of CD players these days, it's far more economical to buy separate units.

There's also a new thing on the horizon called CD-V. Let me tell you about CD-V.

Compact Disc Video

It's called Compact Disc Video or CD-Video or CD-V (I have yet to hear it referred to as Compact Disc-V). Almost everyone who pushes stuff upon us is pushing CD-V like mad. Electronics manufacturers, record conglomerates, movie companies — the very people who are slugging it out on opposite sides of the Digital Audio Tape issue — all want us to have a CD-Video player and lots of CD-Video discs of our own.

Why? Because they *like* us. They want us to have the best in audio and video. They want us to be happy. They want our money.

CD-Video is a disc, the size of a standard Compact Disc, with five minutes of video and twenty minutes of audio on it. What known form of entertainment fits this medium? None, but that's beside the point.

Electronics makers are all excited, you see, because regular compact disc players were such a hit. But now things are leveling off, in terms of new CD players being sold, so the manufacturers are aching to manufacture something new.

As I mentioned before, the recording people don't want the manufacturers to manufacture the new Digital Audio Tape (DAT) machines because people can *record* on them, from *records*, in their *home*! With CD's — and CD-V's — your money buys you one copy and only one copy. You want one for your car? More money please. Your portable player? Ditto. More sales. More profits. More happy record companies.

So they're all together on this one, and when they all get together, it's probably time for the rest of us to watch out.

They may be inundating us with ads, but here are the facts:

★ CD-V discs cannot be played on regular CD players.

★ CD-V players start at about $700.

★ CD-V discs retail for about $8.

★ Although CD-V's can playback five minutes of video, few of them will have five minutes of video. What they will have is a recycled MTV clip (three minutes, in some cases) and then five-or-so audio-only songs.

★ Although it will hold twenty minutes of audio, you're not likely to get twenty minutes of audio. Regular CD's can hold more than 70 minutes of audio. How many 70-plus-minute CD's do you own?

★ After the video is done, the TV screen goes blue for the audio portion of the disc. (I guess at that point we're all supposed to get up and *dance* or something.)

This is all the brainchild of Philips, the Netherlands industrial giant who owns North American Philips, Magnavox, Sylvania and Philco, among others. They also own the patents to the CD technology. They're the ones who convinced Sony and others to hold up on Digital Audio Tape production until CD caught on.

Some say this large and sudden push in the CD-V format is simply a way to force through a standard before RCA can get to market with its CD-V system. (RCA calls it DVI — Digital Video Interactive.) The RCA system has a full seventy-two minutes of video and audio, although not LaserDisc quality. (As we've discussed, inferior formats have never stopped RCA before.)

But who am I to speculate on the motives of industry giants? I know that, deep down, they really have our best interests at heart. Right?

Whatever their motives, the idea was obsolete before it was even shipped. Super-VHS records up to six hours with a picture quality as good as CD-V, and sound quality almost as good. Digital Audio Tape has marginally better sound, with two hours of recording and playback per tape. So who needs yet another machine for five minutes of video and twenty minutes of audio?

According to an official of the Electronic Industries Association, the target market for Compact Disc Video is "... 8 to 16-year-old children of affluent parents."

That leaves me out on both counts.

Pioneer is hoping CD-V will be the stalking horse for a renaissance in LaserDisc players. A teen will go to a store with mommy and daddy in tow. Mommy and daddy will look at the teen's dream, a $750 CD-V player. They will then be shown a $950 player that plays CD-V's, CD's *and* Laser-Discs. For the extra $200 they figure, sure, why not? and another LaserDisc player has entered another home.

Pioneer doesn't much care who makes the multi-LaserDisc player — they want the LaserDisc *format* to survive. The only way for the format to survive is to sell a lot of LaserDisc machines — soon. Besides, Pioneer manufactures most LaserVision movies, and every LaserDisc player is a new market for its LaserVision discs.

"I'll buy you a CD-V player. I'll buy you CD-V discs.
"I'll buy you. . ."

Pioneer LDS1 LaserDisc Player

What can one say about a $2,000 LaserDisc player? It's wonderful, but its wonders obviously have a price.

One of the wonders is the sound. This is the best movie sound available *anywhere*. It's digital, and digital sound for movies is available *nowhere else*. Movie theaters don't have it. VCR's don't have it. Only the engineers who mixed the soundtrack — and you — can hear it in all its digital glory. There's something to be said for that, especially for the audio/visual purist.

The LDS1 also uses digital circuitry to eliminate one of LaserDisc's irritating limitations: no still picture. Now all LaserDiscs have a still picture — sharp, clear, steady. One hopes Pioneer will incorporate this circuitry in all LaserDisc players. It would be nice to say LaserDiscs now have still frame.

If you want the current ultimate in home audio/video, this is it.

Chapter Seventeen

Camcorders

nother word personal electronics has dropped into the lexicon within the past few years is *camcorder*. It, of course, is a contraction of *camera* and *recorder*.

It all started with the first VCR's. It was one of those Beta vs. VHS Battle of the Formats. First there was the BetaMax VCR, followed by the VHS VCR. Then Sony introduced a video camera. It attached to the BetaMax machine and allowed you to record hours of home "movies" for practically nothing. (The alternate was Super 8mm film — at a cost of something like $10 for three minutes.) The video camera/BetaMax combination played back at once, destroying in the process Polaroid's hope for instant home movies. (Anybody remember Polaroid's instant home movies?)

VHS took it a step further. They introduced a battery-operated VHS deck you could sling over your shoulder (although you had to have a rather substantial shoulder). This attached to a video camera and, *voila*, portable video. One was no longer limited to the home — the world was the stage, your friends and family merely actors.

Beta leapfrogged that one by announcing BetaMovie, the first true camcorder. BetaMovie combined camera with video recorder in one battery-operated unit. The BetaMovie was only slightly larger than a video camera. It didn't play back, but who cared? You could video the family outing at Disneyland without looking like a network cameraman.

Then VHS Movie came out, followed by 8mm — Sony's new, smaller format. VHS countered with VHS-C. Sony with SuperBeta Movie. VHS with Super-VHS Movie and Super-VHS-C. And that brings us pretty much up to date. (All of the unusual terms in this last paragraph will be explained shortly.)

Camcorders have opened a new world of capturing the sights and sounds of life. My stepfather, Larry, acquired a BetaMovie shortly before his retirement, and every major and minor event of the last five years has been fully documented in sound and color. ("First snowfall, 1984," "Christmas, 1983, Part One," and "Mary cooking, 7-14-85," are typical notations on his video tapes.)

Family gatherings are now enjoyed in two parts. Part One: The Gathering (birthday, holiday, whatever). Part Two: Watching Larry's Videos of The Gathering. At first, no one wanted to be photographed, but everyone wanted to see everyone else, so everybody has pretty much given up. One hears nary a "Larry, don't take any pictures of me!" anymore.

The funny part of these gatherings is that watching the videos of the first part of the day are often more enjoyable than living it. There's something hypnotic about television — anything on TV is somehow worth watching, whether it's worth watching or not. Hearing people you know say something on television is far more interesting than hearing them say the same thing in person. Strange.

For Larry, this one-step-removed-from-life-is-more-fascinating-than-life-itself quality has taken on epic proportions. One night he lit a fire in the fireplace, set up his camera on a tripod, left the room and let it burn. Then he called my mother into his "editing room" (as he calls the den he converted into a Videophile's paradise). They drank wine and watched the video of the fire on TV — all three hours of it.

Before discussing the basic types of camcorders, let's take a look at the features available on most camcorders regardless of type.

Playback. Here's a major distinction between camcorders. Some attach directly to a TV set and play what they've recorded. Others require a separate player.

Zoom. A zoom lens allows you to move closer to or farther from an object without you yourself having to move. The amount of zoom is known as the *ratio*. Most camcorders have a 6:1 (pronounced "six to one") or 8:1 ratio. The greater the ratio the more powerful the zoom. (You can move in closer using an 8:1 zoom than with a 6:1 zoom.)

Power Zoom. This zooms the lens in and out with the touch of a button. With most cameras you can do this with the hand that's holding the camera. Power zoom allows you to follow a subject without having to look away from the viewfinder. This not only gives greater control than manual zoom, it also produces smoother zooms.

Focus. The focus choices on camcorders are *manual focus* (you do the focusing by turning the lens), *fixed focus* (it has one, maybe two preset focus settings) and *auto focus* (the camera focuses from a few feet to infinity automatically).

Keeping a moving object in focus can be tricky, and if you're trying to zoom at the same time, it's nearly impossible. In these situations auto focus shines. Auto focus is especially useful in low light and for close-ups, the two areas where fixed focus cameras tend to blur.

Fixed-focus lenses have one, maybe two settings — one setting for normal and distant shots, one for close-ups. Deciding what is and is not a close-up while shooting can be difficult. Auto focus is great for video because people and things tend to rapidly and unexpectedly go into and out of the close-up range.

Be careful you're not misled into thinking a fixed focus lens is an auto focus lens. Here's a quote from a camcorder ad: "pan-focus lens requires no adjustment." This statement was followed immediately by, "close-up switch allows you to get close to the action with clear focus and no distortion."

If there were an award for double-misleading advertising, this ad would qualify. In the first place, a "pan-focus lens" (whatever pan-focus means) that "requires no adjustment" implies auto focus. But then they say you've got to flip the "close-up switch" (why didn't they call it the "pan-close-up switch"?) in order to get "clear focus" in close-ups. In other words, the pan-focus lens that needs no adjustment needs adjustment. (The only reason I'm not giving the manufacturer's name is because I saw this in an ad for a local electronics store, and I'm not sure who the guilty party is.)

Lux. Anybody remember the *Lux Radio Theater?* Anybody remember Lux? (Electronics Trivia Question: Who hosted the *Lux Radio Theater?* Answer in a while.) Lux, when applied to camcorders, has nothing to do with soap. It's a unit of measurement indicating the camcorder's sensitivity to light. The lower the lux rating, the less light it takes to make good pictures. Seven to ten lux is common.

Camcorders

With a rating above fifteen lux, you may never notice the difference in bright sunlight, but when photographing little Lisa blowing out the candles on her birthday cake, you will.

Aperture. Also known as *f-stops*. This is a reading of the amount of light the lens lets in when open all the way. The lower the number, the more light is let in. Camcorders frequently have apertures from f1.2 to f1.8.

Lux and aperture combine to indicate how well a camera will perform in low light conditions. A camcorder with an f1.2 aperture and 7 lux would be more sensitive in low light levels than a camcorder with an f1.8 aperture and 20 lux. All other things being equal, it's better to get the lowest f-stop and lowest lux rating available.

Shutter Speed. Until recently, all camcorders had one shutter speed. Now, some of the more advanced camcorders offer a faster shutter speed. The faster the shutter speed, the sharper the picture, especially when the camera or subject is moving fast. In watching a video, you probably wouldn't notice much of a difference in sharpness, but if you were to look at an "action" scene frame by frame, the difference would be apparent.

If you took a video, say, of a horse jumping over a fence and then looked at each frame, the faster the shutter speed the sharper each individual frame would be. You probably couldn't tell the difference in shutter speeds when watching the horse clear the hurdles in "real time" (regular speed). But, there is a difference, and there are those who, when they know the difference is there, want the best.

The tradeoff for faster shutter speed is light — a faster shutter speed requires more light. In bright sunlight there's no problem, but in less-than-ideal lighting conditions, a better picture is usually obtained by not using the high-speed shutter.

Continuous White Balance. Daylight and lamplight, both of which look "white" to us, are seen by the camera as two separate colors. (Daylight has a bluish tint, incandescent lamplight a yellow-orange.) In order to capture colors accurately, the camera has to know, "What is white?" With some early camcorders, the white balance had

"Electronics Trivia Hint: This is his niece."

to be readjusted each time you changed from indoors to out-doors. With continuous white balance, this is no longer necessary. (Electronics Trivia Hint: *The Ten Command-ments, The Greatest Show on Earth* and *The Squaw Man.*)

Hi-Fi. The wonderful sound quality that makes watching *Star Wars* at home so enjoyable can now be ap-plied to The Family Barbecue.

HQ. The four VHS picture enhancements, although manufacturers need only use two of the four to call it HQ. Confusing? Absolutely. Recommended? Yes.

amcorders come in four basic configura-tions. Naturally, there are variations within the configurations. The four con-figurations, along with the pluses and minuses of each are. . .

BetaMovie

The first camcorder, and probably the first to go. The imminent death of Beta is bringing all related Beta products down with it. Until recently, people chose the Beta format for superior picture quality. With Super-VHS and Super-VHS-C (see below), this is no longer the case. Alas, it's bye, bye BetaMovie.

VHS

Full-size, ordinary VHS camcorders are nothing special. They will probably follow BetaMovie to the electronic elephant's graveyard soon. Super-VHS camcorders are something else again.

Super-VHS offers you better quality home video than broadcast television. To get the most out of Super-VHS, you need a high-resolution television (with a resolution of 440 lines or more). But even on regular TV you'll notice the difference between 230 lines (regular VHS) and 330 lines (the limit of ordinary television). And, when you get your high-resolution TV, those extra 100-or-so lines will be waiting for you.

8mm

Eight-millimeter is a popular camcorder format. The picture and sound are great. You can record for two hours on a tape the size of an audio cassette. The small tape allows for smaller camcorders. A great many of the names in still photography have jumped on the 8mm bandwagon: Canon, Nikon, Minolta, Olympus, Elmo (remember Elmo?), Pentax and, of course, the granddaddy of still photography, Kodak.

Eight-millimeter *almost* made it as the standard for camcorders. The challenge came from VHS-C, a format that allowed 8mm-sized VHS camcorders. The problems of the early VHS-C machines were significant: twenty minutes of recording time per tape (vs. 8mm's two hours), poorer picture and poorer sound than 8mm. But VHS-C tapes could be played in a regular VHS VCR (with the use of an adapter), and that proved tempting enough for some.

But not enough: 8mm continued to grow. Then came VHS-C with HQ to improve the picture and a full hour of recording time per tape. Still not 8mm's sharpness and still not 8mm's recording length. Minolta, Olympus and Nikon did not exactly jump the 8mm ship, but they put a few eggs in the VHS basket and came out with VHS-C camcorders.

But now — from my humble vantage point — the fatal blow to 8mm: Super-VHS-C. A little teeny camera that takes better pictures than the great big cameras at CBS (or ABC or NBC or PBS).

VHS-C

Somehow, in talking about 8mm, I told you everything about VHS-C and Super-VHS-C. Oh, well.

VHS-C will probably be around for a while as a camcorder for those more interested in economy than quality. (Aunt Rosejune at 230 lines is every bit as amusing as Aunt Rosejune at 430 lines.)

But my fearless prediction is that Super-VHS-C will be the camcorder format of the foreseeable future.

Large vs. Small

With the constant demand in electronics for miniaturization, the assumed belief is that smaller is better. Certainly this is true of camcorders — or is it?

I took a BetaMovie to Japan a few years ago. (Like taking coal to Newcastle, huh?) It was the smallest, most compact video camera available at that time. I came back with a well-muscled right arm and some very nice videos.

Two years later I took a much smaller 8mm camera to Italy. I brought back some of the most godawful jiggly, jumpy videos you have ever seen.

What happened? Are Japanese cameras designed to photograph Japan better than anywhere else? Did I develop some neurological disorder from eating too much fettucini at Alfredo's? Does sake have a steadying effect and red wine a hyperactive effect?

The difference between relatively steady Japan and *Earthquake II* Italy, it turned out, was the size of the camera.

A large camera is harder to hold up, but easier to hold steady. Large cameras rest on your shoulder, for one thing. This gives two points of support, the shoulder and the hand. The smaller cameras have only one point of support, the hand.

Also, the heavier the camera (within reason) the easier it is to keep steady. The TV news cameras are monsters, are seldom on tripods, and give consistently steady pictures. Even a TV news cameraman would have trouble delivering the same steady picture with a two-pound, hand-held camcorder.

I'm not saying big is better. I'm saying big is not necessarily worse. For most uses, smaller is better. For most people, the portability more than makes up for the difficulty in delivering steady pictures. Smaller camcorders tend to go more places. The 8mm camera became an extension of my hand. The BetaMovie often stayed on the bus.

If, however, you're buying a camera for *serious* use, you might want to rent a larger camcorder and a smaller camcorder and see which you find easier to hold steady.

Frankly, next time I travel I plan to take the smallest camcorder with a zoom and auto focus I can find. I do, however, plan to hold it steadier. Or eat less fettucini.

*The answer to our Electronics Trivia Question is Cecil B.
DeMille. The dancer? His niece, Agnes DeMille.*

Magnavox VHS-C

Three VHS-C Camcorders

I took a look at the RCA CPR-100, the Magnavox Escort and the Toshiba SK60K. They all have auto-everything, and should, considering their prices: $1,399, $1,699 and $1,995, respectively.

The differences between the cameras are small but important. I noticed in a series of short shots that the sound on the Magnavox was slightly clipped at the beginning of each shot. Sound cuts should be as clean as visual cuts. The RCA and Toshiba cameras had good, clean sound cuts.

The Escort includes a high-speed shutter mode for detailing fast action. (The others don't.) The Toshiba offers fade in/fade out to and from a white screen. (The others don't — I prefer fading to a black screen, but what the heck.) The Toshiba also has back-light control for when you're recording against a strong back light, and a view-

Toshiba VHS-C

finder indicator that says "light" when it judges the light to be too low for good contrast. (The others don't.)

The Magnavox is 7 lux, the RCA 10 lux and the Toshiba a disappointing 15 lux.

For the price, the RCA is the winner, but at any price, VHS-C can't begin to hold a candle to Super-VHS-C. Unless prices on regular VHS-C camcorders fall dramatically, there's little reason to get one. You'll ultimately wish you had gotten Super-VHS.

Canon Canovision and Olympus Movie 8

The Canovision was a major disappointment. It's large (too large by 8mm standards), the viewfinder is a separate piece (if you don't take it off before packing the camera you run the risk of breaking it off), and the automatic zoom controls are on the wrong side (usually they're on the right so the camera can be held and operated with one hand). (*All* camcorders, by the way, are prejudiced against lefties. Sorry.)

The Olympus, on the other hand, is almost everything you could ask for in an 8mm camcorder: It's compact, light, the viewfinder is built-in, and the controls are logically placed. The only fault I could find with the Olympus is that it doesn't have a remote control unit for playback. It's a tough life.

The Olympus is more expensive than the Canon ($1,850 vs. $1,699), but, if you ask me, the extra $151 is worth it.

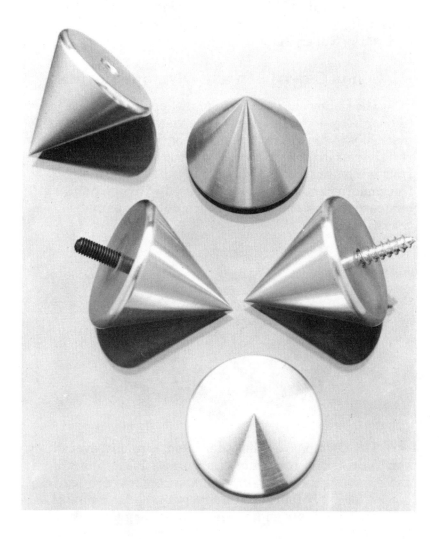

What are these? These are TipToes!
What are TipToes? See page 228

Chapter Eighteen

Audio and Video Accessories

Nitty Gritty Record Cleaner

Earlier I mentioned how valuable our record collections grow as we grow older, not just sentimentally but financially as well. Next to a properly installed cartridge and stylus on a decent tonearm, The Nitty Gritty Record Cleaner, more than anything else, will help keep your records sounding better and lasting longer. (I am assuming you use inner sleeves, touch your records only by the edges, and put them away in a horizontal position immediately after each use — you know, Record Hygiene 101.)

The Nitty Gritty Record Cleaning Machine gently scrubs your records and then vacuums them dry. There are a lot of record cleaning products on the market, but after you use them, where does the dirt go? Maybe a little goes onto the cleaning pad, but, for the most part, the dirt just gets redistributed on the record.

Not with the Nitty Gritty. It works like this: A felt pad is moistened with special record cleaning solution stored within the machine. The record rotates on top of this pad. This loosens the dirt. You throw a switch and a powerful vacuum — the opening of which is located in a narrow slit in the felt pad — sucks the cleaning solution and the dirt right off the record.

The whole procedure takes about two minutes (less than a minute with the Nitty Gritty Mini-Pro, which cleans both sides of a record at the same time) and guarantees you a playing surface that is actually cleaner than new. (Record companies, it is said, add anti-mold agents to their records. Nitty Gritty helps remove this. See next review.)

Nitty Gritty machines start at $259, for the Model 1.0, and gradually escalate to $629 for the Mini-Pro. If you love your records, Nitty Gritty is a must.

SOTA Release Record Cleaner

This stuff amazes me. You put a few drops on a special applicator, rub it around the record for about thirty seconds, and it makes the record sound *much better*. I don't know how, but it does.

I have been told it removes the anti-mold agents record companies add to records. Apparently, unless you live in Jamaica, you don't have to worry about mold on your records, but record companies put it on just the same — some throwback to the 78 days when mold was a big problem. This anti-mold agent, I am told, covers the grooves and mutes the sound of the records.

SOTA Release is a chemical which releases this anti-mold agent — sort of an anti-anti-mold agent agent.

I don't know if that's the reason, but I do know it works. One bottle ($20) treats about fifty records.

Last Products

It's nice to be able to recommend an entire line of products for the care and feeding of all your audio/video products. The company is called Last, and whatever they make is just about the best available. Overall, when in doubt, get Last. ("Think Last First"? I'm glad they don't have much of an advertising budget. We'd all be subjected to slogans like that.)

Here's a rundown of Last products and what they do:

Last All Purpose Record Cleaner. Cleans your records — not as well as Nitty Gritty, but this only costs $8.95 a bottle.

Last Extra-Strength Record Cleaner. Cleans your dirty records — also for new records, to release anti-mold agents and other manufacturing gunk. $13.95.

Last Record Preservative. The box says, "Guaranteed to stop record wear for 200 plays with one application." Such a deal. $16.95.

Last Stylus Cleaner. Cleans your stylus. Yes, your stylus gets dirty, and, yes, it needs more than just brushing. $7.95.

Last Stylus Treatment. Brushed on just before playing a record, it lubricates the tip of the stylus for longer life. $19.95. One bottle lasts forever.

Last Cassette Head Cleaner. Two cleaning cassettes, one for head and capstine, one for tape path, plus a cleaning liquid for both. $13.95.

Last Video Head Cleaner. The only way to clean your video heads is with a *wet* cleaner. (You drip on cleaner before inserting the cleaning cassette.) This one's wet, and, unlike other wet cleaners, you never use the same cleaning surface twice. VHS or Beta. $19.95.

Last CD Protection System. Here I must beg to differ with Last. I consider *all* CD cleaning-protection systems unnecessary. Moderate care in handling is all CD's need. If they get dirty, clean them with distilled alcohol.

Tape

For video and DAT, my favorite tape is Maxell. For audio cassettes, it's Denon. Big deal, right? Well, you're reading my book, and I assume if you're reading my book you're interested in my opinion, so there it is.

Tip Toes

Tip Toes are aluminum cones that lift your speakers off solid surfaces. The result is an open, airier, more resonate sound. Speakers should be considered musical instruments; they're not just boxes from which something comes out of the front. From good speakers, vibrations emanate from all around.

When you set a speaker on a solid surface, you significantly dampen the resonate quality of the speaker cabinet. (It's like holding a bell and then striking it; it makes a noise, but it doesn't ring.) Tip Toes reduce the amount of speaker surface touching earth to almost nothing (the sharp points of three Tip Toes — it only takes three per speaker, by the way). Your speakers virtually float, and so can the music.

Audiophiles believe in TipToeing *everything*: turntables, tape players, even CD players. I don't go that far, but I can hear a difference in TipToed speakers, and I can recommend them for that.

Low profile (half-inch) Tip Toes are $5 each; high profile Tip Toes (one-and-one-half-inch), $7 each.

Monster Cable

Back in the old days, if you used shielded cable you were doing real well. Today, well, whatever you want to spend for cabling, someone will take your money and give you several feet of electron superhighway.

The leader in this industry — an industry it practically invented — is Monster Cable. I remember seeing my first Monster Cable, oh, fifteen years ago and wondering why anybody would pay $10 for a connector that came free with every tape deck, tuner or turntable.

Robert Coyle patiently explained to me that certain metals and certain configurations conduct electrons better than others and these metals and configurations were more expensive than the free ones. Why pay good money for great sound and lose it in a cheap cable? I bought the Monster Cables.

Today you can spend $150 a pair for one-meter Monster Cables. Or, if you're on a budget, how about $50 a pair? Video cables are $24.95 each.

And let's not forget speaker cable. Monster's speaker cable is $9 a foot. In the world of Audiophile speaker cable, that's moderately priced. (And I used to debate over the nickel difference between 16-gauge and 18-gauge speaker wire at the hardware store. Ah, the good old days.) Speaker wire has gotten FAT. One company cleverly calls theirs Music Hose.

Tweek

According to Robert, the single most important improvement you can make to your audio/video system is Tweek. The good news: it takes about fifteen minutes. The gooder news: it only costs $18.

Tweek is a liquid you put between any bare metal contacts in your system: between cables and connector pins, between speaker wire and terminals, between battery terminals and battery receptacles — everywhere. It somehow increases the amount of electrons flowing through that contact, and that increases the amount of audio and video information presented to your senses.

It's a simple process: unplug your cable, brush Tweek on cable and connector, replug cable, twisting slightly. That's it.

Some say a cable and connector once Tweeked is Tweeked forever. Other say it must be reTweeked every time a connection is broken. Whichever is true, an $18 bottle will probably last you until the next century.

Programmable Remote Controls

Some people (like me) have so many gadgets and electronic things that remote controls lie around like so many beached trout. I am constantly fumbling through a stack of remote units looking for the right one that has the right button to do what I need done.

Enter Programmable Remote Controls. They combine the signals of several units into one. I looked at the Onkyo RC-AV1M Universal Remote and the GE Control Central. They do the job well.

They work like this: you place, one by one, each of your original remote controls head-to-head with the Programmable Remote Control. You set the Programmable Remote to programming mode and indicate on the Programmable what kind of remote you are programming (TV, VCR, cable box, etc.). Then, one by one, you press the buttons on the original remote and the corresponding buttons on the Programmable Remote simultaneously. The signal sent by the original is read by the Programmable and stored in the Programmable's memory. You repeat the procedure with all your remotes — or as many remotes as the Programmable will accommodate.

The GE Control Central can duplicate only four remote controls: TV, VCR, Cable, and Aux. The Onkyo has buttons for CD Player, Phono, Tuner, Tape-1, Tape-2, VCR, VDP (Video Disc Player), Cable TV, and Aux, and you're only limited by the amount of memory the Onkyo can store. If you have multi-multi-buttoned original remotes, you may run out of memory on the Onkyo.

Both retail for $119. If you have several remotes or plan to get more in the future (and you will), go with the Onkyo. If you have four or less, and plan to have four or less forever, go with the GE. I found the GE's manual easier to follow, and hence, easier to learn. The GE has an LCD screen. The Onkyo doesn't.

Sonrise Revolving CD Holder

There's something nice about holding the latest in technology in hand-crafted wood. The Sonrise holder holds 40 CD's — twenty per side — in a revolving rack. The rotation is wonderfully smooth — there are more ball bearings at the base of this unit than in most automobiles. $69.95 for oak, $89.95 for walnut.

Monster Cable Zapit

Tired of having to press remote control buttons several times, carefully aiming and reaiming each time until the message is finally relayed? Monster Cable can solve your problem with Zapit. It's a power booster for your remote control. For $24.95, you get a unit about the size of a roll of half-dollars that attaches, with double-sided tape, to your remote control. There's no on/off switch — it works whenever you use your remote. Nothing could be simpler. No more aiming — just be in the same room as your controlled item and push.

CD Mate

This is invaluable for portable and auto CD players. The biggest problem with CD's is, "How do you carry the discs around?" CD Mate answers the question brilliantly. It holds and protects either six or ten CD's in a compact, velcro-sealed holder. The six-CD holder is $9.95, the ten-CD holder is $14.95.

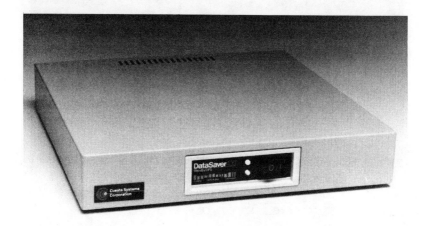

VCR Power Backup

In my former life as a computer reviewer, I discovered, and now use, a power backup system for my computer. The closest I've come to seeing my life flash before me was when I was word processing away — truly great writing, probably my best — when the power went out. The words drained from my screen. My groan could be heard for blocks.

Now, with a power backup, when the house plunges into blackness, my computer stays on. Constant power. I'm happy.

Before I left on my last trip, I programmed my VCR to record *St. Elsewhere*, *LA Law*, and a few other favorites. When I returned a week later, my VCR was flashing "12:00." It flashed because the power, at some point, had taken a trip, too, and the time and programming disappeared from the VCR. None of my programs were recorded.

Now I've installed a second power backup, and my VCR is assured of constant power for the clock and programming. And, if the power goes out while the machine is recording, the power supply should keep it recording for a short while. I'm happy. No, that's an exaggeration. I worry less.

I use Datasaver power backups, made by Cuesta Systems in San Luis Obispo, California. Power backups are not cheap, but the Datasavers are competitively priced: a 90-watt unit retails for $350, 200 watts for $495, and 400 watts for $695. All the units will keep your programming and clocks running for weeks if not months, without house current. The real drain is in recording, but — I'm guessing here — if your VCR takes 45 watts (it probably takes much less), then a 90-watt backup will keep it recording for about 15 minutes, a 200-watt, for about 30 minutes, and a 400 watt, easily for an hour.

When the power comes back on, the units automatically recharge, ready for the next instance of power outage.

Chapter Nineteen

Home Phones

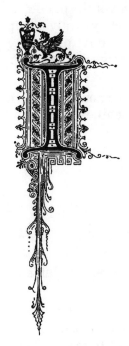 wonder about things. I wonder why television quickly became TV, but the telephone never became TP. I wonder what happened to the "the" in front of television? "I'm looking at television," sounds right. "I'm talking on telephone," doesn't.

In the good old days we never had to worry about buying a telephone. When I got my first phone, the big choice was "Did I want a color?" Ma Bell had colors back then, seven of the worst colors you have ever seen. For — what was it? Two dollars a month? — you could have a color phone. I owned black happily. I would have paid two dollars a month *not* to have one of those colors.

Then came Divestiture (or "The D-Word," as it's known around AT&T). We now have a lot more choices, and with more choices invariably comes confusion.

Some people wish the government had never tinkered with AT&T. "It was so much easier back when there was only one phone company," they say. Easier, but duller.

I remember, in 1971, wanting a telephone answering machine. At that time, it was illegal to add anything to the phone lines. (Even the phone lines in your home were owned by AT&T.) This meant you were forced to use an AT&T phone answering machine. You had to rent one. Fine. Seventy dollars a month. Grumble, grumble, fine. One would not, however, be available for six to nine months. Maybe.

I had to buy an answering machine. To avoid touching AT&T's sacred lines, the answering machine had a device that fit between the cradle and the handset of the phone. In order to answer a call, the machine had to physically lift up the receiver, announce through the mouthpiece my recorded message, and take messages through the earpiece. Cumbersome. Ugly. Unreliable.

Now you own your own phone lines, you own your own phones, you own your own answering machines. I'm happy for divestiture.

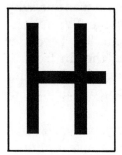

ere are some of the features available on Today's Telephones:

Ringer Cutoff. Absolutely essential. Why people feel the need to answer the phone no matter what else they're doing is a puzzlement to me.

Home Phones

"I was awakened in the middle of the night by a wrong number," people complain.

"Why didn't you turn your phone off?" I ask.

"Maybe somebody has to reach me about something important."

"When was the last time you found out something really important in the middle of the night — by phone, that is?"

"Gee, I can't remember."

"And when was the last time you were awakened by a wrong number?"

"Last month."

"I rest my case."

A ringer cutoff switch is not essential — you can always unplug the phone. But the little plastic thing on the end of the phone cord, the thing that holds the cord in, falls off after about six months of daily plugging and unplugging. Then you have to buy a new cord, which most people don't do, so the cord keeps slipping out of the phone and you wind up missing important calls during the times when important calls usually do come (days and evenings).

If you get a two-line phone, check to see if each line has its own ringer cutoff.

"What the hell sort of convenient new feature is this?"

Auto Redial. Another essential at McWilliams Telephone (or MT, home of "The MT Promise"). One of the most irritating things about a busy signal (other than the actual *sound* itself, which is truly one of the rudest noises on earth) is having to redial. This is especially true if you *must* reach the busy party right away, and particularly true if it's a long distance call (more digits).

Now redialing a busy number is just the push of a button away. Ah, technology.

Memory. Some phones remember numbers and dial them at the push of one or more buttons. If you find yourself calling the same twenty numbers 80% of the time (which most people do), memory dialing is awfully handy.

Emergency dialing. These phones have separate buttons for fire, police and ambulance. What with telephone operators becoming more and more busy and less and less cooperative (blame it on the D-Word, they say), one of these little buttons could save your life.

Illuminated buttons. Dial much in the dark? Nice next to the bed or, if you watch TV with the lights out, the living room.

Speaker Phones. These allow you to talk and listen via a built-in speaker and microphone (also known as "hands free"). Although you can hear the other person just fine, you will, even with the best of speaker phones, sound as though you are talking from the bottom of an empty oil tanker. The other person may be too polite to say anything, but, take it from me, it's damned irritating. I'm generally not too polite. "Would you please get off the speaker phone?" I ask whenever I hear that familiar tinny voice surrounded by echoes.

n addition to features, there are two, uh, philosophical choices to make when buying a phone. They are "Corded or Cordless?" and "One Line or Two Line?" The various moral, psychological and practical considerations of these two weighty issues are considered below.

Corded or Cordless?

Cordless (also known as "wireless") phones have a base station which plugs into the phone line and a portable unit which communicates to the base unit without wires. The idea of a phone with no cord to knock over lamps or disturb the cat seems irresistible at first, but consider the following realities:

1. The range of most cordless phones is limited. Although they may advertise a "50 foot range," that's 50 *uninterrupted* feet. Walls, floors and ceilings all reduce the range remarkably. Consider a cordless phone good for one room.

2. The sound quality is generally not as good, and certainly not as reliable, as wired phones. I can't tell you how many conversations I've had with people who, after zoning out two or three times, say, "Let me get to my other phone." This is invariably followed by, "I'm having so much trouble with that phone," and I am treated to the last five horror stories concerning the cordless phone.

3. Cordless phones operate on battery power and recharge when placed back in their home bases. If you leave the phone lying about (which most people do), it will eventually run out of power and you will have to go running to

a corded phone (see 2). Also, as the batteries fade, so does the effective range of the phone, causing static and drifting (see 2).

4. If you leave the phone lying about (which most people do), you might not know where it is to answer it. Yes, you can listen for the ring, but those electronic rings often sound as though they're coming from *everywhere*. Not only do you have to run to the room where the phone is, you also have to find the phone — all before the caller hangs up or the answering machine kicks in. The whole thing can be amusing to the observer. It looks like *Beat the Clock*. (Remember Beat the Clock?)

This may sound as though I am down on cordless phones. I am not. They're good for back yards. And ballrooms. And tennis courts. And polo fields. (I have one in each of mine.) But for ordinary rooms, wired phones work better.

Cordless phones are a great idea. The technology hasn't caught up yet.

Home Phones

One Line or Two Line?

Certainly by now, if it's available in your area, you have Call Waiting. Call Waiting is one of the great inventions of the twentieth century. But perhaps you've outgrown Call Waiting. The solution — get a second line. Here are some of the advantages of having two lines:

1. Two people can make calls at the same time. Naturally they have to use separate phones, but, unlike Call Waiting, each can make separate calls.

2. You have two numbers. This means you can give different numbers to different people. One number can be for close friends, the other for relatives and everybody else. You can turn off, or not answer, the second line any time you wish. The "private" line can also be unlisted.

3. If you're talking on an important call, the second line can be answered by an answering machine. With Call Waiting, if you don't interrupt your important call to answer, you have no idea who called.

4. Your phone conversations are not interrupted by annoying clicks, beeps and boops — the mating calls of Call Waiting. The other line rings, and, if you have the ringer turned off, you'll never know — until you check your machine.

5. There must be a Law of the Universe which states, "If you get two phone calls in any twenty-four hour period, and if they're both important enough, they will both come at the same time."

With one answering machine and Call Waiting, the message from the first call is punctuated by the little beep that indicates another person is calling. The first caller doesn't know this, and continues with the message. "The number is 570-BEEEEEEEPP! and it's real important that you call because the number is unlisted and I'll be waiting, so call soon, 570-BEEEEEEEEPP! Okay? Bye." Meanwhile, the second person calling just gets a ring — no answering machine — and assumes you're too lazy to turn your machine on or have gone to Acapulco for a month.

With two lines you can have an answering machine attached to each, and both messages will be recorded. Further, you can have two different messages, one for each line. On the "private" line you can tell your intimates that you *have* gone to Acapulco. On the "public" line you can say, "I'm in the shower. I'll be right out." It tends to confuse burglars.

Naturally, all these wonders come at a price. In Los Angeles, for example, Call Waiting costs $5.00 to install and $3.50 per month. A second line costs from $34.50 to $47.50 to install and $12.05 a month.

"But they'll have to run new wires all over my house," you may say. Not so. Almost all indoor phone lines consist of four wires, but today's phones only require two. If you have a standard modular jack, your house is already wired for a second line. When the second line is installed, the phone company will connect the second line to your existing wiring.

All of your single-line phones will work on your original number as usual, but if you plug in a two-line phone, it will be able to use both lines. You can also buy an adapter that allows any single-line phone to access only line two (the new, second number).

I was delightfully surprised to learn I already had the wiring to add a second line to every room in my house. I had visions of cable being run over, under, around and through everything, which had always been the procedure in the pre-D-Word days whenever I wanted more than one line. Ah, progress.

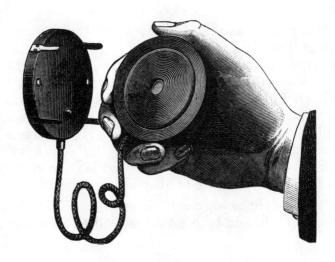

Colonial Data AP2002

I've been using this phone for about two years and like it a lot. It has a typewriter-style keyboard. All I do is type the first three letters of the person I want to call, and it automatically dials the person. It's also a speaker phone (a good one), makes conference calls (on the two-line model) and has a built-in clock. It comes in high-tech dark grey or warm and friendly beige. $179.95.

Telko 803 Radio Phone

A phone, an AM-FM clock radio, a hold button, a ringer turn off button. What more do you need next to your bed? $59.95.

Telemania Quacky Phone

This phone began quite seriously. People collect duck decoys, it seems. The idea, a few years ago, was to have a high-quality duck decoy — the sort one would proudly display on one's mahogany desk — and, hidden inside, a phone. It cost several hundred dollars and was supposed to appeal to people who thought a phone cluttered up a desk.

Well, it was such a silly idea from the start that people bought them as gag gifts — not quite what the original designers had in mind. Then came the inexpensive imitators, and it was all over. Duck phones have joined the ranks of Pet Rocks. $89.

Phone Censor

Here's a nifty phone accessory. Imagine this scenario: You want to take a nap for at least two hours. At the end of two hours, you don't mind being disturbed by a phone call, but if no phone calls are forthcoming, you'd just as soon keep sleeping. A problem. The solution? Phone Censor.

Phone Censor allows you to turn your phone off for from one to fifteen hours, in one hour increments. At the end of that time, the ringer will be turned back on, and whoever wants to can get through.

I find this feature of Phone Censor heaven. I can't tell you how many times I've gotten up at 8 AM to turn on the phone for a call scheduled to come, "Sometime tomorrow morning," only to have the call come at 11:59. Now I just set the phone to go on at 8 AM and I can, if I need to, sleep until the 11:59 call.

But what about the bill collectors or encyclopedia salespeople who call at 8:01? If you so choose, another feature of Phone Censor comes into play. The Phone Censor will screen calls and only put a call through if the person on the other end knows the code. (The code is simple, something like: call, let it ring twice, hang up, call back within a minute. The code is something *like* that. It may not *be* that. You may be one of those bill collectors out there trying to break my code.)

The Phone Censor has four different ring patterns. Each ring pattern has a different incoming code. You can give different people different codes. Business acquaintances can have one code, friends another, really close friends a third, and mother the fourth.

Each uses their code when dialing, and you know who's calling (or at least which group is calling). You can choose to answer or not, as you please.

The Phone Censor replaces the ringer on one telephone only. (The Phone Censor has its own built-in chime.) Other extensions in the house ring as usual (unless, of course, you turn them off).

At $39.95, the Phone Censor is a true bargain. It's available only from the manufacturer, Chrono Art, 9175 Poplar Avenue, Cotati, California, 94928; (707) 795-1834.

Telephone Headsets

Headsets are great if you need your hands free and hate the boxy sound of speakerphones. I tested three different models and their quality varied widely.

The headset from ACS Communications plugs into your phone where your handset does. Your handset then becomes a weight which you use for hanging up at the end of a call. This model has a volume control, but I found the microphone sat too close to my mouth so that any sibilant sound became a hurricane of noise. ("Ssssay, isss Ssssam there?") There's no way to extend the microphone, but when I aimed it at my chin, it worked better. With a list price of $131.90, it's extraordinarily overpriced.

The model from National Teletronics, called the Featherweight Phone, offers more than the ACS. Instead of attaching at the handset, the Featherweight Phone joins on the phone line side. (You connect the phone line to it, and it to your telephone.) The microphone on this one worked much better than the ACS, even though the microphone couldn't be extended.

The Featherweight also leaves my handset available, so I can still use my phone as a regular phone. While the ACS has a dial for volume control, the Featherweight has a switch: low and hi. Low was low, high was normal. On high, I could also hear a faint hiss. Not a plus, but the price is: $19.95 mail order.

Gemini Industries makes a headset called Model TA-240. It has the best of both of the above headsets: You can switch from headset to handset at the push of a switch, permitting you to use either one, depending on the call. The Gemini also has a dial volume control. Unlike the others, the microphone can be pulled away or pushed toward the mouth, as well as adjusted up or down. My callers thought I sounded just as good with this as with my regular handset. The best part, the Gemini retails for just $12.95. Wow.

One last note: None of the three had speakers-on-the-ear as good as the handset. That is, I could hear the person I was talking to better with my handset than with any of these headsets.

Speakerphones are easier to use, but those who you call will like the sound of the headsets over the hollow echo of speakerphones. If you want a headset, the Gemini TA-240 is by far the best buy.

Brookstone Telephone Hearing Booster

The Brookstone installs simply enough. You plug your handset into the hearing booster, and the booster into your phone. The booster has a sliding switch, one end is marked "Loud," the other end, "Soft." The booster softens wonderfully (for the one person in America who has too *loud* a telephone), but, at full max "Loud," the booster only increases the volume marginally. Because it works without batteries, I suppose it can only do so much.

The only good thing about the hearing booster is that it has, like all Brookstone products, a lifetime satisfaction guarantee. For instance, suppose you bought a hearing booster, despite this review, and used it for ten years. Then you decide, "You know, that McWilliams was right. I shouldn't have bought this. I can't hear a damn thing better." You take it back to a Brookstone store, and, if you have a receipt, you'll get cash back. If you don't have a receipt, they'll give you store credit. If you haven't seen a

Home Phones

Brookstone store, they're fun places — lots of gadgets and other useful stuff. Brookstone also has a catalog.

The Doctor is Always Within Reach

...because of the
MALLORY VIBRATOR'S
Contribution to the Mobile Telephone

Thanks to the mobile telephone, the family doctor is always within reach of his patients. In emergencies, he can give directions over the phone as he speeds to the side of the stricken!

As you check over the many uses for two-way radio and mobile telephones—in trucking, trains, shipping, police cars and ambulances—remember that it was a Mallory achievement, the Mallory Vibrator, that made possible this miracle. It also made possible your automobile radio set.

Mallory makes many other parts for modern electronic equipment, which though hidden from the user's eye, perform vital services. Mallory supplies the indis-

pensable parts—condensers, filters, resistors, controls, capacitors, relay switches, jacks, plugs and rectifiers— that make the miracles of modern electronics dependable and practical.

In the fields of electronics, electrochemistry, and metallurgy, Mallory has pioneered many new ways. The creative research, knowledge and experience that Mallory has amassed in more than three decades of pioneering stand ready now to assist manufacturers with design or production problems in these complex fields.

You are invited to consult with our engineering staff. Their record for making so many new ideas work is strong evidence they can be of important assistance to you.

Chapter Twenty

Car Phones

think of car phones as the ultimate automotive luxury. To be driving down the street, chatting away, doing business, placing bets, er, talking with your broker — that's life in the moderately fast lane. (In the fast lane, somebody else drives and your broker rides with you.)

A short while ago, car phones were outrageously expensive. Only so many were allowed in a given metropolitan area. Like taxicab medallions, rent-controlled apartments or Cristal champagne, when demand outstrips supply, prices soar. In some areas where prices were controlled, the wait for a car telephone was more than ten years.*

---

* Which reminds me of a joke Ronald Reagan told my brother (and about twenty million other people because my brother saw it on TV). I can tell it here because (A) it's funny and (B) it has to do with technology — mostly (A).

A man in Russia went to buy a car. He filled out all the necessary papers and filed them with all the necessary departments. At the last department the Commissar of Transportation told him, "Congratulations, comrade. You have successfully filled out all the necessary forms and your car will be ready in ten years."

"Will that be in the morning or the afternoon?" the man asked.

"It's ten years from now," the Commissar said, "What difference does morning or evening make?"

"The plumber's coming in the morning."

In the past, all the car phones communicated with one central transmitter/receiver, usually located in the downtown area. To use the phone in the suburbs required lots of power.

There were only so many lines, and if all were engaged, that was that. It sometimes took hours just to get a line, or hours of trying for a call to come in. A rider leaning out of his limo talking on a pay phone was not an uncommon sight.

Now, rather than one giant transmitter/receiver for a city, there are dozens — sometimes hundreds — of smaller transmitter/receivers, each covering a one-mile radius. These circles overlap, blanketing an area in a cell-like pattern, hence *cellular* phones.

As you drive from one cell to another, your call automatically transfers from one cell station to the next. It's seamless, for the most part — you never know that in a twenty-minute call you might have used twenty different cells.

The cellular concept allows tens of thousands of phones in areas formerly limited to a handful. This has sparked the electronics industry to mass-produce car phones. (Before they were a specialty item manufactured by a few companies.)

Also, because the phone only has to transmit a maximum of one mile, the cellular phones need to be less powerful, making the concept of a phone that can fit in your pocket (if you have a rather large pocket) a reality. Dick Tracy's two-way wrist phone is not too far off.

Most car phones today come with optional battery packs. The whole unit is about the size of a shoe box, and it can be carried around by a strong arm. (The smaller "pocket-sized" portable phones don't have the power of the larger ones, hence the smaller ones are plagued by poor reception.)

A portable phone's signal strength is measured in watts. Three watts is the maximum. Three watts should also be considered the minimum. What you save by getting less than three watts will be more than spent in frustration and excess phone time. (You are charged by the minute, and the minute it takes to reconnect is a minute you pay for).

The cost of operating a car telephone varies from city to city, but, to use Los Angeles as an example, it costs $50 for "service establishment" (don't you love Phonese?) and a $45 "monthly access charge." "Peak airtime" calls cost 45 cents per minute and "off-peak airtime" costs 27 cents per minute. Toll calls are, naturally, extra.

If you dial a number and it doesn't go through, these are known as "incomplete calls" and are "charged at 1/2 rate." This means that if you call someone and they don't answer, you pay 23 cents (peak) or 14 cents (off peak) for the privilege. Unless you let it ring for more than a minute, in which case you pay more.

At these rates, you can see why some people keep the phone number in their car confidential. You pay 45 cents a minute whether you call out or someone calls you.

Most of the features found on home phones can be found on car phones, too. (Please see the previous chapter.) The hands-free feature is a good idea in the car — you never know when you're going to need both hands. Unlike the built-in microphones in regular speaker phones, most car phones have a removable microphone that can be mounted close to the user's mouth. (The sun visor, for example.) This closer miking eliminates some of the tunnel effect common on ordinary speaker phones.

Mitsubishi DiamondTel Phone

To the car phone installers I talked with, the Diamond-Tel is the Mercedes of cellular phones. I haven't begun to figure out all the things it does. It has more buttons on its keypad than I know what to do with.

I do know it sounds awfully good — very few people ask, "Are you in your car?" Even the hands-free microphone works. (I had someone call me from my car so I could hear.)

The DiamondTel also has a battery pack and portable antenna. If you're willing to carry it around (or willing to pay someone to carry it around for you), you'll never be out of touch. $1,830.

Chapter Twenty-one
Answering Machines

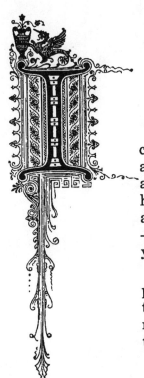 cannot imagine life without an answering machine. Coming home after a long day of, well, not being home, and finding the little light on the answering machine blinking, blinking — somehow it says, "Someone loves you, someone loves you."

I also cannot imagine why some people consider it discourteous to let their phone be answered by "a machine." What, pray tell, are the alternatives?

Nothing? Just let it ring and ring. A friend called and left a frantic message on my machine. He needed a yes or no from me *right away*. I called and called and called. He doesn't "believe" in answering machines. (What's there to believe in? It's a machine, not a religion.) It took thirty calls to communicate a message that, with a machine, would have taken only one.

An answering service? Talk about discourteous. "Seven, seven, four, nine," a distant voice intones, "One moment please." Click. Pause. More pause. Still more pause. And a little more pause.

Eventually the voice returns. I can hear someone being murdered — or maybe it's just the TV — in the background. "Seven, seven, four, nine," the voice says again.

"I'd like to leave a message for Alex, please."

"Is Alex the last name?"

"First name."

"Alex what?"

"Bell."

"Bill? What is Bill's last name?"

"Bell."

"Bell?"

"Yes, Bell."

"Bill Bell?"

"No, Alex Bell. B-E-L-L."

"Bell is the last name?"

"Yes."

"Alex is the first name?"

"Yes."

"I'll check."

The voice checks. Voices take longer to find things than, say, eyes and hands. The murder continues unabated, or perhaps it's just a satanic rite. The voice finally finds Bell.

"Mr. Bell, you have three messages. Your mother called. She says you have the number. . ."

"I am not Mr. Bell. I want to leave a message for Mr. Bell."

"Your name?"

"McWilliams."

"Nick Williams?"

"No, McWilliams."

"Mick Williams?"

"No, McWilliams. One word."

"Could you spell that please?"

"M-C-W-I-L-L-I-A-M-S. McWilliams."

"Oh, McWilliams."

"Yes."

"Is that the first name or last name?"

"Last name."

"One moment, please."

I am on hold again. I wonder why, why is this operator so busy? I wonder if maybe this is the number people call when ordering Popeil's Pocket Fisherman and maybe one of those irresistible ads was just on TV. I wonder if I should continue holding. I wonder if I should order yet another Pocket Fisherman. The voice returns.

"No messages, Mr. Williams."

"*Mc*Williams, and I want to *leave* a message."

"For whom?"

"Alex Bell."

"Is that the first name or last name?"

"I'd like to order a Pocket Fisherman, please."

"Will that be C.O.D. or major credit card?"

I'm sure there are wonderful answering services. I had one in New York, The Belles, who treat you like family. They were the basis of the musical *Bells Are Ringing*. But I have left lots of messages with lots of services in my time, and although most are good at name and phone number, few are good at much else. If I leave an intricate message on someone's machine, I know at least they'll hear it, word for word, with verbal gestures.

I suppose, for those who consider answering machines discourteous, the only truly courteous thing to do is to never leave home.

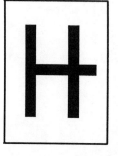

ere are some of the features available on answering machines:

VOX. Some machines will record, say, thirty seconds of message even when the person only has five seconds of message. This means you are treated to twenty-five seconds of phone company clicks, static and dial tone at the end of each message. Conversely, these machines will also cut someone off at thirty seconds, even if they have forty-five seconds worth of message. Machines with VOX record a message for as long as the person keeps speaking, and then stops. There may be a few seconds of clicks at the end, but not as many as on a non-VOX machine.

Most VOX machines allow you to set a maximum time for incoming messages — three minutes, for example — so pesty calls don't consume your whole incoming tape.

Message Only. On a machine without this feature, if someone calls and hangs up, it counts as a message. On a non-VOX machine you listen to twenty or thirty seconds of dial tone (etc.) for each hang up. It's demoralizing to have the machine say "5 Messages Waiting" and find it's four hang ups and a computer calling to sell you insurance. I don't *want* to know how many people called who didn't bother to leave a message.

Remote. This allows you to get messages and sometimes even change your outgoing message from any phone in the world. The earlier models used a little box called a "beeper." You would hold up to the phone and beep your desire to the answering machine. The newer models — known, not surprisingly, as "beeperless" — use the beeps of any touch-tone phone to communicate with the answering machine. If you travel to places where dial telephones are still the rage, you may need a beeper (or a device that simulates the touch-tone beeps).

Toll Saver. After the machine is reset, it will answer the phone after the fourth ring for the first message and after the second ring for all subsequent messages. If you're calling to check on messages and the phone rings three times, you know you have no messages, and you can hang up, saving yourself the toll.

Auto Reset. If the machine answers *just* before you get to the phone (and doesn't it always?), you have to yell over the outgoing message "I'm here! Hold on! Don't hang up!" and wait for the message to complete itself — all the while listening to yourself trying to sound real cheerful on that message, which was a failure. Then your conversation is recorded as a message, which you forget about until you see the light blinking. Then you think somebody called, but it's just a transcript of your last call. Is that what's troubling you, bubbie?

Well, auto reset will turn off the answering machine and reset it the instant you pick up the phone. If you like call screening (listening to who's calling before letting them know you're home), be sure the auto reset feature can be turned off.

(If auto reset is not part of your current machine and you'd like it to be, see the review of FoneAlone at the end of this chapter.)

Clock/Calendar. This records the day and time of each message and displays it when the message is played back. It's great for catching those slippery people who call at 4:45 and say, "It's after five and you're not here so I have to do something else." Now you'll know.

Built-In Phone. I believe in combining things only if (A) there's a real good reason for it, and (B) the items being combined tend to last the same amount of time. Adding a phone to an answering machines satisifies neither.

Answering Machines

Telephones and answering machines have two different functions. Answering machines have their own microphones and speakers and therefore don't need to share the microphone and speaker of the telephone. And, you can certainly use a telephone without any help from an answering machine.

Telephones also tend to last longer than answering machines. If you buy the two welded into one (albeit attractive) unit, when the answering machine answers its last call, you may find yourself with a large, unattractive telephone. Further, if the *telephone* breaks first, you're out an answering machine while getting the phone repaired.

The only reason for getting the two together is style, and for style we often sacrifice a certain degree of practicality. And thus it goes.

Two-Line Answering. Not recommended unless it can answer calls coming into *both* lines *simultaneously*. I haven't yet found a machine that can do that. It's better to have two less-expensive machines, one for each line.

Record A Call 2100

Simple, basic phone answering machine. A little screen tells you how many messages you have. Push one button (there is only one button) and your messages are played. Pushing the button again while a message is playing plays that message again. For more elaborate control, the top opens and an additional series of buttons — far more difficult to comprehend — are available. Beeperless remote, VOX, toll-saver. $99.95.

PhoneMate Performance Series 7650 Telephone and Answering Machine

I was alone one evening and decided to review the PhoneMate 7650. I plugged it in, according to directions, and went on to do something else. About two hours later, a voice from behind me said, "You have a phone call." The PhoneMate 7650 does not ring. It has a voice that says, "You have a phone call." It scared the hell out of me. I unplugged it and never plugged it in again. It's sitting in the corner now. If it says anything else, I'm sending it to Stephen King.

FoneAlone

This one wins my mother's Seal of Approval. For two years now, my mother has been in a race with her answering machine. Will she pick up first or will it? If it picks up, she has to either turn it off or yell over the outgoing message, "I'm home! Hold on!" and then have most of the conversation recorded. At one point she actually fell and hurt her shoulder while racing for the phone.

Enough was enough. FoneAlone to the rescue. FoneAlone attaches between the answering machine and the telephone jack. If the answering machine gets to the phone before you do, all you have to do is pick up any phone in the house and FoneAlone instantly turns off and resets your answering machine. This, for my mother, was roughly the equivalent of the invention of 300-calorie frozen entrees — in other words, a major scientific advance.

If you like using your answering machine to screen calls, just plug a phone into the answering machine. Any phone connected to the answering machine will not interfere with the machine's function. For this phone, it's as though FoneAlone's not there.

FoneAlone is also handy for multiple phones. If a FoneAlone is connected to every phone in the house or office, the first phone picked up will automatically block out all others. This saves the "Hello?" "Hello?" "I've got it." "You've got it?" "I've got it." dialogue that goes on when more than one person gets to the phone at about the same time. FoneAlone is $29.95. Mom, to whom almost nothing I own is worth what I paid for it, thinks FoneAlone is worth it. From manufacturer, or from Sharper Image, 800-344-4444.

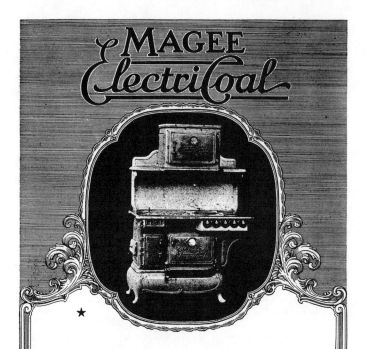

MAGEE *ElectriCoal*

★

MAGEE Combines Coal and Electricity

by using EDISON Electric Equipment with their Coal Ranges

THE MAGEE ElectriCoal Range is dual in its make-up, comprising a perfect coal range and a complete electric range. The electrical equipment (Edison) includes an oven, broiler and three cover units. The electric oven, insulated on all sides, is a fireless cooker. The coal range is complete, from the large baking oven to the efficient brass coil for heating water.

The Magee ElectriCoal Range is made in Gray Por-cel-a or in ebony black, both nickel-trimmed. with polished top.

These ranges are carefully crated, with complete instructions, so that they can be installed anywhere.

Sold through local dealers or direct. Send for illustrated booklet

MAGEE FURNACE COMPANY
(Dept. H) Boston, Massachusetts

Chapter Twenty-two

Small Kitchen Appliances

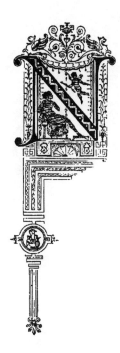

o, I'm not going to divide kitchen-users into three categories: Snackers, Cooks and Gourmets. No, I'm not going to make comments, such as, "The Gourmets cut their teeth on *The Art of French Cooking* and their fingers on Sabatiers." No, I'm not going to point out that Gourmets need to eat well, Cooks like to eat well, and Snackers like to eat.

No, I'm not going to do any of that. (Cheers from the general populace.)

Historically, kitchens got more electrical gadgets, and sooner, than any room in the house. While the phonograph was still being hand-cranked in the parlor, waffles were being electrically grilled in the kitchen.

In most homes, this is still true. Even setting aside major appliances — refrigerator, stove, dishwasher — a modern kitchen is a cornucopia of electronics: toasters, blenders, microwaves, crock pots, Cuisinarts (and the various chopping, dicing and slicing Cuisine Clones), knife sharpeners, mixers, can openers, Mr. Coffees (and all the Mr. Clones), popcorn poppers, woks, electric knives (remember electric knives?), ice cream makers, deep fryers, and that latest craze, macrowave freezers.

Let's take a look at some of these gadgets.

263

The first microwave, 1947.

Microwave Ovens

The joys of microwave ovens are well known: leftovers heat in a minute and, magically, don't taste like leftovers; frozen anything becomes hot anything in two minutes; food can be heated right in the serving dishes, saving a lot of wash up.

The most popular use for microwaves, however, is boiling water for instant coffee. People spend $300 for what an immersion heater could do for $3. Ah, life in America.

The old joke about, "He's so bad in the kitchen he can't even boil water," is becoming a reality. I'm sure if I were visiting someone and he or she asked me to boil some water, my first question would be, "Where is the microwave?"

Microwaves work by speeding up the movement of water molecules within foods. The friction of the speeding molecules heats the water, which in turn cooks the food.

Everything cooked in a microwave is essentially "steamed in its own juices."

Here are some features you're apt to come across when shopping for microwave ovens:

Carousel. Microwaves are generated in uneven patterns. Various electronic "stirrers" have helped to even this unevenness out, but most microwaves still have a "hot spot" — an area in which food cooks faster than others. This is why most microwave recipes say, "Turn every five minutes," or "Turn once during cooking." A carousel turns the food for you, assuring even heating of whatever you're cooking.

The drawback of the carousel is that it reduces the total usable space for large items, such as turkeys. Something turning around cannot use the corners of a rectangle. (That sounds too much like geometry to me; I'm getting sleepy.)

Timer. The question is not whether you get a timer or not (all microwaves have a timer), the question is how elaborate a timer do you want. I bought a microwave with an elaborate timer. I'm sure it can independently turn on and off every light in the neighborhood, if only I'd take the time to read the instruction manual to find out how. As it is, in three years I have learned how to turn the microwave on and off, for as much as ten minutes, in ten-second increments. I feel I'm doing Real Well.

Temperature Probe. This is inserted into whatever you're cooking (usually a roast) and signals the microwave to turn off when the food reaches a certain internal temperature.

Browning Coil. Microwaves do not brown food. Browning food requires radiant heat. Some microwaves have added radiant heat in the form of a coil on the roof of the oven. The coil glows and browns whatever is under it.

Convection Oven. A few top-of-the-line microwaves include a convection oven. These cook food using regular (non-microwave) heat. Convection ovens cook food faster than regular ovens because the heat is blown around the oven by a fan. This method of cooking is said to produce juicier roasts with crispier outsides. It is, however, a whole new form of cooking, and whatever regular oven recipes you have will have to be adapted.

Frankly, unless you're a gourmet looking for new culinary mountains to scale, if you already have an oven, you probably won't use a convection oven. To learn microwave cooking is a whole new world. (And most people don't even learn that; they use the microwave for reheating, not cooking.) To learn yet another form of cooking, well, you have to love cooking a lot.

Microwave Recommendation: Buy cheap. Most people use their microwaves for boiling water and reheating food. *All* microwaves do this with equal precision. Some may take a few seconds longer than others, some may require a turn here and there, but, for the most part, a microwave is a microwave is a microwave. Of all the features above, the most valuable for me is the carousel.

I eat because I'm a glutton. I use a microwave because I'm impatient. I use a carousel because I'm lazy. A carousel microwave gratifies three of my seventeen deadly sins, all at once. Few electrical appliances (found in the kitchen) can make that claim.

Macrowave Freezer

For a while, it seemed as though Korea was going to become the perennial "me too" of personal electronics ("Let Japan invent it and we'll make it cheaper," seemed to be their national motto). Now they've invented not only a new kitchen appliance, but a whole new *technology*, with applications as far-reaching as medicine and climate control.

It's known as the macrowave. Microwaves heat food by speeding up water molecules. Macrowaves chill and freeze food by slowing down the water molecules. You can make Jell-O in thirty seconds, turn hot tea into iced tea in forty-five, make ice cubes in a minute, and ice cream in less than a minute-and-a-half. (The cream in the ice cream slows down the freezing process.)

Although developed by a consortium of Korean industries, the first macrowave to be available in the United States is from Munsoon Electronics. Models from Kum Doo

Wae, Sung Hoo and Ram Too are expected shortly. But don't look for models with Japanese names on them any time soon.

The Japanese have been holding back the Super-VHS technology from the Koreans, and the Koreans, in retaliation, are withholding all macrowave licensing from Japan. This has the Japanese terribly upset. The Japanese have been spreading rumors that macrowaves are unsafe, don't work well, and some are even saying macrowave technology doesn't exist at all!

All these rumors are, of course, falsehoods, and the Japanese companies spreading these mistruths are going to feel as sorry for spreading them as U.S. manufacturers did when they finally recognized the full potential of the transistor.

The future looks bright for the macrowave technology. Already in the prototype stage:

Macrowave air conditioning. Because the waves can pass through the air and only cool objects containing large amounts of water (such as human beings), macrowaves can be generated to cool stadiums full of people at, say, sporting events or Weight Watchers conventions. (On the drawing boards: battery-operated macrowave hats that transmit macrowaves for ten to fifteen feet. Result: True portable air conditioning you can share with family and friends. The term, "He's cool," will take on new meaning.)

Macrowave refrigerator. Any cabinet, closet or room in your home can be turned into a refrigerator and/or freezer. Macrowave refrigerators require no insulation: A closed door is enough to keep the waves inside. (Unlike microwaves, which are small waves, macrowaves tend to be big waves and don't go through even large cracks around the doors.)

Macrowave Beer Cans. A small, disposable, battery-operated macrowave generator, located inside the can, keeps beer cold up to twelve hours, even after opening.

Climate Control. Sending macrowaves into clouds causes condensation which in turn causes rain, or, in ski areas and on Christmas, snow.

Of course, the applications of macrowaves in medicine are too obvious to mention.

But, until then, there's still the Munsoon Macrowave Freezer. The basic model (BM49995) is $449.95; the deluxe model (DM54995) with two ice trays, assorted Jell-O molds and ear muffs is $549.95. As with all new personal electronics items, the prices are likely to drop over time.

And the big question continues to be: Will the Koreans be able to permanently freeze the Japanese out of the macrowave market?

Toshiba My Cafe Coffee Maker, Braun Coffee Mill and Braun Coffeemaker

The secret of good coffee is freshly ground beans. It's hard to get any fresher than the Toshiba My Cafe — it grinds the beans and makes the coffee all in one operation.

You fill My Cafe with the correct amount of water, then measure the beans and put them in the grinder/brewing section. Close the top, push the appropriate button (it makes regular, demitasse and espresso), and the grinding starts. The grinding takes no more than twenty seconds. Hot water begins to drip on the now-ground beans, and freshly brewed coffee is collected in a pot below.

The brewing takes a while longer than Mr. Coffee — about ten to fifteen minutes for an eight-cup pot — but you can remove the pot at any time during brewing process to pour a cup or two. Put the pot back and the brewing continues.

Small Kitchen Appliances

The Toshiba My Cafe has a built-in timer and displays time of day when not occupied with coffee making. The timer lets you wake up to freshly ground, freshly brewed coffee every morning.

The primary drawback of this machine is cleanup. The grinder/brewing assembly needs to be removed and cleaned each time it's used. The Toshiba reuses the same metal-screen filter, unlike most drip coffee makers that use disposable paper filters. The screen must be at least rinsed off between brewings. This takes a bit more effort than discarding and replacing a paper filter. The Toshiba's grinder assembly and metal screen are dishwasher safe.

If you don't mind grinding and brewing your coffee in two steps, there's the Braun Coffee Mill and Braun Coffeemaker. You put beans in the top of the Coffee Mill and ground coffee collects in a removable plastic container at the bottom. (The whole thing looks remarkably like the Braun Peanut Butter Maker. Do you think they might be the same machine with different names? I haven't had the nerve to try.)

After grinding beans in the Coffee Mill, you dump the coffee in the Braun Coffeemaker and brewing commences at the rate of one cup per minute. The Braun Coffeemaker uses paper filters. Although it's a two-step process, it saves time in cleanup (unless you clean the Coffee Mill every day, which really isn't necessary).

The coffee taster at *Consumer Reports* liked the coffee from the Braun best. (The Toshiba came in 19th, but then Mr. Coffee, who started it all, came in 20th.)

When I heard *Consumer Reports* had a coffee taster, I immediately called Kelly Services (they're not Kelly Girls anymore) and asked if they had any temporary coffee tasters. They said yes.

The next morning a middle-aged man arrived with a rich Columbian accent. I poured a cup of coffee from the Toshiba and a cup from the Braun and put them on the table, carefully remembering which cup was which. I also put a glass of water in front of him so he could rinse out his mouth between tastings. (I saw a documentary about wine tasting on PBS. I assumed coffee tasting was pretty much the same.)

He tasted the first cup. "This is coffee," he said. He took a sip of water. "This is not coffee," he said. He tasted the second cup. "This is coffee," he said.

"Which is better?" I asked, leaning closer in anticipation.

"I don't know," he said, "I only taste it and tell you whether it's coffee or not."

So much for my reviews of food and drink.

The Braun came with incomplete instructions. Nowhere was I told how much coffee to put in. (Maybe this is something everyone is just supposed to know, like how long to boil an egg before it's hard inside.) The Coffee Mill never suggested which grind (it goes from very fine to very coarse) works best with the Coffeemaker.

The Toshiba, on the other hand, included a measuring device for beans and two instruction-recipe books that told me more about coffee and its uses than I'll ever want to know.

If you want to awaken to the smell of freshly-ground, freshly-brewed coffee, the Toshiba is your best choice. If you don't mind waiting five minutes for your first cup, and you believe the *Consumer Reports* taste tester, get the Braun. (The Braun Coffeemaker has a timer and can be set ahead to brew. You will, however, miss the freshly-ground quality.)

The Toshiba My Cafe is $160. The Braun Coffee Mill is $50. The Braun Coffeemaker is $80.

Braun Multipractic Food Processor

This little thing does just about everything you can ask from a food processor — and all for only $85. It has the standard metal cutting/mixing blade, a dough hook, a whisk, plus four slicing blades. Three of the slicing blades are two-sided, giving you a total of seven slicing/grating choices.

Small Kitchen Appliances

This not only has more features for less money than a Cuisinart, it also has something Cuisinarts don't have: a variable speed control.

Unlike the Braun Coffeemaker, the Multipractic comes with a complete, full-color user guide and cook book. It's bilingual, so you can brush up on your French while learning a new appliance.

Braun Hand Blender

On the other hand, here's a product from Braun in desperate need of a variable speed control. The Braun Hand Blender is, well, a blender held in the hand. The blade is lowered into the container to be blended. Unfortunately, it only goes on and off. The on goes on fast and furious. In the first split-second, half the contents of an eight-ounce glass are all over the kitchen.

If the Hand Blender had a variable speed control, one could begin slowly and then gradually build up speed. It seems to be the initial jolt of power that sprays things around the room. Maybe Cuisinart will come up with a hand blender with variable speed. $24.

Braun Citromatic Juicer

Fresh orange juice is one of the joys of life. This machine makes that joy easy. You can squeeze a whole glass of juice in about a minute. The top half of the unit detaches and can go to table as an attractive juice pitcher. (It holds about eight ounces of juice.) A few seconds of rinsing is all the cleaning it needs, or you can throw it in the dishwasher.

It also makes tangerine juice (talk about heaven) and lemon juice. (Really, when was the last time you had a glass of *fresh* lemonade?) There's no on/off switch — the pressure of the orange against the router turns the machine on; releasing the pressure turns it off. It's quiet, gentle and seems safe enough for children to use (once the oranges are cut). $24.

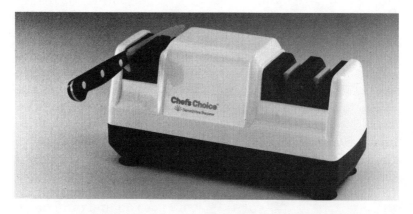

Chef's Choice Diamond Hone Sharpener

One of the safest tools in a kitchen is a *sharp* knife. With a dull knife you have less control; one tends to push too hard. A dull knife is an invitation to an accident.

The Chef's Choice is the finest knife sharpener on the market. It sharpens knives in three stages, just as professionals do. Stage one gives a deep, but shallow angle to the edge of the knife. Stage two gives a more acute angle. Stage three hones the very edge of the knife to almost-razor sharpness. Chef's Choice calls it the Trizor Edge. After three-stage sharpening, keeping knives sharp should take only stages two and three.

It's easier to use than it is to describe. Magnets hold the knife at the right angle. All you have to do is pull the knife through the slots the recommended number of times. You might want to practice on your cheaper knives, however, until you get the hang of it.

The Chef's Choice is recommended for all kitchens, even if your knives don't have fancy French or German names. All knives cut better when sharp, and nothing sharpens knives better than the Chef's Choice. $79.99.

Rival Crock Pot

The lowly crock pot. What a fad it was. One decade as famous as Barry Manilow. The next decade as famous as Barry Manilow. (I'm sorry. Some company sent me a video tape to demonstrate the magnificence of its Surround Sound. It was Barry Manilow singing *Memories*. I was surrounded. I haven't quite yet recovered.)

Rival produced the first crock pot, then it seemed as though everybody except Ford Motor Company produced a crock pot, and now it's back to Rival, alone, producing crock pots.

The crock pot is invaluable for stews, soups, sauces and vegetables. It makes remarkable hot dogs, and the best fish. (Fish only needs an internal temperature of 140 degrees to be fully cooked. Almost all fish is overcooked. Crock pots on low don't get much hotter than 140 degrees. Fish can't be overcooked.)

For smaller quantities there's the Crock-ette. It's a little teeny crock pot, just the right size for double-servings of main dishes, or multiple servings of side dishes.

Maxim or Oster Toaster

Here's the best toaster. It toasts anything in thickness from a pocket of pita bread to a bagel. It has a special rack inside that closes down on the food and holds it tight and upright for even toasting. It also does two slices of ordinary bread, for those run-of-the-mill mornings. About $50.

Chapter Twenty-three

The Home Office

he devices we normally associate with a business office are creeping their way into the home. Typewriters, copying machines, leather reclining chairs — all once the domain of the office are now coming home.

The reasons for this phenomenon include:

★ Prices have dropped on a lot of "semiprofessional office equipment" in the past few years, thanks, mostly, to microchips. A $2,000 copier might be an unnecessary luxury; a $300 copier a necessity.

★ More people are working out of their homes: starting businesses, freelancing, and climbing the corporate ladder harder and faster.

★ More people are working outside of their homes: With two breadwinners away all day, the work of maintaining a house needs to be done faster and more efficiently.

★ More people are realizing that running a house is a business in itself: writing checks, answering letters, maintaining mailing lists and just plain keeping track of things are the stuff of both big business and little apartments.

Some of the tools of a home office are covered in other sections of this book (telephones, answering machines, and, if it's anything like my office, stereo, CD's, VCR's, TV's and popcorn poppers). Here are some of the items that weren't.

Canon PC3 and PC5 Copier

Canon sort of invented home copying. They came up with a relatively low-cost, high-quality copying system, dubbed it the Personal Copier, and hired Jack Klugman to promote it. It seems to have worked, as Canon copiers are everywhere.

The primary difference between the PC3 ($695) and the PC5 ($845) is paper feeding. With the PC3, you have to feed paper in one sheet at a time. The PC5 holds about forty sheets and feeds them automatically.

Both make crisp, clear copies. Both can copy from books, magazines or any object which can be placed on a flat surface. (The original lays on a horizontal, glass surface. It never goes into the machine, so your original is never in danger.)

My only complaint is that when the copy button is pushed, nothing at all happens for one to seven seconds (depending on when the last copy was made — the longer time between copies, the longer the first copy takes to make). During that time I wonder, "Did I push the right button? Should I do something else? Should I push it again?" Seven seconds can be a long time for an apprentice neurotic. A screen saying, "Patience, dear heart, I'm warming up so I can make you the best copy you've ever had," would be appreciated.

A Few Words (Very Few)
About Personal Computers

I have written entire books about personal computers, so I could go (and have gone) on and on about them. But I will not. This will be a concise look at personal computers in the home office at the end of the second-to-the-last decade of the twentieth century.

When considering a computer, the first choice you must make is Apple or IBM? Let's look at IBM first.

When people talk about IBM computers, in almost every instance they're talking about IBM *compatible* computers. For whatever reason, IBM let dozens of other companies copy their computer so closely these other companies openly advertise "100% IBM Compatible."

This remarkable tolerance on IBM's part has created a highly-competitive market for IBM compatibles. Today you can buy IBM compatibles for prices that would have been considered science fiction only a few years ago.

IBM is the standard for computing in this country. It is certainly true for business — more than 95% of all personal computers used in business are IBM compatible. This dominance of the business place, combined with falling prices, has made IBM compatibles the most popular computer for the home as well.

Mom and dad used to buy the kids an Apple because it was the computer the kids used in school. Now mom and dad are buying IBM compatibles for themselves because IBM is the computer they're using at work.

There are two IBM models computer manufacturers tend to copy, the PC/XT and the AT. The PC was the first IBM personal computer, the XT is a PC with a hard disk. Together they're considered one level of compatibility.

The AT (for Advanced Technology) is a faster IBM. It's more powerful, and tends to be more expensive. For most home office applications, a PC/XT is more than sufficient. But the prices of AT compatibles is falling, so if you can get an AT compatible for about the price of a PC/XT compatible, get the AT.

The Apple world is divided between the Apple II and the Macintosh. For a home office, you can forget the Apple II — it would be like buying a VCR that records for one hour: remarkable in its day, but that day has passed.

My early predictions that the Macintosh wouldn't make it were, frankly, wrong. The Mac has established a cozy little niche in computing, and people who use Macs think of them as people, not computers. You don't buy a computer when you get a Macintosh, you join an extended family.

A Macintosh can handle the workload of a home office just fine. If, however, you plan to use your home computer to interact with the "real" business world, it's probably best to go IBM. Certainly, if you use an IBM at work, it's best to go IBM at home.

My only complaint about the Macintosh is that it's overpriced. Apple, and only Apple, makes the Macintosh. They are quick to sue any company that so much as hints of Macintosh compatibility — or even the Mac's "look and feel."

The funniest one was when Apple sued a company for trying to put a picture of a garbage can on an IBM screen. Apple claimed it was copyright infringement because the Macintosh uses a picture of a garbage can on its screen. The other company removed the offending can. Apple now has proprietary use of all the garbage cans in computing.

This complete lack of competition gives Apple a virtual monopoly on the Macintosh. Apple sets its own prices, which are much higher than they would be if Apple had to compete with others in the making and selling Macs.

So, in buying a Mac, you've got Apple to buy from, and that's about it.

If you're buying an IBM compatible, consider IBM. IBM has introduced a new series of computers (don't worry: they won't affect the home office for years), and they're selling off their "old" computers (PC's, XT's and AT's) rather cheap. Owning a genuine IBM might be within your reach.

I also like Kaypro. Kaypro makes good computers at low prices. Also, the Epson Equity series is inexpensive and popular.

If space is a problem, consider the Zenith Laptop Computer series. It's small (portable, actually) and has a great screen. When you're done with it, you can put it in a desk drawer.

The Home Office

The best family personal computer is the Leading Edge with Bernoulli removable drive. For $1,995 you get a complete computer (less printer) with a removable 20 megabyte disk drive. It uses Bernoulli technology to store 20 megabytes of information on a removable cartridge about the size of a Compact Disc holder.

Additional cartridges are $50. This means, for $50 additional per person, every member of the family can have his or her own 20-megabyte IBM-compatible computer. There's no fighting about which programs go on the disk and in what order. Everybody get's their own disk, full of their own programs and data. No disagreements — and complete confidentiality to boot.

"Standard" PLUMBING FIXTURES

In a Bathroom Five Feet Square.
Standard Sanitary Mfg. Co.
Pittsburgh

Chapter Twenty-four

Bathroom

here's an old saying (you see it on souvenir plaques in highway gift shops a lot, right next to Hamlet's soliloquy), "No matter where I take my guests, it seems they like my kitchen best."

Well, I have a nice kitchen, and people say, "Oh, you have a nice kitchen." But so many people have *spectacular* kitchens these days, it's hard to impress anyone with a kitchen.

The room people gasp over is my bathroom. What they like especially is the tub. The tub, in fact, is one of the reasons I bought the house. It's a large, white, tiled tub. I mean large: six feet by four feet, and two feet deep.

As soon as I arrived to spend the first night in my new home, I filled the tub for a long, hot soak. There wasn't enough hot water. The hot-water heater filled it maybe a quarter of the way. It was more like a hot pan than a hot tub.

I had a solar hot-water heater installed with a 110-gallon storage tank. I couldn't stand the guilt of consuming all those natural resources every time I took a bath. Besides, where I live, solar pays for itself in a few years. I also had a 55-gallon gas hot water heater installed as backup.

I went again to fill my tub. It leaked.

Experts came, experts on unleaking tubs. They agreed: It was hopeless, beyond repair, I needed a new tub.

New tubs of this style are not cheap. They are called Roman Spas. To replace this one would cost $2,000. To replace it and add Jacuzzi jets would cost $2,750. Guess which extravagance I chose?

Bubbles

Let me tell you about bubbles. No, not Beverly Sills — *bubbles*. Hot water with bubbles in it. Bubbles make hot water even more therapeutic than hot water already is. Some of the reasons...

1. It keeps the water moving. When water is not moving, the body forms a thermal shield around it — it keeps the hot water away. That's why, after laying still in a hot tub, it feels as though it's not hot anymore, but when you move, it feels hot again. When you move, you break the thermal shield and the hotter water comes into contact

with the skin again. With bubbles, the water does the moving for you — you can luxuriate in laziness.

2. A Jacuzzi jet with enough power has a massage-like therapeutic action. This is what most people think of when they think of a Jacuzzi. Moving a sore neck or foot or arm in front of a powerful Jacuzzi jet seems to knead out the tension in no time at all.

3. There's something psychologically soothing about bubbles. Standard, in their (overpriced, if you ask me) Jacuzzi bathtubs, calls the bubbles-only effect, "Champagne Action." They sell this *in addition* to the jets, and people pay the extra almost $1,000 for it. There is something floaty and airy and festive about bubbles, especially when you're *in* them.

Kenney Needle Shower
Four Models to Choose From
A Connection for Every Style of Tub Faucet

Bubbles are available in basically three formats:

Roman Spa. This is a tiled enclosure of any size, shape and proportion. The number of jets is limited only by your imagination and budget. These include any tiled tub, including the ones attached to swimming pools.

Hot Tubs. These began as tubs (usually of redwood) filled with hot water. Now most are made of fiberglass or acrylic, although wooden ones are still available. They generally hold from one to eight people, have two to eight jets, and are usually outdoors.

Interior Add-Ons. There are companies that will add Jacuzzi jets to whatever enclosure (usually bathtub) you already have.

Exterior Add-Ons. These are the fairly inexpensive units (compared to the alternatives). They are usually used in conjunction with the bathtub you already own and lower into the water from outside of the tub.

Hot Springs Indoor/Outdoor Spa

A spa indoors? Sure, why not? What else are you doing with that extra bedroom, rec room, basement or glassed-in porch? Storage, I bet. I had a spa indoors for over a year. It was in a two-bedroom apartment. The living room had a dining area, so I used the formal dining room for seven-foot-square hot tub. Sure it was eccentric, but then so are my visitors. There was never a problem with excessive humidity as you might suppose.

The Hot Springs Indoor/Outdoor Spa (from Watkins Manufacturing), true to its name, will operate fine either indoors or out. I have mine outside, now that I have an outside to put it in.

It comes with a variety of jets, a heater, filter and light. It requires practically no maintenance — dump a little chlorine in every week or so, rinse off the filter every few months. The thermostat regulates the temperature accurately, and, I am told, never adds more than $20 a month to the electric bill. (It operates on regular household current.)

Watkins is one of the largest manufacturers of self-contained spas. They're owned by a big conglomerate (Masco), so if something happens during your guarantee period, at least there'll be *somebody* to complain to. This is important, because spa companies seems to go in and out of business more often than massage parlours. The place I bought my last tub at was a hot tub dealer one week, a patio furniture dealer the next.

The spa itself carries a five year structural guarantee, and a two-year guarantee on the plumbing and moving parts. The Indoor/Outdoor is $4,495. Other models start at $3,495. They can be delivered anywhere in the U.S.

Well, that was an interesting trip outdoors and underwater. Let's get back to the bathroom....

Plaque Never Sleeps

No, I'm not going to drag out Mr. Toothbrush. Nor am I going to go on like Jerry the dentist on the old (and better) Bob Newhart Show. ("What is orthodontia?" he would ponder. "Orthodontia is like Life. . . . ") I am going to explore a subject I am uniquely unqualified to explore: teeth and gums.

So why am I exploring it? Because there is a new electrical device which makes, as they say, "old fashioned brushing a thing of the past." (I should write ad copy, huh?) It's the **InterPlak**. (It's not even the InterPlak 9000 or InterPlak Deluxe, just good old InterPlak.) It's one product from a company that makes only one product, and it's my favorite thing in the whole book.

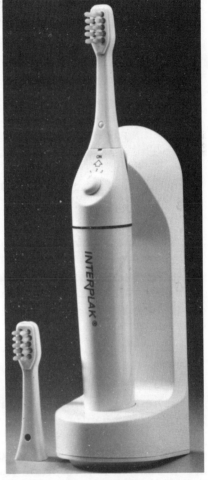

But before I can tell you about the InterPlak, first I have to tell you about plaque. (I can just hear you squealing with anticipation.)

Plaque is a soft, sticky-waxy substance which forms naturally on tooth surfaces. If it is not removed within 24 hours, it begins to harden. Fully hardened, it is called tartar or calculus.

Tartar is porous, like a miniature coral reef. It becomes home to whole colonies of bacteria. The bacteria, being alive, produce waste products, and, being bacteria, are not too fussy about what they do with it. Some of it winds up in the mouth (causing bad breath), some of it is swallowed, and some of it drips onto the gums, causing irritation, inflammation, and, eventually, open sores.

The overwhelming odds are that this is going on in your mouth, right now, and you aren't even aware of it. (And who wants to be aware of it anyway? Well, let's be aware of it for a brief while.)

Tartar builds up first in the areas where plaque is not removed: just below the gum line, especially between teeth. This is the famous area where "ordinary brushing doesn't reach." Gradually, the "coral reef" builds and extends to areas just below and above the gumline around the entire tooth.

There are 18 inches of gum-tooth surface in the average mouth (the distance around each tooth, multiplied by the number of teeth in your mouth). Some people have irritation along the whole length of it. It's like having an 18-inch open wound in your mouth. (It's not *like* having one. It *is* having one.)

That's the bad news. The good news is that this form of gum irritation is easily prevented and quickly cured. It takes maybe five minutes a day (every day), and an hour or so every six months.

The five minutes a day is spent flossing and Inter-Plaking. Most dentists will tell you flossing is just as important as brushing. So, why don't we all know this? Advertising. A year's worth of dental floss will set you back a few dollars. If you "brush regularly after every meal," a few dollars is probably your toothpaste budget for a month. There's more profit in selling toothpaste, so we're all instructed to brush, brush, brush.

Flossing is simple. Use unwaxed dental floss. Wind it around your fingers. (Those little plastic "dental floss applicators" are a waste of time, money, floss, plastic, etc.) Thread the floss between your teeth. Pull it back and forth and travel down the length of one tooth. Be sure to get under the gumline. Then, without removing the floss from between the teeth, guide it down the opposite tooth, pulling back and forth.

Flossing between teeth is two separate motions: down one tooth and back up, then down the opposite tooth and back up. Do not just go down and up in the middle of the opening between the teeth. You're not trying to dislodge a stubborn fragment of food. You're pulling the floss below the gumline at the base of each tooth to remove plaque. If you go straight down between the teeth, you will miss the gum-line of both teeth and risk damaging the papillae, the pointed part of the gum between the teeth. ("Papillae" — great word, huh?)

Remove the floss, either by pulling it through the teeth like thread through a needle, or back out the top. Persevere until all teeth have been flossed.

When flossing, there should be no bleeding. If there is, it's a sign your gums are not in the best of health. You need the flossing. Red floss should clear up in a week or two of "good oral hygiene and regular professional care." If not, call your dentist. (Vitamin C is said to strengthen gum tissue. Perhaps an increase in C will reduce the bleeding.)

Flossing may take a while to master, but once you do, it takes less than three minutes to do the whole mouth.

Follow flossing with a good brushing, or, better yet, InterPlaking.

The regularity of flossing and brushing must be stressed, so I'll stress it: You have 24 hours to remove the plaque before it hardens into low-rent bacterial housing.

Every six months, have a cleaning by a dental hygienist. The hygienist will scrape off and polish away the tartar and calculus that has eluded your flossing and brushing. If you haven't had your teeth cleaned in a while, make an appointment. It's dull, but worth enduring.

Hydrogen peroxide is the best mouthwash I've found. Dilute it half and half with water. Swish it around your mouth and hold it there for a minute. You'll feel it begin to foam. That's bacteria being evicted — permanently. Gargle. Spit it out. Do this a couple of times a day.

And now, high-tech anti-plaquers: the Interplak. It's an electric toothbrush, but completely unlike Broxident's, which is really nothing more than a vibrator with bristles.

With the InterPlak, each individual bunch of bristles (there are ten of them) twist back and forth. They swirl clockwise, stop, swirl counterclockwise, stop, and swirl clockwise again — 4,200 times a minute! (Who counts things like this?)

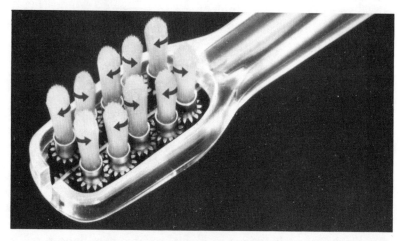

This twisting action gets at plaque between teeth and under gumlines. You don't really *brush*, you just *guide* the InterPlak around your mouth for a minute or two and your teeth are clean. Very clean.

The InterPlak doesn't replace flossing. If, however, you don't floss and know you're not going to floss, the Inter-Plak will get at more tooth surfaces than brushing alone could ever reach. Still, the best combination is flossing and InterPlak.

The InterPlak costs $99 and comes with two inter-changeable brush heads. The brush heads take a second to change, so the whole family can use the same handle. Additional brush heads are $12.95 each. It comes with its own recharging stand.

The InterPlak is so effective, you don't need tooth-paste. (After the age of fourteen you don't need toothpaste anyway — the only value in toothpaste is fluoridation, and adults don't need fluoridation, hence, don't need toothpaste. Radical thought, I know, but toothpaste is one of the most profitable consumer products around, and I'm afraid our brains have been washed more effectively than our teeth by billions of dollars of advertising.)

I went to see a new dentist for an emergency (a filling had fallen out) and I asked him about the InterPlak. His initial reaction was reserved skepticism — there are apparently dozens of worthless mouth-oriented gizmos invented and sold every year. He researched it, however, and was impressed. He now uses one himself and recommends it to all his patients.

After the age of fourteen, gum disease is the cause of more tooth loss than decay. Plaque-free, tartar-free teeth are the cornerstone of healthy gums. The InterPlak is the best daily method of plaque-free, tartar-free teeth.

I've been using an InterPlak for about a year. Prior to that, my teeth would need a professional cleaning every six months. My last cleaning was more than eight months ago. The dentist examined my teeth and said he couldn't find any plaque or calculus — I didn't need a cleaning! (A dentist saying you don't need a cleaning is like McDonalds saying you don't need a Big Mac.)

I can't be too enthusiastic about this product; I can't recommend it enough. If you buy only one thing as a result of reading this book, let it be the InterPlak. (For more information, call 1-800-537-1600.)

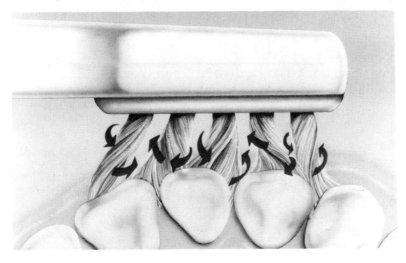

Norelco vs. Remington

Here's a controversy that been going on in shaving circles for years: Which gives the best shave, the Norelco or the Remington? Answer: The Remington. *But the* Remington Microscreen is fragile, whereas the Norelco Floating Heads are almost indestructible. If you travel a lot, or are not very careful with your implements of ablution, Norelco may be the better choice. (It's no slouch on close shaves, either.) Or, you can do as a friend does: Remington for the home, Norelco for the road.

By the way, if you're a blade man and decide to try an electric, give yourself two weeks before deciding if an electric's for you. When you shave with a razor, the hair tends to grown down. That makes it hard for the electric to shave closely. Within two weeks, the hair is growing straight out, the best position for the electric to clip it off.

Talking Scale

This scale not only talks, it remembers what you weighed last time you weighed in, and tells you how much you lost or gained since your last trip to the scale. It then says, "Have a nice day," or, of you prefer, simply, "Goodbye." It remembers the weight of five different people, plus a guest.

I don't see much point in this, except for people who have trouble reading the numbers on a scale. My mother doesn't like this scale because it's *loud*. Now loud is fine, because people who have trouble seeing — especially due to age — often have trouble hearing, but mother didn't like it at all. When she came to visit me, the talking scale could be heard throughout the house. Every time she went into the bathroom we listened carefully. She didn't weigh herself for a week. $99.

"Tell it to shut up."

What Would You Give FOR A PERFECT, HEALTHY BODY?

WOULD you spend 10 minutes a day using this wonderful instrument to obtain a perfect, healthy body? The delightful, pleasing touch of NEW LIFE VIBRATOR sends a thrill of energy and vigor rushing through your veins. When you apply it to your body you instantly feel the soothing, invigorating, vitalizing effects of increased blood circulation and transform your entire being into one that glows with health. Use the

NEW LIFE VIBRATOR

and you will feel Strength, Energy, Vigor, and ncreased vitality the instant it starts the free flowing circulation of blood and distributes the strength and building power of the food you eat.

RHEUMATISM in practically every case, no matter how severe, is instantly relieved with the NEW LIFE VIBRATOR. We guarantee this and if after a three day |trial, you feel we have failed, you may return us the instrument, as provided in our written guarantee, and we will return your money cheerfully.

DEAFNESS—The ear presents a perfect labyrinth of tiny organs each of which demands its quota of perfect blood supply. You who suffer from defective hearing or even absolute deafness, will find that a conscientious use of the NEW LIFE VIBRATOR will stimulate the stagnant flow of blood and transform your defective ear drums into useful organs.

INDIGESTION even in chronic cases yields almost instantly to the wonderful effects of the NEW LIFE ▼IBRATOR. Why suffer from this curse of humanity when we guarantee immediate relief or return your money in exact accordance with our written guarantee that goes to every purchaser.

Nature is the greatest of all physicians; do not use drugs but aid nature by stimulating your worn tissues with the NEW LIFE VIBRATOR; reconstruct your entire body by causing a proper flow of blood and you will see a weak, unshapely arm or limb transform itself into a rounded member of beauty and health; a haggard face look younger and above all you will

RENEW AND ENERGIZE YOUR ENTIRE BODY

A poor circulation causes weakness, because you eat strength-giving foods without distributing their blood-building qualities. THE NEW LIFE VIBRATOR instantly helps nature in a distribution of all the food values and the pure blood of the body.

The leading physicians of America recognize the NEW LIFE VIBRATOR as a scientific means of quickly correcting nature's irregularities.

INTERESTING HEALTH BOOK FREE

Write for a copy of our free Booklet, which illustrates with actual life photographs just what this wonderful vibrator will do. Remember the book is free, and is yours for the asking.

AGENTS WHO DESIRE A PERMANENT INCOME

will find the NEW LIFE VIBRATOR a seller of such remarkable rapidity that no energetic man or woman can fail to make it a source of permanent income. Everyone is interested in his or her health and a simple five minutes demonstration of the NEW LIFE VIBRATOR convinces the most sceptical. We still have open territories waiting for some live agent to come along and reap a big harvest of unusual profits.

Write for agents' proposition; it will show you a way to a permanent income of a size that will astonish you. Territories going fast, so drop us a post card today.

HAMILTON - BEACH MFG. COMPANY

104 A Street   Racine. Wisconsin

Chapter Twenty-five

Everything You Need to Know About Cardiovascular Fitness Including What Cardiovascular Means

 hate exercise. Fitness is something to admire in others. I'm not quite as bad as Oscar Levant ("The only exercise I get is when I fall into a coma"), but I'm close.

I tell you this because I don't want you to think I have anything to convince you of. I won't tell you how well you will be, look and feel as a result of "working out." The only time you should pump iron, from my point of view, is when your clothes are wrinkled. I am not a physical fitness fanatic. I am, if anything, an antifanatic.

I have, in fact, done extensive research on how to do as *little* exercise as possible. Here are my findings:

First, we have to set our goals. If your goal is to have a well-defined body, flat stomach, chiseled thighs and a tight ass, this is not the chapter, nor the book, nor the writer for you.

The goal here is fitness — *inner* fitness, not outer ripples. The goal is a healthy heart and all the tubes connected to it, not becoming Jane Schwarzenegger or Arnold Fonda.

("Cardiovascular," by the way, refers to the heart and its attendant arteries, veins and capillaries. "Cardio" is Italian for "heart." Cardio Toarmina was a famous lover in ancient Rome, before he moved to Grand Rapids. Actually, the word comes from the Greek, "kardia," or heart, but I like the Italian version better.)

Cardiovascular fitness takes only thirty minutes, three times a week. Yes, preparing for the thirty minutes takes a while, as does cleaning up afterward, so figure three hours a week, tops. But the hard work (exercising) part will take thirty minutes, three times a week.

It's called aerobics, a term I'm sure you've heard before. The idea behind aerobics is simple and scientific: You gradually get your pulse up to your "target zone," keep it there for twenty minutes, and gradually return it to normal. (The target zone is a range, measured in pulsebeats per minute, within which your heart is working harder than normal, but not too hard.) Do this three times a week, and all those benefits of exercise you've heard about — except the overtly cosmetic ones — will be yours.

Really. That's all you have to do. I've checked it out with all sorts of experts. Of course, before beginning *any* kind of exercise program, you should check it out with *your* expert: your doctor. Naturally, whatever your doctor says overrules anything I might tell you here.

Cardiovascular Fitness

You can find your target zone by consulting this handy chart:

Age	Target	Age	Target
25	140-170	46	124-149
26	140-169	47	123-148
27	139-168	48	122-147
28	138-167	49	121-146
29	137-166	50	120-145
30	136-165	51	119-144
31	136-164	52	118-143
32	135-163	53	117-142
33	134-162	54	116-142
34	133-161	55	115-140
35	132-160	56	115-139
36	132-159	57	114-138
37	131-158	58	113-137
38	130-157	59	112-136
39	129-156	60	111-135
40	128-155	61	111-134
41	128-154	62	110-133
42	127-153	63	109-132
43	126-152	64	108-131
44	125-151	65	107-130
45	124-150	66	107-129

Find your age. Next to your age is your target zone. After five minutes of warming up, your pulse should be within your target zone. Keep your pulse within your target zone for twenty minutes, then spend five minutes gradually "cooling down."

How you get your pulse up is entirely up to you. (Hot baths do get your pulse up, but, do not count for aerobics. I already checked. You have to *move* in some way or another.) Dancing, walking briskly, jumping, bicycling, swimming — the method of activity is up to you.

Personally, I use one of those little trampolines and lots of loud music. I make tapes with five minutes of fairly fast music, twenty minutes of hot and heavy music, and five more minutes of moderately fast music. Then I reward myself with a favorite slow piece which plays as I put the trampoline away and look forward to *not* doing *this* again for *at least* 48 hours.

I picked the trampoline because it was the easiest on my body. Jogging, dancing on a hard floor or jumping up and down I found to be too jarring. After a week, my feet hurt, my knees hurt, my back hurt, my hips hurt. I'm just your basic cream puff, you know. On the trampoline, wearing a good pair of running shoes, I get none of those hurts. (And swimming is even easier on the body than dancing on a trampoline.)

I was surprised how relatively easy this regimen really is. (Of course, my earlier images of exercise parallelled Madame Tussaud's Chamber of Horrors.) Keeping the pulse within the target zone keeps you breathing hard, but not panting. Remember: The more out of shape you are, the more quickly your pulse soars to your target zone. After a month of this program, I was working a lot harder to keep my pulse within the zone, but that harder work was no more difficult than the not-as-hard work when I began.

What does all this have to with personal electronics? you ask. Good question.

Somehow, you've got to keep track of your pulse. Counting it for fifteen seconds and multiplying by four doesn't work too well when you're jumping up and down. The answer is an electronic one: Pulsemeters.

Pulsemeters monitor your pulse and give you an ongoing digital readout of how you're doing. They come in a variety of shapes and styles (reviewed soon), but they all perform the same basic task: letting you know how many times your heart is beating each minute.

Cardiovascular Fitness

Pulsemeters have revolutionized exercise. In the past, people tended to *over* exercise, which, in many ways is *worse* than not exercising at all. (The weekend athlete syndrome.) That's why most of us who have instinctively avoided exercise our entire lives are currently in such good shape. Now you can exercise just right — lowering your risk of heart attack and stroke, gaining more energy, and feeling more "alive" (whatever that means) — thanks to pulsemeters and the microchip that gives them life.

Casio Pulsemeter Watch

Alas, this watch, and other watches like it, don't work well for exercise. It'll tell you your pulse, but to get it you have to push a button on the watch's face and then wait, motionless, for five seconds. These five-second pauses don't fit well into the rhythm of aerobics. It also doesn't tell you when you're exceeding your target zone so you can slow down. $59.95.

I am told by Patrick Netter, author of *High-Tech Fitness* (Workman, $12.95) and owner of the High-Tech Fitness store in Los Angeles, that the fit-on-your-finger pulse meters are worthless as well. That takes care of the low-cost alternatives. Now...

Computer Instruments Pulsemeter

Now here's a pulsemeter designed especially for exercise. I've been using one for almost four years, and it works fine. You set the upper and lower limits of your target zone, strap it to your chest, and disco down. If your pulse falls below the set target zone, it will beep. If your pulse rises above the set target zone, it will beep in another way. If it's quiet, you know you are within your target zone and all is well.

It comes with an earphone, so you can use it in an aerobics class without disturbing your fellow participants, or you can use it while fast walking without beeping on the street. At $179 it's not cheap, but, considering the benefits, it's a great buy.

The No. 1A Folding Pocket
Kodak *Special.*

Just as good as a camera can be made—so small as to never be in the way.

There has never before been so much quality put into so small a camera—in lens and shutter and mechanical precision it is right. Making the popular 2½ x 4¼ pictures, the camera itself measuring but 2 x 3¾ x 8 inches and with a high speed lens and shutter equipment it fills every requirement of those who demand a perfect combination of convenience and efficiency.

No. 1 A Folding Pocket Kodak *Special* with Rapid Rectilinear Lens, speed *f* 8 and
F. P. K. Automatic Shutter, - - - - - - - - $15.00

ALL DEALERS.

EASTMAN KODAK CO.

*Catalog of Kodaks free
at the dealers or by mail.*

Rochester, N. Y., *The Kodak City.*

Chapter Twenty-six

Still Cameras

hat is he doing reviewing still cameras?" you might ask. "Photography is an optical-chemical process. What do still cameras have to do with electronics?" If you ask these questions, you haven't had a look at a still camera in a while.

Still cameras have more microchips, electronic meters, batteries and motors than, say, a Walkman. Electronic exposure, auto film advance and now auto focus put still cameras soundly in the personal electronics arena. (Besides, I like still photography, okay?)

In still photography there are three categories: serious 35mm cameras, pocket-sized 35mm cameras, and Kodak.

Kodak is in a class by itself. They're a mass merchandiser of pictures; sort of the K Mart of photography. Anything taken with a Kodak camera is not a photograph, it's not even a picture; it's a snapshot.

This is odd, because Kodak makes what is generally considered to be the best film (for both still and motion picture photography) and the best slide projector (the Carousel) in the world. Why, then, they should make the world's worst still cameras is beyond me. (There is one exception to this, which I'll get to a little later.)

I am particularly disturbed by the Kodak Disc System. Have you seen the *quality* of these pictures? Unless you've taken an extreme close-up, the grain is larger than most people's heads. The images are fuzzy, the colors muddy.

Why Kodak abandoned their Instamatic system, which gave passing fair pictures, for the Disc system is beyond me.

It, of course, is not beyond me. Kodak makes money by selling cameras to a certain segment of the population (everyone who's gone to or dreams of going to Disneyland, for example). Once all ninety million of these people bought an Instamatic, it was time to market something new. Not better, just new.

NEW KODAKS

" You press the button, we do the rest."

Seven new Styles and Sizes
ALL LOADED WITH *Transparent Films.*
For sale by all Photo. Stock Dealers.

THE EASTMAN COMPANY,
Send for Catalogue   *ROCHESTER, N. Y.*

My friend Virgil Thomson, the noted composer and music critic, teases me with the notion that the electronics industry introduces a new system of music reproduction every twenty years so that the record companies can sell everyone the Beethoven Symphonies all over again. He says the perfect recording medium has been available all along, but the companies have been simply releasing better and better systems on a predetermined schedule so that we have to repurchase our record libraries over and over again.

I'm not that cynical about the audio industry, but I am occasionally that cynical about Kodak. I have seldom seen as unnecessary an "improvement" as the disc system — or should I say I have never seen such a dramatic leap *backwards* promoted as a major technological breakthrough.

As you can probably tell from the above diatribe, I am not a fan of the Kodak Disc System. In fact, for almost everyone I recommend 35mm. Here are the reasons:

1. Although 35mm cameras initially cost more than Disc cameras, eventually they cost less. Here are the economics of 35mm vs. Disc:

I priced film and developing at two popular locations: a one-hour photo store and a discount drug chain. All prices include film and developing. At the one-hour store, 35mm prints cost 51 cents each; Disc prints cost 71 cents each. At the discount drug chain, 35mm prints cost 28 cents each; Disc prints 40 cents each.

2. The quality of a 35mm image is far, far superior to either Disc or Instamatic. Not only will your regular snapshots be noticeably sharper and clearer, you can also blow up small areas quite large with excellent results.

3. There is a broader range of films (made, ironically, by Kodak) for 35mm cameras. Faster films, finer grain films, even black & white films — all unavailable in the Disc or Instamatic formats.

Kodak's right about one thing: Pictures *are* Forever. Thirty-five millimeter preserves forever best.

PHOTOGRAPHIE · PHOTOGRAPHIE · PHOTOGRAPHY. 24

Pocket 35mm Cameras

My childhood was documented by a Brownie. Brownie cameras were for people who didn't want to fiddle with light meters and focusing and f/stops. It took clear, sharp pictures. (My mother has several drawers full, some of which surfaced in this book — yes, that little boy is me.) Some of its drawbacks were size (it wouldn't fit in dad's pocket, although it would fit in mom's purse; but then, *everything* fit in mom's purse), difficult film loading (it used paperbacked roll film) and fiddling with flashbulbs.

My mother later switched to a Kodak Instamatic, which was smaller, had film in a cartridge and a flash cube. Alas, the quality of the pictures deteriorated remarkably.

Today, well, don't let on, but for her birthday I plan to get her one of those new 35mm auto-everything. It's as easy to use as the Instamatic, with a picture that's even better than the Brownie. But which one to give her?

I chose three to look at: The Minolta Freedom III, the Nikon One-Touch, and the Kodak VR35, Model K12.

All three cameras have electronic flash. (No more flash cubes; the flash will last as long as the camera, or so we're told.) All three have automatic loading. (Put the film cassette in the left side, pull the leader to the right, and close the back. The leader will then attach itself to the take-up spool and advance to the first frame.)

When you load, the camera "reads" from the cassette the type of film you're using and sets the film speed automatically. The film speed is the ISO/ASA number. All Kodak film has the number emblazoned on the front and sides. You buy "100" film, "200," etc. The higher the number, the more sensitive the film is to light, that is, the higher the number, the less light you will need to take pictures. Higher speed film, however, tends to be grainier than lower speed film.

For auto-everything cameras to work, your film cassette has to have what's called "DX markings" on the cassette. Most film nowadays has DX markings. To be sure, look for a "DX" on the box before you buy. When you've taken your allotted number of photographs, the camera will automatically rewind the film back into the cassette.

All three cameras have automatic focus. With Instamatics, the lens is fixed-focus (one focus fits all) and not particularly sharp. These new cameras have extremely sharp lenses that require focusing, but the camera does the focusing for you — within limits.

An important point to look for in a camera is how close it will focus. The Kodak can focus as close as 3 feet from the subject; the Minolta, 2.1 feet; and the Nikon, 1.5 feet. At 1.5 feet, you can capture a person's face. At 3 feet, the person's head and shoulders. So if you like to move in close, the Nikon has the advantage. The Minolta isn't bad at 2.1 feet, but the camera doesn't have an out-of-focus indicator. The other two cameras do. With the Nikon and Kodak, if you've moved in closer than the camera can focus, a light blinks in the viewfinder. All you have to do is move back until the light stops blinking — foolproof.

The cameras come with nonremovable 35mm lenses. A 35mm lens is considered wide-angle: good for getting both people and the environment around them. Keep in mind, however, that wide-angle lenses tend to distort in close-ups. If you like to take portraits of people's faces, expect the proportions to be off. (For perfect portraits you need an 85mm lens or higher.)

With all the cameras, the viewfinder is just above the lens. The cameras, therefore, are not SLR's (single lens reflex cameras), which are more expensive. In an SLR, you look directly through the lens: what you see is precisely what you get. Here, what you see is close to — but not exactly — what the lens sees. You'll only notice a difference in close-ups.

All three have auto-flash: the camera automatically activates the flash unit when it senses the light is too low. Some of them also can sense when the subject is in heavy shadow — in relation to the background — and will use the flash for fill light ("fill-flash"). Of the three cameras I used, the Nikon was the only one that automatically activated for fill-flash. With the other two, I had to manually ask it to flash. I guess that's why Nikon calls theirs a "Smart Flash."

All auto-everything pocket cameras set the shutter speed and aperture settings for automatic exposure. The three I tried did this job quite well. Not one picture had the wrong exposure, despite some tough situations (deep shadows, sunlight reflecting off water, dark people against white walls).

The Nikon has the ability to take filters, such as a haze filter to protect your lens, or a polarized filter to bring out the blue of the sky or reduce reflected images. The Minolta offers a "sequential mode." If you hold down the shutter button, it will take a picture every two seconds. If you're shooting an action scene, this can be helpful.

Because the three cameras performed so well, mom would be happy with any one. I prefer the Nikon One-Touch for its extra-close focus and its Smart Flash. The Nikon retails for $259, The Minolta Freedom III for $265, and the Kodak VR35, Model K-12 for $229. You should be able to find all of them for under $200. (Two stores I called sold the Nikon for $159.) Happy birthday, mom!

One other camera to consider, which I didn't have time to look at, is the Fuji DL-300 QD. It comes with a "Databack," meaning the camera will expose, on the bottom right corner of your pictures, the date you took the picture. In later weeks or years, when looking at pictures of a vacation or the family, you'll know exactly when it was. ("He's not three years old here, he's two — look at the date!") If you don't like it, you can turn it off. The Fuji DL-300 focuses as close as 2.6 feet, and you can get an optional close-up lens for shooting at 1 foot (and only 1 foot). You can also get a telephoto attachment. The camera retails for $260. (I found it for $179.)

Serious 35mm Automatic Cameras

"God is in the details," said Mies van der Rohe. Mies was, of course, referring to architecture, but the same can be said of photography.

I use my camera almost exclusively for portraits. In my estimation, people's faces are the most amazing and beautiful surfaces on earth. Especially the eyes. (What do they say? Windows of the soul? Mirrors of the soul?)

To get a good portrait requires an 85mm lens, or greater. Also, you have to look directly through the lens so you can frame and focus *exactly* what you want. This requires a single-lens reflex (SLR) camera.

For those who have the desire, but haven't been particularly handy with 35mm SLR cameras, there's a new generation of automation. Topcon and Konica offered the first automatic cameras over fifteen years ago. Canon, with its AE1, popularized automation, and many manufacturers have improved on it even more. Automatic exposure setting is not big news, but automatic focusing is.

I looked at the Canon EOS 650, the Minolta Maxxum 7000, and the Nikon N4004. All are marvels of technology. All have slightly different features and personalities.

As to the commonalities, the three cameras come standard with a 50mm f1.8 lens (a "normal" lens, neither wide angle or telephoto), automatic film loading, automatic film speed setting (when you use DX-coded film), automatic winding and rewinding, automatic exposure setting, and automatic focus. It's all just as simple as the smaller auto-everything pocket cameras. With the SLR's, you also have the benefit of additional lenses, filters, varieties of electronic flash attachments, and the advantage of taking closer pictures.

Why autofocus over manual focus? Automatic focus is particularly helpful in low light situations, and for those who simply have no aptitude for focusing. It also allows you to focus your attention on the subject being photographed, not on focusing the subject. (Did that last sentence make sense?)

Autofocusing is a two-step process. First you place the subject in the middle of your frame and press the shutter release button half way. The lens focuses. When it's finished — a mere split second or so later — a green LED in the viewfinder lights up. (You may also hear a beep.) Second, still holding the shutter half way (to lock your focus in), you adjust your framing, placing the subject wherever you want. Press the shutter all the way. The picture is taken; the film advances to the next frame.

There are times, however, when you will want to switch to manual focusing. (The cameras all have manual override.) If you're shooting fast action, such as a moving vehicle or almost any sporting event, your subject may be moving too fast to give you the luxury of two steps. (Also, with the focus always changing by the second, the camera might not stop focusing long enough for you to lock in.) Manual is better in such instances.

Also, some objects play havoc with the focusing apparatus. While the autofocus pocket cameras use infrared beams, these cameras use more sophisticated, optical systems. This system allows for interchangeable lenses, but it has its quirks. I was taking a picture of a white, metal bathroom scale for this book with the Nikon, and the lens kept zooming in and out, never stopping at a focus. The manual said the camera has trouble focusing on surfaces with no contrast (like my all-white bathroom scale).

The Canon manual said the same thing, but got even more specific. It has trouble with: misty scenes, light-colored or white objects, subjects in extremely low-light situations, subjects having generally horizontal patterns (window blinds), subjects with an object in front of them (such as bars in front of convicted felons), and fast-moving subjects. So I focused the bathroom scale manually.

I tried the Minolta with a telephoto lens and found the autofocus to be temperamental. It's because the little rectangle in the center of the screen (where the focus locks on) would be on an area of poor contrast, such as the cheek of someone's face. With a telephoto lens, areas of poor contrast are more common. As I said above, the autofocus mechanism needs varied contrast. It's true with all the cameras. If I focused on my subject's eyes, locked in the focus, and moved my framing, it all worked fine.

Once I understood the need for varied contrast within the rectangle while focusing, all three cameras focused quickly and accurately all the time.

Because they are all completely automatic, God is in the batteries, as it were. The cameras are dead without good batteries. When the Minolta became low on batteries, the internal mirror froze up. Low or dead batteries mean

you won't be taking pictures, even manually. (Or, as James LaPine had one of his characters saying in the remarkable *Sunday in the Park with George*, "No electricity, no art.")

As to which camera I think is better, I prefer the Canon EOS 650. I like its styling, and, more importantly, its features and accuracy in exposures. The Nikon and Minolta tie for second. The Nikon N4004 does not offer any exposure information. This may not be important to many people, especially those new to photography, but I always want to know the shutter speed (to stay away from fuzzy, camera-jiggled pictures), and, if I'm concerned about depth-of-field, I want to know the f/stop. Nikon does not tell me either. I have to trust in its ability. The Nikon gave me great pictures, for the most part, but I'd like to have the extra control. But that extra control costs more, as you'll see below.

The Minolta and Canon not only give exposure information within the viewfinder, but also on top. I love that. What I don't like about the Minolta is that the lock button and some of the other buttons look fragile and collect dust easily. Maybe I'm just paranoid, but I can imagine it gumming up.

The Canon EOS 650 (all cameras are quoted with 50mm, f1.8 lens) is $649; the Minolta Maxxum 7000, $659; and the Nikon N4004, a bargain at $504.

Polaroid Spectra

There's something gratifying about instant gratification. At a whim's notice, I can have Instant Rice, Instant Pudding, and microwave popcorn. And when family or friends visit, there's instant photography, thanks to Polaroid.

Still Cameras

I've always thought of Polaroid as snapshot time and not a system particularly designed for "photography." Ansel Adams didn't trip around the mountains with a Sun 600, and, despite Polaroid's campaign of displaying Polaroid photographs taken by professionals, I doubt if any photographers produce the slick ads in magazines with an SX-70 or a Spectra (except the Polaroid ads, of course).

This isn't to say the Spectra isn't a fun camera — it is. It has a nonremovable, wide-angle lens, like the auto-everything pocket cameras: great for capturing people within their environment. You can get as close as 2 feet, and the camera beeps a warning if you get any closer. It will also beep if you're beyond the 16-foot range of the automatic flash.

The Spectra produces rectangular pictures — a nice advancement since the SX-70. A rectangular frame is easier to compose than a square frame. The Spectra is $224.

As for the Spectra film itself, I find the pictures are not as sharp as with 35mm film. The colors do often appear as vivid as advertised, but using this film differs from shooting with 35mm color. With 35mm, for the best color, shoot your subject in the shade. Although the colors may seem muted to your eye, the pictures produced will appear rich in color. If you shoot people in the sun, your pictures may be too contrasty, the shadows may be dark and deep (and the people squinty-eyed).

Spectra film, on the other hand, works just the opposite. The pictures I took of people in the shade came out with muted colors. The pictures I took in the sun came out well — not overly contrasty at all — with the colors rich and varied (and the people squinty-eyed). The best pictures were produced in the full sun — with the automatic flash engaged to soften any deep shadows.

Spectra pictures come at a price. The film lists for $12.40 a ten-pack, meaning each shot costs $1.24. My local discount store sells a pack at $9.99, bringing the cost down to a dollar a shot. That's still two to four times more expensive per shot than using a 35mm camera (depending where you buy and develop your 35mm film). As with pudding, rice and popcorn, instant is always more expensive.

EVERYTHING ELECTRICAL FROM SOUP TO NUTS

Chapter Twenty-seven

Stuff

This is a catchall chapter of things I did not know where else to put. They don't fit into any other categories, and to create more categories would require more chapters and this book already has twenty-seven.

So here goes, *stuff*...

Bionaire   Ionizers

Air molecules are charged either positively or negatively. People tend to feel better around negatively charged air and feel worse around positively charged air.

Negative ions are created naturally by falling water, lightning and green plants. This explains why people tend to feel better in nature, or why the air seems so clean after an electrical storm.

Positive ions are created by electrical machinery. This whole book has been enticing you to invite various electronic gadgets into your home. To counterbalance their positive-ion effect, you might want to invite a negative ionizer home as well.

Negative ion generators do just that: They generate negative ions by the billions. The problem with most negative ionizers is that they tend to collect dirt on the surfaces surrounding them. (I had one on a white wall. Within six months, the area around the ionizer had gradations from gray to black in concentric circles, getting darker as it approached the ionizer. It looked like some sort of esoteric target.)

The Bionaire Room Ionizer eliminates most of this dirt by filtering it from the air before it has a chance to affix itself to the surfaces surrounding the ionizer. The Bionaire uses a disposable filter. You replace it once every six months or so. When you replace it, you'll be glad all those black pollutants are in the filter and not in your lungs.

The Bionaire Room Ionizer makes electronic indoor living easier, with cleaner air, filled with lots of positive-producing negative ions. The Bionaire 1000, $369.95; the larger 2001 is $499.95. Consider each of these units good for one room; negative ions are short-lived and do not travel well.

For the car there is a smaller ionizer, the Bionaire 300. It's small enough to fit on the dashboard, just above the speedometer. It can spew negative ions directly on your face as you drive. It does not have the air filtering capabilities of the home unit. $44.95.

Stuff

Braun Voice-Control Alarm Clock

Here's my favorite alarm clock. At the appointed hour it begins to beep, gently at first, then more assertively. Any loud noise will get it to stop beeping -- for five minutes. Then it begins again: softly, then loudly. Another loud noise will make it silent again -- for five more minutes. Then . . .

The loud noise could be almost anything: yelling, "Shut up," clapping your hands, hitting a table, throwing a shoe against the wall, etc. I just say, "Thank you," to mine. I try to treat my machines with respect. If I say "Shut up" too often, I'm afraid it will shut up permanently one morning when I need it to not shut up.

It's small, about the size of a Kit-Kat bar, and fully portable. It's battery operated, one AA battery lasting at least six months. It's not digital: the clock face has second, minute and hour hands, invaluable when trying to show a youngster what "clockwise" means.

My only complaints are: It has a 12-hour, not 24-hour, alarm. If you set it for 7:00, it will go off at 7 AM *and* 7 PM. It also makes a slight -- almost imperceptible -- ticking. I know some will find an electronic gadget that ticks refreshing, but I sometimes find myself putting it a bit further away from the bed so the princess won't be bothered by the ticking pea. About $30.

Nikry Music Machine

This is a wristwatch that doubles as a keyboard instrument, or a keyboard instrument that doubles as a wristwatch. You decide. It's worn on the wrist. It's a rectangle, about two inches by one inch and not quite a half-inch thick. The top flips open, like a little piano, to reveal a 13-key keyboard and a little digital clock.

Believe it or not, this thing actually works. The keys are minuscule (five keys to the inch), with even smaller keys for sharps. ("The black keys.") But they work. Put your finger (which is the width of three keys) over a key, and it plays only the center note. Remarkable.

This is not a concert grand, you understand. It makes those sounds we now associate with pocket calculators playing *Swanee River*. But for $17.95, it's lots of fun.

The Eye of the Storm

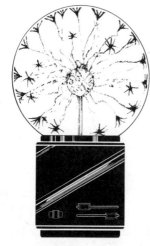

This is a globe of clear glass, within which patterns of electrical energy randomly play. The rays of energy (they look like the static electrical displays from old science fiction movies) are bluish and pinkish.

You can set the intensity and speed of the patterns using two sliding switches on the front. It will generate random patterns, or it will respond to sound vibrations in the room. (The louder the sound, the brighter the "storm.")

It's especially fun to put your hand on the glass. The rays begin attacking your hand. There's no sensation of being shocked, but it does startle some people. Others take to it like ducks to drakes. They put a hand on either side of the globe and fulfill their *Master of the Universe* fantasies.

A few years ago, I bought one just like this, except slightly larger, for $1,200. Within a week I realized the thrill had worn off. Friends were still amazed by it, at first, but I realized it wasn't worth $1,200 to amaze the few friends who hadn't seen it yet. I returned it for a refund.

This one costs $199. That's more in the acceptable range of the things-to-keep-around-to-amuse-your-friends budget. These are fascinating for the first few hours, but, ultimately, they're electronic Lava Lights. Within two years they'll be a cliché, but by then you'll have gotten your $199 worth of fun out of it. The thing to do then is to put it away for a decade or two. Imagine how much fun a Lava Light would be today.

Stuff

Burglar Alarms

It seems altogether fitting and proper that we end a book on how to get electronic goodies with a little advice on how to *keep* the electronic goodies got.

Most people still think of burglar alarms as something for The Rich Folk on the other side of the tracks. And it's little wonder: Professionally installed burglar alarms can be expensive.

A few years ago I bought a "basic system" (so described by the installer). It cost $1200 for the equipment and $650 to install. All it had was one door contact, two motion detectors, a panic button, a dialer (to the security company) and a very loud horn. It did the job. Two attempts were made to break in, but the intruders ran at the horn's blast.

Now such security systems can be found much less expensively and installed by yourself. Several companies offer wireless systems. You place battery-powered entry sensors on your doors and windows and/or screw in battery-powered motion detectors on your walls. If someone breaks in, the offended sensor will send a digitally-coded radio signal to your base unit (locked in a closet), which will then trigger a loud alarm and/or call a security company. When you enter (through a selected door), you have anywhere from twenty to forty seconds to go into your closet and type in a disarm code. Otherwise, the alarm goes off.

You need to replace the 9-volt batteries yearly in each sensor. If a battery runs low, the sensor will beep softly.

I looked at basic systems by Schlage, Universal Security, Tandy, and Black and Decker. All the systems have optional goodies, such as signal relays (for large homes), dialers (to call a security company and/or friends, relatives, neighbors, etc. of your choice), base-unit backup batteries (to power the system if the house current is out), remote-control panic buttons, outside horns, smoke detectors, house light controllers, and extra sensors.

There are two basic ways to set up a security system. One is to cover all possible entryways by placing sensors on every door and window. For your windows, you have a choice of two types of sensors: one that detects a window

317

THE PERSONAL ELECTRONICS BOOK

being opened, and another that detects the breaking of glass. Most systems only come with the former. With your windows and doors guarded, you and your pets are free to roam the house with your system armed.

The other way is to rely more on motion detectors. A motion detector is a cigarette-pack sized unit that mounts on your wall near the ceiling. It's an infrared sensor and can detect movement within a wide path. A motion detector does its job extremely well -- even a cat will set it off.

I prefer motion detectors over window sensors because, one, I have a lot of windows, and, two, motion detectors are more difficult, if not impossible, to fool. The down side is that you can't roam in an area that's armed. (If you have pets, they'll have to be either outside or in a room without a motion detector when the system is armed.) The Black and Decker system doesn't yet offer motion detectors. The Black and Decker system was also the most expensive, at $649.

Schlage's Keepsafer system retails for $179. For that, you get a base unit and three entry sensors for doors or windows. The base unit has an internal speaker that will let out an 85-decibel siren when triggered. You can also add an external speaker. It's particularly suited for apartment dwellers. Schlage also has a $349 Keepsafer Plus system that's meant more for those in houses. You get three entry sensors, a remote control, and a larger base unit that has expandability. With the Keepsafer Plus, you can add any or all of the goodies mentioned above.

Tandy's $59 Ultrasonic alarm unit is inexpensive but almost worthless. It's a stand-alone motion detector that screams either instantly or after a 15-second entry delay. When you come in, you hit a shutoff switch on the unit before the alarm goes off. A burglar could do the same thing or simply pull the plug.

Tandy's Burglar and Fire Alarm Center is much more useful, and a basic system retails for $214. For that, you get a smoke detector, four magnetic window/door sensors, a siren horn, 100 feet of wire, a lock and two keys, and the main control box that covers up to four alarm areas. Each alarm area can have several sensors wired in series. If "in

318

series" goes over your head, you can see how complicated this system can be; it's *not* a wireless system, but uses wire, as do professionally installed systems. It means a lot of work to set up, and probably more than you want to tackle.

Tandy offers a variety of sensors for the system: vibration detector, glass breakage detector, panic switch, infrared motion detector, active beam sensor (it shoots out a narrow invisible light beam, and if the beam is broken, the siren sounds), magnetic door/window sensor, concealed magnetic switch, foil contacts and more. If you prefer to disarm the alarm by punching in a code number, you can install a digital keypad to replace the lock and key. A phone dialer and battery backup can also be added to the base unit.

These choices in the Tandy system are high-end system choices. If you have a lot of time and know-how, the variety is here. I wouldn't consider this system simple, so I don't recommend it for most people.

Universal Security's Perim-a-tron system lists for $299 and comes with three entry sensors, a base unit that can cover two different alarm zones, a battery backup, and an external siren. Each sensor also contains a panic button. This can be handy in that you always have a panic button near you. If you have small children, this handiness quickly evaporates as their curiosity expands and they like to push things. (If you mount the sensors high enough, say, twenty feet off the ground, you can avoid this.) The system has unlimited expansion, and can use any of the goodies mentioned in the sixth paragraph.

In sum, if you want a good burglar alarm and easy installation, look at Schlage's Keepsafer Plus or Universal Security's Perim-a-tron. If you want a complex system of sensors, consider either the Tandy system, or call an alarm company.

Chapter Twenty-eight

Seven Suggestions for Buying Personal Electronics

ry Before You Buy. I don't care what the spec sheets or the advertisements or the salespeople say, try it before you buy it. See it in operation. You will be told, "This one on sale works just like the more expensive model we have set up." Uh-huh. "Would you mind setting up the one on sale?" you can ask, fingering your checkbook. (If for some reason you can't see a demonstration, make sure you can get your money back. See number six.)

Naturally, this rule doesn't apply to small appliances. You can't expect a store to demonstrate every crock pot in stock. They should, however, have one on display for you to tap, poke, fondle and otherwise explore. They should also be willing to open the sealed carton of the one you're buying so you can check for breakage, mislabeling, color, etc.

2. If You Can't See the Difference or Hear the Difference, Don't Pay the Difference. I don't care what the spec sheets or the advertisements or the salespeople say (Is there an echo in here?), there is no point paying $700 for a TV that looks the same to you as a $500 TV or $1,000 for a

Sometimes you meet an electronics salesman you just <u>know</u> you can trust.

While others, somehow, you know you can't.

No, this isn't a personal electronics store,
but you just won $10,000.

pair of speakers that sound the same to you as a pair of $250 speakers. So much of personal electronics is subjective. What sounds and looks good to you, not what looks good on paper, is what matters.

3. If You Can See the Difference or Hear the Difference, Pay the Difference. You'll be living with your personal electronics purchase for a long time. To the degree your budget can tolerate it, get what looks and sounds best to you. On a day-to-day basis, home video and audio is one of the best entertainment values around.

Let's take an extreme example. Let's say you fall in love with one of those $5,000 Super Home Entertainment Systems. If you finance it at 10% for three years, that brings the total purchase price to $5,800. A system such as this, with proper care and repair, should last ten years. Let's add $1,500 ($150 a year for ten years) for repair (or a service contract). That brings the total cost of the Super System to $7,300. Sounds high, but what it figures out to is $2 a day. It's hard to find a better entertainment value than that.

4. Wait Two Weeks Before Buying. *Never* go browsing and buying in the same day. I don't care how many sales, specials, deep discounts and this-is-the-last-one-left-in-the-country-and-we-don't-know-when-we'll-be-getting-any-more-like-it-certainly-not-at-this-price—and—probably—not-this-year pitches you're given, don't buy. Look. Shop. Compare. Decide. *Then* wait two weeks. Forget about it. If in two weeks you still want it, it's probably right for you. If not, your patience has saved you a lot of time and money.

If you're *really rich* you may think this rule does not apply. Well, if you're real rich with *nothing else to do*, then it doesn't apply. But most rich people I know are also busy people. Think of the *time* it will take to learn to use this new gizmo, and if you seldom or never use the impulsively purchased item again, that's time wasted. If you still want it in two weeks, send the upstairs butler down to pick one up.

5. Don't Pay More Than You Have To. I know this sounds stupid, but any number of people buy things at full-

They're waiting for you.

price audio, video and small appliance stores when they could get precisely the same equipment for less at a discount store or by mail. The full-price stores might be a good place to shop, but just because you shop there doesn't mean you have to buy there. (If you're taken by a particularly helpful salesperson, hire the person as a consultant or buy them a thank-you CD or something.)

To get the best price on a personal electronics item, shop by phone. Know the precise brand, model number, color, etc., you want. Start with the mail order discount houses. Their ads can be found in the back of *High Fidelity*, *Stereo Review* or most wide-circulation consumer magazines. Get the best price.

Then call your local discount stores. Many will say, "We don't quote prices over the phone, but come in and we'll

Unprepared personal electronics buyer (with albatross).

meet or beat any price." To which you can respond, "I'm not coming in, but can you beat $_____," and give the lowest price quoted from a mail order house. If yes, great. If not, buy by mail.

There are only two major questions you need to ask when buying by mail: "Is this new merchandise in factory-sealed cartons?" and "Does it have a full U.S. warranty?" (Some "gray market" imported goods come without a U.S. warranty. Steer clear.)

6. Get a Money-Back Guarantee. In writing. Most reputable merchants (including mail-order houses) offer, at the very least, a 7-day refund policy. If you return the item in the original carton with all the packing material, you get your money back. "Money back" is the key here, not an "exchange" or "store credit." The refund should apply for any reason, including "I don't like it." You might not.

7. Once You've Bought It and Like It, Forget It. Don't second guess yourself. Don't keep checking the ads to see if the prices drop on the very item you bought (they will). Don't keep looking for improved versions to come out (they will). Just look at and/or listen to and/or purée with whatever you chose and enjoy it.

" I thought these were just suggestions!!"

What's Next?

What's next? Frankly, I don't know. After almost a year's worth of work, this book is being assembled the last week in August, 1987. It'll be in the stores by October, 1987, thanks to a Herculean effort by the folks at Prentice Hall Press. (Usually it takes nine months from manuscript to finished book.)

The 1989 edition of this book will be in the stores by October, 1988. Until then, there are apt to be some changes in the world of personal electronics.

To keep up with these changes, I publish a newsletter, cleverly entitled *The Personal Electronics Newsletter.* It's especially for people who have read this book and are looking for the latest in products, trends and projections.

The Personal Electronics Newsletter is $50 per year (ten issues), and has a full money back guarantee.

This being a book of buying advice, I must advise you *not* to subscribe to the newsletter if your local paper carries my syndicated column on personal electronics. There's too much duplication of information between the two to make it worth your while.

If you subscribe to the newsletter and your local paper later picks up the column, we'll be happy to refund you for all the issues you haven't received.

If you'd like your local paper to carry the column, please ask them. Newspapers do respond to readers' requests, more than any other medium I know. The column is called "Personal Electronics" and it's syndicated by Universal Press.

But until your paper gets it, you can subscribe to *The Personal Electronics Newsletter* by sending $50 to: Prelude Press (my company) Box 69773, Los Angeles, California, 90046.

Or, if you want to charge it to your VISA or MasterCard, please call (213) 650-9571.

Thank you.

Addresses

Acoustic Research
330 Turnpike Street
Canton, MA 02021
(617) 821-2300; (800)
225-9847

ACS Communications
250 Technology Circle
Scotts Valley, CA
95066
(408) 438-3883

AKG
77 Selleck Street
Stamford, CT 06902
(203) 348-2121; (800)
243-7885

Alpine Electronics of
America
Car Audio Division
19145 Gramercy Place
Torrance, CA 90501
(213) 326-8000; (800)
ALPINE 1

Altec-Lansing
Route 6 & 209
Milford, PA 18337
(800) 258-3288 ; (717)
296-4434

American Acoustics
(Mitek)
1 Mitek Plaza
Winslow, IL 61089
(815) 367-3000

Audio Pro / Sonic
Research
180 Sunny Valley
New Milford, CT
06776
(800) 243-2673

Audio Products
International (Refcon)
135 Torbay Road
Markham
Ontario, Cana L3R 1G7
(800) 387-4260

Bang & Olufsen of
America, Inc.
1150 Feehanville Drive
Mount Prospect, IL
60056
(312) 299-9380; (800)
323-0378

Bionaire
901 North Lake
Destiny Drive
Suite 215
Maitland, FL 32751
(305) 660-0265; (800)
524-0086

Black & Decker
10 North Park Drive
Hunt Valley, MD
21030
(301) 683-7000; (800)
235-2000

Bose
The Mountain, Dept.
SR
10 Speen Street
Framingham, MA
01701
(617) 879-7330

Braun
66 Broadway, Route 1
Lynnfield, MA 01940
(617) 592-3300; (800)
633-0035

Brookstone - Main
Headquarters
920 Vose Farm Road
Peterboro, NH 03460
(603) 924-9511

Canon USA
One Canon Plaza
Lake Success, NY
11042
(516) 933-6300

Casio (Pulsemeter
Watch)
15 Gardner Road
Fairfield, NJ 07006
(201) 575-7400; (800)
227-1000 or (800)
272-0272

CD Mate
989 Coronado Drive
Glendale, CA 91206
(818) 500-8303

Celestion Industries
P.O. Box 521 Kuniholm
Drive.
Holliston, MA 01746
(617) 429-6706; (800)
235-7757

Chef's Choice
(Edgecraft Corp.)
407 Meco Drive
Wilmington, Delaware
19804
(302) 992-0383

Chrono Art (Phone
Censor)
9175 Poplar Avenue
Cotati, CA 94928
(707) 795-1895

Colonial Data Services
Corp.
80 Pickett District Road
New Milford, Conn
06776
(203) 355-3178

Computer Instruments
Corp. (Pulsemeter)
100 Madison Avenue
Hempstead, New
11550
(516) 483-8200; (800)
227-1314

Conrad-Johnson ·
Design, Inc. (Motif)
1474 Pathfinder Lane
McLean, VA 22101
(703) 698-8581

Cuesta Systems
Corporation (Data
Saver)
3440 Roberto Court
San Luis Obispo, CA
93401
(805) 541-4160; (800)
332-3440

Addresses

Data Saver (see Cuesta Systems Corporation)

DBX
71 Chapel Street
Newton, MA 02195
(617) 964-3210

Dental Research Corporation (Interplak)
1726 Montreal Circle #14
Tucker, GA 30084
(800) 334-4031

Desktop Publishing With Style
P.O. Box 480265
Los Angeles, CA 90048

Eastman Kodak Company
Communication & Public Affairs
343 State Street
Rochester, NY 14650
(716) 724-4000, 724-2575; (800) 242-2424

Energy Refcon (see Audio Products Intl.)

Eye of the Storm (see Rabbit Systems, Inc)

FoneAlone (see Sparrevohn Engineering)

Fosgate
55W South Street
Heber City, UT 84032
(801) 654-4046

Gemini Industries, Inc,
215 Entin Road
P.O. Box 1115
Clifton, NJ 07014
(201)471-9050;
(800)526-7452

General Electric Company
600 North Sherman Drive
Indianapolis, IN 46201
(317) 267-3110; (800) 626-2000;
(317)267-5000

Goldstar Electronics Int'l, Inc.
1050 Wall Street West
Lyndhurst, NJ 07071
(800) 255-2550

Hitachi Sales Corp.
401 West Artesia
Compton, CA 90220
213-774-5151; (800) 262-1502

Hot Springs Indoor/Outdoor Spa
(see Watkins Manufacturing Corp.)

InterPlak (see Dental Research Corporation)

JVC Company of America
41 Slater Drive
Elmwood Park, NJ 07407
(201) 794-3900; (800) 526-5308

Kash 'n' Gold (Telemania)
360 Smith Street
Farmingdale, NY 11735
(516) 756-0020

Kenwood (PR Freeman McCue)
1315 E. Watson Center Road
Carson, CA 90745
(213) 639-9000

Kodak (see Eastman Kodak Company)

Koss Corporation
4129 North Port Washington Avenue
Milwaukee, WI 53212
(414) 964-5000; (800) 872-5677

Laser Disc Corp. of America (LDCA) (Pioneer)
200 West Grand Avenue
Montvale, NJ 07645

(201) 573-1122 X-250; (800) 421-1404

LAST
Box 41
Livermore, CA 94550
(415) 449-9449; (800) 223-5278, 223-5278 in CA

Luma
Telecom/Mitsubishi Electric
3350 Scott Blvd. Bldg. 49
Santa Clara, , CA 95054
(800) 422-5862

Magnavox (see NAP)

Maxell Corporation
Consumer Products Division
60 Oxford Drive
Moonachie, NJ 07074
(201) 641-8600; (800) 631-2540

Maxim
164 Delancy Street
Newark, NJ 07105
(201) 344-4600

Minolta Audio-Visual
101 Williams Drive
Ramsey, NJ 07446
(201) 825-4000

Mitek (see American Acoustics)

Mitsubishi Audio/Video Division
5757 Plaza Drive
Cypress, CA 90630
(800) 421-1140; (800) 262-1299 in CA

Mitsubishi Mobile Electronics and Car Audio Divisions
800 No. Biermann Ct.
Mount Prospect, IL 60056
(800) 323-4216; (312) 298-9223 in IL

Monster Cable Products
101 Townsend Street

Addresses

San Francisco, CA
94107
(415) 777-1355; (800)
331-3755
Motif (See
Conrad-Johnson
Design, Inc.)

NAD USA
675 Canton Street
Norwood, MA 02062
(617) 762-0202

Nakamichi
19701 South Vermont
Avenue
Torrance, CA 90502
213-538-8150;
800-223-1521

Nakamichi/Pacific
Cassette Labs
20655 South Western
Avenue
Suite 116
Torrance, CA
(213) 618-9267

NAP (Phillips) /
Magnavox / Sylvannia /
Philco
Consumer Electronics
P.O. Box 14810
Knoxville, TN
37914-1810
(615) 521-4316; (615)
475-0317

National Teletronics
Paoli Corp. Center
16 Industrial Boulevard
Paoli, PA 19301
(215)640-9944

NEC Home Electronics
1401 W. Estes Avenue
1255 Michael Dr.
Wooddale, IL
60191-1094
(312) 860-9500; (800)
323-1728

Nikon, Inc.
623 Stewart Avenue
Garden City, NY
11530
(516) 222-0200; (800)
231-1389 or (213)
516-7124

Nikry Company
7751 Burnet St.
Van Nuys, CA 91405
(818) 989-5084

Nitty Gritty
4650 Aero Highway;
Unit F4
Montclair, CA 91763
(714) 625-5525

Olympus
145 Crossways Park
Woodbury, NY 11797
(516) 364-3000 x-267

Onkyo
200 Williams Drive
Ramsey, NJ 07446
(201) 825-7950

Oster (Sunbeam)
Milwaukee, WI 53217

Panasonic / Technics
One Panasonic Way
Secaucus, NJ 07094
(201) 348-7000

PhoneMate, Inc.
325 Maple Avenue
Torrance, CA 90503
(213) 618-9910; (800)
247-7889

Pioneer Electronics,
Inc.
P.O. Box 1720
Long Beach, CA 90801
(800) 421-1404 ; (213)
835-6177 in CA

Polaroid
3232 West MacArthur
Blvd.
Santa Ana, CA 92704
(213) 515-1633; (800)
854-8038

Pulsemeter (see
Computer Instruments)

Pulsemeter Watch (see
Casio)

Rabbitt Systems, Inc.
(Eye of the Storm)
100 Wilshire Boulevard
Santa Monica, CA
90401
(800) 772-7012

RCA
RCA Distributing Corp.
12889 Moore St.
Cerritos, CA 90701
(213) 404-3044;
(800)626-2000

Record-A-Call
19200 South Laurel
Park Road
Compton, CA 90220
(213) 603-9393; (800)
421-2461

Refcon (see Audio
Products Int'l)

Samsung Electronics
America
301 Mayhill Street
Saddle Brook, NJ
07662
(201) 587-9600; (800)
524-1302

Schlage Lock Co.
Box 3324
2401 Bayshore Blvd.
San Francisco, CA
94119
(415) 467-1100

Sharp Electronics Corp.
Sharp Plaza
Mahwah, NJ 07430
(800) 223-2121

Shure Brothers
222 Hartrey Ave.
Evanston, IL 60204
(312) 866-2374, (312)
866-2200

SME (see Sumiko)

Sonrise
13622 NE 20th Street,
Suite F
Bellevue, WA 98005
(800) 231-8663

Addresses

Sony Corporation of
America
Corporate
Communications Dept.
9 West 57th Street
New York, NY 10019
(800) 222-7669

SOTA Industries/Sales
P.O. Box 7075
Berkeley, CA 94707
(415) 527-1649,
Factory: (415)
632-0394

Sparrevohn
Engineering
(foneAlone)
143 Nieto Ave. #1
Long Beach, CA 90803
(213) 433-7240

STAX
940 East Dominguez
Carson, CA 90746
(213) 538-5878

Sumiko (Tweek)
P.O. Box 5046
Berkeley, CA 94705
(415) 843-4500

Talking Scale (see
Technasonic)

Tandy
1700 One Tandy Center
Fort Worth, TX 76102
(817) 390-3011

Technasonic (Talking
Scale)
869 W. Buena
Chicago, IL 60613
(312) 679-6666

Technics (see
Panasonic)
Telemania (see Kash 'n'
Gold)

Telko
Consumer Telephone
Division
23041 Alcadle Drive
Laguna Hills, CA
92653
(714) 770-9644

Thorens \ Concorde\
Epicure Prod. Inc.
8500 Balboa Boulevard
Northridge, CA 91329
(818) 893-8411; (800)
225-7932 Thorens

Tiptoes (Mod Squad)
542 Coast Highway 101
Leucadia, CA 92024
(619) 436-7666

Toshiba America
82 Totowa Road
Wayne, NJ 07470
(201) 628-8000; (800)
221-0314

Tweek (see Sumiko)

Universal Security
Systems, Inc.
10324 So. Dolfield Road
Owings Mills, MD
21117
(301) 363-3000

Velodyne Acoustics
2565 Scott Boulevard
Santa Clara, CA
95050
(800) VELODYNE,
(408) 748-1077

Watkins
Manufacturing Corp.
(Hot Spring Spa)
6225 El Camino Real
Carlsbad, CA 92008
(619) 438-3334; (800)
331-5832 CA
/(800)854-2271

Yamaha Electronics
Corp., USA
6660 Orangethorpe
Avenue
Buena Park, CA 90620
(800) 854-3262

If you were
free to *live*..

WERE you today to throw off the restraints of social conformity . . . would you, too, first satisfy that inborn craving for Ultraviolet? Would you discard the trappings of civilization to spend strenuous health-

brimmed days in the beneficent sunlight?

For most convention-ridden people such action is denied. But the vital Ultraviolet portion of the sunlight can be brought right into the home by means of the justly-famous *Alpine Sun Lamp*. For years this apparatus has been used by physicians for the application of Ultraviolet as a powerful remedial agent. Now, with the growth of the preventive ideal, physicians are making it available to their patients for regular irradiation as a means to complete physical fitness.

To those who accept the obligation of a healthy body for themselves and their family...who glory in a robust tan throughout the year...the *Alpine Sun Lamp* has a vitally interesting message.

Ask your physician about it...and write for the treatise *"Ultraviolet for Health."*

Modern bathroom fixtures by courtesy of the Crane Co.

The Original ALPINE SUN LAMP *Luxor Model*

Send today for this free booklet and for the economical terms upon which the Luxor Model may be rented for home use under your physician's direction.

HANOVIA CHEM. & MFG. CO., Dept. D2, Newark, N. J.
Please send me, free, a copy of the book "Ultraviolet for Health."

Name _____

Address_____

City_____ State_____

My Physician's Name _____

Index

Index

Index

Index